The Admiral's Secret Weapon

The Admiral's Secret Weapon

LORD DUNDONALD AND THE ORIGINS OF CHEMICAL WARFARE

Charles Stephenson

THE BOYDELL PRESS

First published 2006
The Boydell Press, Woodbridge

ISBN 1 84383 280 1

The Boydell Press is an imprint of Boydell & Brewer Ltd
PO Box 9, Woodbridge, Suffolk IP12 3DF, UK
and of Boydell & Brewer Inc.
668 Mt Hope Avenue, Rochester, NY 14620, USA
website: www.boydellandbrewer.com

A catalogue record of this publication is available
from the British Library

This publication is printed on acid-free paper

Typeset by Pru Harrison, Hacheston, Suffolk
Printed in Great Britain by
MPG Books Ltd, Bodmin, Cornwall

CONTENTS

To my wife, Pamela,
who has lived for several years with
a 'third person in the marriage',
albeit one who has been dead for
around a century and a half

ILLUSTRATIONS

FOREWORD

When Charles Stephenson approached me some time ago to ask for access to family papers relating to my ancestor's secret plans I thought little of it. It was, I thought, an obscure story in an otherwise intriguing and eventful life. How wrong can you be; strangely enough, it always seems to be those closest to you that can most surprise, and so it is with this story of Thomas Cochrane.

I have grown up in a home filled with family memorabilia left behind by many generations, some famous and many that have passed on leaving little imprint at all. Thomas Cochrane, later the 10th Earl of Dundonald, certainly left his mark on the world, and his shadow stretches longest in our family hall.

The author makes no claim to understand my great-great-great grandfather in this book, but his painstaking research uncovers the very essence of the man. He plots the very single-minded thoughts of one man through the prime of his life to his grave, and he does so eloquently following the story of Thomas's 'Secret Plan'.

From a personal perspective it is good to know that Thomas and his Grandson, the 12th Earl of Dundonald, were not directly responsible for the first use of chemical weapons on a grand scale at Ypres during the First World War, but also I am pleased that the mystery the author reveals towards the end of this book still leaves a few questions unanswered.

The story itself is intriguing, being played out over one whole century, weaving a path through some of Britain's most eminent scientists, politicians and military. It illuminates a tenacious and single-minded person who, at times, seems driven to the point of paranoia as a result of the reception he receives from his peers.

What I find most intriguing is how little the world has changed in 200 years. We are today actively engaged in discussing weapons of mass destruction, only now they are biological and nuclear, with chemical paling into a poor third place. The discussions are, for the most part, ill-informed and driven by the politics and politicians of the day. As always nobody wants to pick up the bill to deliver measured scientific reasoning.

I wonder if the story will be re-told in another 100 years and find that the world players are still engaged in the same game but with higher stakes. I hope not, but fear it will be ever so.

Douglas Dundonald
July 2005

INTRODUCTION

Thomas Cochrane, the 10th Earl of Dundonald, as well as being a sea-warrior of almost unparalleled prowess, was an inventor. At the time of his death he had some fourteen patented inventions to his name covering a variety of fields – steam boilers, gas-lighting, and the use of compressed air to facilitate tunnelling operations being just a sample. This work, however, is concerned with just one of his inventions, the definitely unpatented methodology behind his Secret War Plans.

Surprisingly, given the number of biographers who have made Cochrane their subject, this is one facet of his life that has been, if not exactly ignored, then not subjected to overmuch scrutiny. It is difficult to say exactly why this should have been, as the Plans, which were really several developments upon a more or less constant theme, were formulated to overcome specific tactical difficulties, and are illustrative of the original thinking that their author was capable of. His virtually lifelong quest to have them adopted, an ultimately unsuccessful venture, further gives an insight into his tenacity and the confidence he had in his own judgement, while also demonstrating his unqualified lack of tact when dealing with superior authority. These are all characteristics that have attracted the attention of previous writers, yet, for reasons that are obscure, this particular embodiment of those characteristics has received scant attention.

The methods embodied in the Secret War Plans, involving the generation of massive amounts of poisonous gas, accompanied by saturation bombardment and smoke screens, were revolutionary at the time of formulation, and remained so at the time of the author's death some forty-nine years later. They also remained a secret – being considered by two subsequent generations of the Dundonald family as too sensitive to divulge – for a further forty-eight years following the 10th Earl's demise; a remarkable length of time even if they were, probably, obsolete towards the end of the period.

This work, then, seeks to trace and explain the history of the Secret War Plans of Lord Dundonald from their inception in 1811, through their various manifestations as investigated by several committees during the nineteenth century, and their subsequent disclosure to a small readership in 1908, and a wider public in 1924. Along the way they, or versions of them, had been scrutinised by some famous names: among them Sir William Congreve, whose 'rockets red glare' remain immortalised in the 'Star Spangled Banner'; Michael Faraday, one of the founding fathers of electrical engineering; and Winston S. Churchill, who needs no introduction here. It is the intention that anyone with an interest may now be able to follow these famous names and learn the story of the Secret Plans, or at least as much of that story as it is possible to tell, for it is a truism that when researching any matter historical, there is always more to discover. This work, then, cannot claim to be definitive – no work can – but it does, for the first time, present previously unseen evidence, and thus tell a fuller story than any previous work, including that published by the present author.

In writing this account the practice has been to use primary sources wherever possible, that is, texts produced by the principal actors contemporaneously. Fortunately this has proved possible for the greater part of the core of the work. On occasion, however, it has been necessary to rely on accounts by those principals produced retrospectively, accepting all the caveats inherent, and only, when no other course was available (fortunately rarely), have secondary sources been utilised.

With the exception of Chapter 6 – which is also the sole departure from the philosophy outlined above – a chronological approach has been adopted, from the biographical and contextual first chapter up to the final chapter, which deals with the post-Great War period. Chapter 6 was, as first conceived, written with the object of demonstrating that the Secret War Plans were not unique and were merely a facet of a methodology that had been conceived, and occasionally developed and used on a small scale at least, on several occasions since ancient times. However, when comparing these other attempts at 'chemical' warfare with the schemes put forward by Dundonald it became apparent that the War Plans were not just on a different scale from any previous, or indeed later, proposal or attempt, right up until the German gas attack at Ypres in 1915 and the subsequent outbreak of general chemical warfare, but were qualitatively different as well. Dundonald had not merely conceived an idea, but had translated it into a workable – in the utilitarian sense – scheme utilising readily available contemporary technology to achieve specific objects. He had, in short, invented chemical or gas warfare, and not invented it in the way that, for example, Leonardo da Vinci 'invented' the tank or helicopter, or Arthur C. Clarke 'invented' the communication satellite, where the concept was arrived at, but the method, the ability to put the concept into practice, was absent. Dundonald conceived both the concept and the methodology necessary to realise that concept. These having been arrived at, only the will to put them into action was needed, and this was, of course, the factor that was consistently lacking. Whether, had the will been supplied, the Plans would have worked in the sense Dundonald always believed they would is of course a different question, and one that is addressed, or at least as far as conjectural matters can be, in the work.

The work also deals with another mystery concerning the Secret War Plans; the role that they played in inspiring the German gas attack at Ypres in 1915. It was the case that the 12th Earl of Dundonald genuinely feared that he had been the unwitting catalyst for this event, through the Plans being stolen and delivered to Germany, whereupon the concept behind them had formed the basis of the German adaptation of chlorine for military purposes. This second Dundonald family secret was first revealed in 1978 by a biographer of the 10th Earl, Ian Grimble, and it is investigated in some depth in the final chapter.

The task of tracking down the source material associated with the War Plans would not have been possible without the expertise and professionalism of those who are entrusted with the keeping of various archives. I am indebted therefore to Mr David Brown and the staff of the National Archives of Scotland for assistance in tracing the papers of the Dundonald family, which are held in their collection. I also owe a great debt to Ms Andrea Clarke of the British Library who cheerfully put up with innumerable queries regarding obscure texts. Mr A. Khan of the House of Lords Record Office provided me with information on a little-known nineteenth-century MP, while Mr Paul Gibbons of the same establishment traced various entries in the House of Lords records and interpreted Parliamentary expressions; grateful thanks are extended to them both. For providing me with difficult-to-locate documents I also owe thanks to Dr Gail Nicula, Chief of the Library Division of the Joint Forces Staff College, National Defense University, Norfolk, Virginia.

The Public Record Office has also yielded up much useful information, but with its catalogue and document-ordering service now available online the human interface has gone into decline somewhat. Nevertheless a great deal of thanks is due to that institution as well. On a personal level, I am indebted to Mr Bob Paterson and Mr Kevin Ryan for applying the ultimate test to any work of this nature – does it make sense and is it intelligible to the intelligent layman? – and to Mr Steph McCrossan and family for similar assistance, as well as for putting up with my presence while researching in Edinburgh. A work dealing with members of the Dundonald family could hardly have been completed without the active assistance of the current members of that family, so I extend my thanks also to Douglas Dundonald, who currently heads the clan as the 15th Earl and was kind enough to write the Foreword.

I have previously published condensed accounts of the Secret War Plans, and thankfully the further information garnered for this work does not, in any meaningful way, render them inaccurate. For their backing in the publication of these previous efforts I am grateful to Mr Hugh Andrew, Mr Marcus Cowper, and Mr Martin Robson.

As related earlier, it is axiomatic among historians that there can never be a definitive account of any historical matter. There are always other sources to discover, and no doubt I have failed to unearth many important documents that bear upon the subject. Nevertheless, there has to be a time when one draws the search to a close and tries to assemble the material into a meaningful account. In terms of material, then, this work, though I will claim it as the fullest account so far, does not claim to be the final word on the matter – there probably never will be a 'last word'. It does, though, lay before the reader, as stated, the most detailed and accurate, insofar as the current writer has been able to make it, story of the Dundonald Plans yet to appear. Any faults in the presentation of this material, the greater portion of which has not been published previously, or its interpretation are, despite the number of others who have been involved, mine and mine alone. I can only trust that they will not be too many.

Charles Stephenson
Ellesmere Port
November 2005

1

Diabolical Engines of Warfare

> The French admiral was an imbecile, but yours was just as bad. I assure you
> that, if Cochrane had been supported, he would have taken every one of the
> ships.
>
> Napoleon Bonaparte on the Battle of Aix/Basque Roads

THOMAS Cochrane can be fairly categorised as belonging to that select group
who possessed, in Clausewitz's phrase, 'the genius for war'.[1] It would be a
futile exercise to draw up a list of similar such people, but it would surely include
several of those who share the distinction with Cochrane of occasionally being as
frightening to their own side as to the enemy. Cochrane was undoubtedly a
maverick whose qualities were enormous, with the almost inevitable corollary that
so were his faults. His genius for making war was counterbalanced by his utter
failure to exhibit even a modicum of discretion when dealing with his superiors,
and, predictably, the latter defect led to the negation of the former quality. Probably the greatest, perhaps because it was backhanded, tribute to him concerns the
vetoing of his appointment, late in life, to an independent command. As it was
stated: 'Age has not abated the adventurous spirit of this gallant officer, which no
authority could restrain; and being uncontrollable it might lead to most unfortunate results.'[2]

Clearly, the fact that the subject was seventy-nine years old at the time of this
statement did nothing to alleviate the writer's concern – quite correctly in all probability. In his comparative youth, however, Cochrane seemed set fair to become an
authentic national naval hero, perhaps second only to Lord Nelson. Indeed, he has
been described 'without hyperbole' as 'after the death of Nelson, the greatest naval
commander of that age of glory'.[3] This may be so, but in fact Cochrane and Nelson
fought in quite different types of warfare; Nelson was a fleet commander, while
Cochrane, basically, gained his reputation as a warrior in single-ship or small-ship
actions. There is, however, no doubting, and a perusal of his exploits can only
confirm this, that he had utterly mastered the art of frigate warfare and what would
later be termed combined operations, and put this mastery into practice with
deadly effect. As he himself was to state it with regard to the latter:

1 Thomas Cochrane in 1809

Thomas Cochrane, 'painted after his nose was shattered by Shell whilst commanding HMS Imperieuse', by James Ramsay. Cochrane was wounded by a shell-splinter at Fort Trinidad, Rosas, Catalonia, on 25 November 1808. It may have been an application of artistic licence, but the Cochrane nose, which was a not unremarkable feature, appears undamaged in this rendition.

Picture courtesy of the 15th Earl of Dundonald

I had completely disorganised the telegraphic communication of the enemy [. . .] and had created an amount of terrorism on the French coast, which, from inculcating the belief that it was intended to be followed up, prevented the French government from further attempts at throwing a military force on the Mediterranean coast of Spain.[4]

His outlook on war and methods of fighting it were akin to those of a later generation, and if Admiral Sir John 'Jacky' Fisher's 1899 observation that 'Moderation in war is imbecility!'[5] places him squarely among the early advocates of what we now call 'Total War', then Cochrane had such a modernistic outlook on his profession almost a century before such ideas began to gain common currency. 'War, to him, was about killing the enemy while preserving his own men, and any means to hand – including any infernal device, fiery or explosive – was welcome.'[6]

One of the prime exemplars of this outlook was his conception, adoption, and unremitting urging of unique methods of chemical warfare over a century before they became commonplace on the battlefields of the Great War. Evidence that he was no mere dreamer can be adduced from the fact that they were, in almost their original form, still considered at that later date, in fact his life story amply vindicates the cliché concerning 'truth being stranger than fiction':

A brilliant inventor and tactician, he won gallant victories, received the highest decorations for valor, and held major commands in the navies of five different countries: Britain, Chile, Peru, Brazil, and Greece. Yet in his turbulent career, he was also discredited, imprisoned for fraud, financially ruined, stripped of his rank, degraded from his knighthood, expelled as a member of Parliament, and repeatedly involved in litigation and legal squabbles.[7]

However, since this is not a biography of Cochrane, here is not the place to explore in depth his improbable life and work; here we are only concerned with one aspect of that work. Here we are concerned only with, as his first biographers were to put it, 'the device known as his "secret war-plans" for capturing the fleets and forts of an enemy by an altogether novel process, attended by little cost or risk to the assailant, but of terrible effect upon the objects attacked'.[8] However, in order to be able to place the value of his plan in its proper context, it is necessary to understand something of the author of that plan. To that end an examination of certain aspects of his career is necessary.

Thomas Cochrane, later the 10th Earl of Dundonald, was born at Annsfield, Lanarkshire on 14 December 1775. His father, Archibald, was a scientific speculator and inventor who had lost a large fortune in his ventures, thus greatly impoverishing himself and his family. The Dundonald family (motto: *By Courage and Labour*) could boast of having several of its members make the ultimate sacrifice while fighting for Sovereign and Country: three of them had been killed during the war of the Spanish Succession and the 7th Earl had met his end during the Seven Years' War.

Thomas Cochrane went to sea in 1793 under his uncle, captain, later a knight and admiral, Alexander Cochrane. He swiftly demonstrated great ability, passing his lieutenant's examination at the first attempt and gaining promotion. A stint aboard the flagship of the American station was followed by his return to European waters and duty aboard the *Thetis*, then the *Barfleur*, which was among those ships blockading the Spanish Fleet off Cadiz. During his service thus far Cochrane had managed to establish a reputation for himself as an outspoken and abrasive individual, which, in a system that to a large extent depended on patronage, or 'interest', for advancement, meant he risked retarding progression of his career. His promotion might have been encumbered and other less able, but more amenable, men advanced ahead of him had he not displayed remarkable talent. This undeniable ability resulted in him being awarded the command of a vessel in the Mediterranean Fleet, the somewhat inappropriately named *Speedy*. It was while in command of this vessel, with the temporary rank of commander and the courtesy title of captain, that he established his reputation as something approaching a naval genius following his engagement of the Spanish frigate *El Gamo*.

On 6 May 1801, off Barcelona, the *Speedy*, with fourteen 4 lb guns and a crew of forty-eight, took on the Spaniard, with thirty-two 32 lb guns and a crew of some three hundred, and forced her surrender. Such disparity in size and gun power meant that the smaller vessel could have surrendered with no attending disgrace. Cochrane, however, determined to attack. Running up the colours of a US vessel, a permissible *ruse-de-guerre*, allowed him to get alongside despite the enemy firing two broadsides as they determined the true nationality of the little ship. Once alongside, the guns of the *El Gamo* could not be brought to bear, allowing the British ship a moment of safety, which was used to devastating effect. The guns of the *Speedy*, double shotted and at maximum elevation, fired up through the Spaniard's side and decks, inflicting some fifty casualties on the enemy crew. Crucially, many of these were officers, including the captain, who had been fighting the vessel from the quarterdeck.

Being safe from the Spanish guns by virtue of its proximity left the British ship open to a danger just as great: being boarded by the enemy. Cochrane overcame this particular hazard by the simple expedient of getting his blow in first. Leading virtually his entire crew on to the *El Gamo*, the ship's boys remained and the doctor manned the wheel, and adopting another ruse in shouting back for reinforcements, he managed to affect the surrender of the much larger vessel.

Such a feat meant Cochrane's stock rose dramatically yet still promotion to post rank – that is, to Captain as a rank rather than as a position, for whatever the actual rank of an officer in command of a vessel, they are inevitably known as the 'captain' – was denied him. This was a subject upon, and around, which he engaged in an acrimonious correspondence with no less a figure than the First Sea Lord, Admiral John Jervis, Earl of St Vincent. This was, to put it mildly, a fool-hardy thing to do, especially when, after being informed that his recommendation for promotion for *Speedy*'s second-in-command had been refused owing to the small number of men killed aboard the vessel, he reminded the admiral that 'his own Earldom had been awarded for an action in which there was only one man killed on his flagship'.[9] This was a calculated, and, it must be said, gratuitous insult as St Vincent was known to be ultra-sensitive to the charge that his ship suffered little damage because he kept it out of the thick of the action.

Such imprudent behaviour to those who had control over his career and advancement had one immediate result; he, and the *Speedy*, were relegated to monotonous duties. It may have had more harmful long-term effects, however, in that he had gained further notoriety as an insubordinate and reckless officer. Of the first charge he was undoubtedly guilty, and of the second, in spheres other than what might be termed the diplomatic, entirely innocent. Cochrane's apparent impetuosity in battle was nothing of the sort, and he was possessed of the ability to size up complicated situations almost instantly and then to act decisively. No matter how fraught the situation he always maintained a cool head and took his decisions accordingly – and, apart from when caught unawares, he never acted precipitously, but always carefully planned for all contingencies. In fact he was caught unawares in July 1801 and forced to surrender in the face of overwhelming odds, but only after he had, as the officer who took him captive remarked, 'for so many hours struggled against impossibility'.[10] His captivity was hardly onerous, lasting no more than two weeks, before he was exchanged, a common occurrence in those days, and then belatedly promoted to full captain. It mattered not, however, as in the same year peace temporarily broke out with France and Spain, formalised in the Treaty of Amiens signed in 1802. Cochrane was put ashore on half-pay.

The temporary peace lasted some fourteen months before hostilities resumed and Cochrane, eventually, for his earlier behaviour had not been forgotten, took to the sea again. It was during this period that his worst suspicions about the Admiralty's persecution of him were, at least to his satisfaction, confirmed vis-à-vis the case of the convoy lamp: in 1798 an act, the Compulsory Convoy Act, was passed that gave the Admiralty the power to enforce convoy on all ocean-going ships. This act was repealed in 1872, and, despite the historical precedent, the story of the difficulty in reintroducing the system during the Great War is well known. However, the system was put to good use during the wars with Republican France. Cochrane was assigned to convoy duty and, as was his wont, had applied his mind to the difficulties of keeping a convoy in some kind of order at night – the merchant captains found it difficult to keep station with the leading frigate owing to the lack of a distinctive light displayed on that vessel. Cochrane devised a powerful lamp that would act as a beacon for the following vessels and allow them to keep station on the leading ship, a device he offered to the Admiralty but which was rejected, only for the same Admiralty to shortly afterwards offer a prize of £50 for the design of such a light. Cochrane submitted his invention, but under the name of another, and it duly won the competition. However, when he revealed himself as the true designer the consequence was that 'not a lamp was ever ordered'.[11]

Reassigned to his former corsair-like activities, he continued winning fame and, not altogether of negligible account to him coming as he did from an impoverished family, fortune by way of prize money. This was also a major point in his favour as far as his crew was concerned. He also developed during this period an expertise in what would be known later as combined operations. In 1808 his taking and holding of Fort Trinidad, near Rosas, is an example of his original and unconventional methods. This type of audacity, coupled with success, had made him a public hero, but it was only the following year that his downfall came, during the aftermath of am operation that could, paradoxically, have caused him to rise to the highest degree of acclaim. This was the first occasion for Cochrane to practise what might be termed a set-piece plan for the destruction of shipping in a protected anchorage. Its importance in the context of his future 'secret war plans' lies in the fact that these plans were evolved to carry out exactly this type of operation. Indeed, Cochrane's plan for the destruction of a French fleet can be considered as a precursor of those methods, and as such is worth considering in some detail.

It was arguably the most famous action that Cochrane ever undertook and was known, somewhat confusingly, as either the Battle of Basque Roads or the Battle of Aix Roads. Whatever the nomenclature, however, the location and object of the action are clear: a set-piece assault upon a flotilla of French vessels in a secure yet difficult to blockade anchorage. The British tactic of closely blockading the ports and anchorages of Revolutionary France had as its object preventing the various dispersed portions of the enemy fleet from combining into larger groups, when they would have been able to make mischief. However, utilising a period of rough weather that had driven the Royal Navy off station, a force of some eight ships-of-the-line had sailed from Brest, joined with other vessels from L'Orient, and, along with yet more ships from Rochefort, combined, on 23 February 1811, at anchor in the Aix Roads. It was thought that their commander, Admiral Allemand, proposed to break out and sail for the West Indies in an attempt to relieve Martinique, 'one of the last unpicked plums of the French overseas empire remaining'.[12]

The Aix Roads anchorage was protected by shore batteries in masonry fortifications on the surrounding islands and, unbeknoken to the Royal Navy, by a boom. A

British blockading force under Admiral James Gambier had taken station some miles off the coast and had, so far, prevented the French from leaving their haven. The possibility of further rough weather dispersing the British fleet made the destruction of the French vessels imperative, and it was for this reason that Captain Cochrane, on 21 March 1809, was summoned to the Admiralty in London, and told that he was to carry out such destruction:

> There is an undertaking of great moment in agitation at Rochefort, and the Board [of Admiralty] thinks that your local knowledge and services on the occasion might be of the utmost consequence, and, I believe, it is intended to send you there with all expedition; I have ventured to say, that if you are in health, you will readily give your aid on this business.[13]

Writing many years later, Cochrane was to recount his doubts concerning the operation, which he had raised with Lord Musgrave, the First Lord. Musgrave had received a letter from Admiral Gambier outlining the difficulties of effecting operations against the French ships:

> The enemy's ships lie much exposed to the operation of fire-ships, *it is a horrible mode of warfare, and the attempt hazardous if not desperate*; but we should have plenty of volunteers for the service. If you mean to do anything of the kind, it should be with secrecy and quickly.[14]

This letter sets out the rather curious position that appertained with regard to the necessity to destroy the enemy vessels; the Admiral on the spot was placing the onus for the operation on the Admiralty, implicitly refusing to undertake the operation with the resources at his disposal. As Cochrane was quick to realise:

> It was now clear to me why I had been sent for [. . .] The Channel fleet had been doing worse than nothing. The nation was dissatisfied, and even the existence of the ministry was at stake. They wanted a victory, and the admiral commanding plainly told them that he would not risk a defeat [. . .] as a last resource, I had been sent for, in the hope that I would undertake the enterprise.[15]

He wryly noted that if he succeeded then the fleet and government would take the credit, and if it failed then he would be left to take the blame. He also calculated that great offence would be caused by him, a junior officer, being placed in such a responsible position, but, reassured (wrongly) on the last point he agreed to undertake the enterprise and submitted his plan for the Admiralty's consideration. It was approved with the entire concurrence of the Board.

His arrival at Gambier's fleet did not, as he had accurately forecast, please many of the officers there; 'Every captain was my senior [. . .] all regarded me as an interloper, sent to take the credit from those to whom it [legitimately belonged].'[16] The diary of William Richardson, an impressed seaman at the scene, relates the following entry for 5 April 1809:

> In consequence of some reproachful words uttered by Rear-Admiral Harvey against Lord Gambier, because his lordship could not grant him the command of leading in the fire-ships (as Lord Cochrane was sent here expressly by the Admiralty for the purpose), Rear Admiral Harvey was ordered to England, and there he was tried by a court-martial which dismissed him from the service. He was however, after some time reinstated.[17]

The disgruntled naval officers considered themselves quite capable of carrying out such an operation, and, it has to be admitted, very likely could have. Though perhaps invidious in the context of hierarchy and etiquette, Cochrane's position operationally was, at least potentially, highly favourable. Here he was, a junior officer, given virtual *carte blanche* to carry out what by any standards was a major operation of war. That he would be successful was, at least in his own estimation, a foregone conclusion. As he had put it to Musgrave with regard to his plan:

> There was no risk of failure whatever [. . .] On the contrary, its success on inspection must be evident to any experienced officer [. . .] [and the destruction of the enemy's squadron] would not only be certain, but, in fact, easy.[18]

Cochrane wasted no time. Arriving at the Basque roads on 3 April 1809, he immediately made a night-time reconnaissance of the enemy positions in a small boat, assuring himself that the enemy batteries were of short range and thus relatively harmless. Having completed this he decided that rather than wait for fire-ships to arrive from Britain they could more rapidly be constructed on the spot from available materials. He also went about building devices that were to later feature in his secret war plans: explosion vessels.

> I worked hard at the explosion vessels, two, at least, of which I determined to conduct personally; not because I deemed myself more competent to conduct them that others, but because being novel engines of warfare, other officers could not have given that attention to their effect which long deliberation on my part had led me to anticipate, if directed according to the method on which their efficacy depended; it being certain, even from the novelty of such a mode of attack, that the officers and crews of the line-of-battle ships would be impressed with the idea that every fire-ship was an explosion vessel.[19]

Terrorism of the enemy personnel was his goal, a 'main feature of the plan', as he put it, and from this terror would come the confusion and paralysis that would allow the enemy ships to be destroyed – in fact they would virtually destroy them-selves in their 'attempt to escape from such diabolical engines of warfare'. Cochrane's description of the construction of the explosion vessels is worthy of note:

> The floor of the vessel was rendered as firm as possible, by means of logs placed in close contact, into every crevice of which other substances were firmly wedged, so as to afford the greatest amount of resistance to the explosion. On this foundation were placed a large number of spirit and water casks, into which 1500 barrels of powder were emptied. These casks were set on end, and the whole bound round with hempen cables, so as to resemble a gigantic mortar, thus causing the explosion to take an upward course. In addition to the powder casks were placed several hundred shells, and over these again nearly three thousand hand grenades; the whole, by means of wedges and sand, being compressed as nearly as possible into a solid mass.[20]

Seaman Richardson relates how he was detailed to help in the conversion of the third explosion vessel:

> We stowed thirty-six barrels of gunpowder (90 lb each) in her hold upright and heads out [open], on each one was placed a 10-inch bomb shell, with a short fuse in order to burst quickly. A canvas hose well filled with prime powder was laid for a train from the barrels to a small hole cut in her quarter for the purpose, and the train was led through it to her outside, which was well fastened – a port fire which would burn twelve or fifteen minutes so as to give the people alongside in the boat who set it on fire sufficient time to escape before she exploded.[21]

Cochrane's plan mixed audacity, originality, and an awareness of human psychology into a potent brew. The explosion vessels were to lead the attack, with Cochrane in personal command, and were to be followed by the fire-ships. The French of course would have been aware of the danger of attack by these incen-diary methods, and would have evolved precautions against them: obviously containing only a small crew they were liable to be boarded by enemy seamen before they reached a position where they could be safely fired and abandoned to drift in the requisite direction. Cochrane had calculated, however, that if the explosion vessels led the attack, and one or more was fired, then the enemy would have no way of knowing if the following vessels were floating mines or not. Under the impression that they might be, he noted that 'however gallant the enemy, there was little chance of the fire-ships being boarded'.[22] To add to the confusion he intended to cause, Cochrane planned to attack under the cover of the obscurity of darkness; visual obscurity was to be a feature of his later plans.

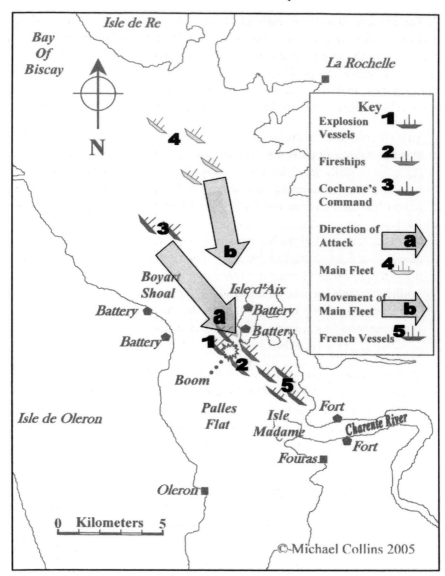

The map shows the following labels:

Isle de Re

Bay Of Biscay

La Rochelle

N

Key
Explosion Vessels **1**
Fireships **2**
Cochrane's Command **3**
Direction of Attack **a**
Main Fleet **4**
Movement of Main Fleet **b**
French Vessels **5**

Boyart Shoal

Isle d'Aix

Battery

Battery

Battery

Battery

Boom

Palles Flat

Isle de Oleron

Isle Madame

Fort

Charente River

Fort

Fouras

Oleron

0 Kilometers 5

©-Michael Collins 2005

2 Cochrane's attack on the French Fleet at the Battle of Basque/Aix Roads,
11–12 April 1809

This was arguably the most famous, and controversial, action that Cochrane ever undertook, featuring a set-piece assault upon a flotilla of French vessels in a secure yet difficult-
to-blockade anchorage. The anchorage was protected by shore batteries in masonry
fortifications on the surrounding islands and, unbeknown to the Royal Navy, by a boom.
Map courtesy of Michael Collins

The attack went in on the night of 11 April 1809, Cochrane having calculated that the weather, though somewhat rough, would prove no impediment. He led the attack in the largest of the explosion vessels and, having judged time and distance as well as was possible, the fuses were kindled and its crew of six abandoned it for a small boat. The results, though not according to plan, were at least spectacular to the escapees rowing, literally for their lives, against wind and tide.

> To our consternation, the fuses, which had been constructed to burn fifteen minutes, lasted little more than half that time, when the vessel blew up, filling the air with shells, grenades and rockets; whilst the downward and lateral force of the explosion raised a solitary mountain of water, from the breaking of which in all directions our little boat narrowly escaped being swamped [. . .]
> The explosion vessel did her work well, the effect constituting one of the grandest artificial spectacles imaginable. For a moment the sky was red with the lurid glare arising from the simultaneous ignition of 1500 barrels of powder. On this gigantic flash subsiding, the air seemed alive with shells, grenades, rockets, and masses of timber, the wreck of the shattered vessel; whilst the water was strewn with spars, shaken out of the enormous boom, on which [. . .] the vessel had brought up, before she exploded.[23]

Though the most formidable part of the French defences, the boom, had been fortuitously overcome the rest of the plan went awry, and out of all the fire-ships, 'upwards of twenty in number', only four reached the enemy position and none actually set alight any of the enemy vessels. The other explosion vessels detonated with as spectacular effect as the first one, but again did no physical damage to the French vessels. Richardson corroborates this:

> On April 11, at half-past eight in the evening, it being very dark, and a strong tide setting with blowing weather right towards the enemy's ships, the explosion vessels set off [. . .] [They] soon blew up with a dreadful explosion [. . .] Shells and rockets were flying about in all directions, which made a grand and most awful appearance. All hands were up that were able on board all our fleet, to behold this spectacle, and the blazing lights all around gave us a good view of the enemy, and we really thought we saw some of their ships on fire. But it seems they had been prepared for this business, for as the fire-ships closed on them, they slipped or cut their cables and ran their ships on shore.[24]

The damage was caused via the psychological effects of the methodology employed; as Cochrane had calculated, after witnessing 'one of the grandest artificial spectacles imaginable' the defenders were apt to attribute such properties to each and every vessel that approached. The result, though achieved in a way far different from that which was intended, was nevertheless of decisive importance: the French ships, in attempting to escape either cut their cables and drifted aground, or, in attempting to sail to safety, ran aground. Daylight revealed the spectacle of the entire fleet, with only two exceptions, in a position of complete helplessness, compounded by the fact that the tide was receding, leaving them completely high and dry.

Cochrane had meanwhile retrieved all the stray men from the fire-ships and explosion vessels and returned to his command, the frigate *Impérieuse*, which he proceeded to sail into the Aix Roads. Undoubtedly his unorthodox methods had achieved victory, but he wished to make this an even more stunning success by the complete physical destruction of the stranded enemy ships, and it was at this point that he once again courted controversy. From Cochrane's point of view, the view that has become the generally accepted orthodoxy, what was required was for Gambier to send several heavy ships to support him. To Cochrane, Gambier seemed unable to comprehend this and despite him signalling on no fewer than four or five occasions (the actual number is disputed), he was unable to elicit any positive response from what one of Cochrane's latter-day biographers, accepting the orthodoxy, has termed the 'non-combatant admiral'.[25]

This adverse judgement of Gambier is a recurring theme in almost all of the biographical works that deal with Cochrane and the Aix/Basque Roads operation, at which time he had been an admiral for some fourteen years. Further, it is in the context of his performance at the battle, and in his relationship with Cochrane, that Gambier has become largely defined. For example, in 1807 he had commanded the Baltic Fleet during its bombardment of Copenhagen, an act subsequently condemned by another of Cochrane's biographers as nothing more than vandalism and one requiring 'neither nautical skill nor a gift for strategy'.[26] Gambier had, though, compelled the surrender of the Danish Fleet through this action and was thus, artificially in the orthodox view, credited with being a competent commander. After elevation to the peerage he was, in 1809, appointed commander of the Channel Fleet, which, again according to the orthodox view, he reduced to 'as dismal a condition of disarray as could well be conceived'.[27]

Some rather unattractive features of the man buttress this perspective of Gambier; for example, he seems to have been something of what might be termed a religious maniac, obsessively distributing fundamentalist tracts to his subordinates and holding services aboard his ship. More importantly, as may be evidenced by the letter to the Admiralty concerning fire-ships already quoted, he displayed a distinct lack of decisiveness, a trait that saw, again from the orthodox perspective, its culmination in his failure to support Cochrane at an important moment – 'one of the most contemptible acts of any commander-in-chief in British naval history'.[28]

So, despite Cochrane's victory over the French fleet being substantial, with four of the enemy vessels completely destroyed and the rest badly damaged and in no condition to put to sea for a considerable time, and thus the threat posed by a 'fleet in being' disposed of, it had not been annihilating. Consequently, Cochrane was furious with Gambier. This would perhaps have been of little moment but for two other considerations: firstly, Gambier's reports on the battle seemed to him to first understate, and then ignore, his decisive role in it:

> Lord Gambier, in his first despatch to the Admiralty, gave me credit for everything but the success of my plan, and in his second despatch *omitted my name altogether as having had anything to do with either planning or executing it* [. . .] the whole merit of which was ascribed to Lord Gambier, who was never nearer than nine miles to the scene of action.[29]

Secondly, and more fatefully, Cochrane had been chosen, in 1806, by the electors of Westminster to be their Member of Parliament. It was in this latter capacity that he, in effect, became undone as the phrase has it, for he let it be known that he would oppose the traditional motion of thanks to Gambier in the House of Commons, 'on the ground that the commander-in-chief has not only done nothing to merit [it] but [. . .] neglected to destroy the French fleet in Aix Roads, when it was clearly in his power to do so'.[30] In perhaps unknowing support of Cochrane's case, the great Napoleon Bonaparte later put it thus vis-à-vis the action: 'The French admiral was an imbecile, but yours was just as bad. I assure you that, if Cochrane had been supported, he would have taken every one of the ships.'[31]

Lord Musgrave was appalled, seeing as Cochrane could not, that such a move would be interpreted as an attack on the governing establishment and that this establishment would close ranks on Cochrane. He was known as a 'radical' MP and was outspoken about the abuses perpetrated by the governing elite – despite being an aristocrat himself – on those further down the social scale. Moreover the war that Cochrane had distinguished himself so well in was, it must be remembered, a war against the France that had dispossessed and executed most of its own aristocracy and governing elite – a war against a revolutionary state. Those who had lost their power, and in many cases their heads, in France were from the same class as those who constituted the governing elite in Britain. The social system in Britain was not, to the undiscerning eye, markedly different from that which had pertained in Royalist France. The net result could be little other than to make those at the top in Britain somewhat nervous. They would be hardly likely to countenance what they might conceive of as a great British victory being downgraded by a 'class traitor', as a later age might have termed him, with the lack of confidence in the infallibility of government and establishment authority that this would imply.

In a battle between Cochrane and that establishment there would only be one winner. This was precisely what happened; Gambier, upon hearing that his conduct was being questioned, demanded a trial:

> 'I request that you will be pleased to move the Lords Commissioners of the Admiralty to direct a Court Martial to be assembled as early as possible, for the purpose of enquiring into my conduct as Commander in Chief.'[32]

Cochrane's unrivalled abilities as a warrior were not matched by his abilities in courtroom or parliament. He was completely outmanoeuvred in both by those who regarded him as a greater enemy than the French. To the end of his life he was still bitter about what he considered to be the rigging of Gambier's court martial; his autobiography, published half a century later, contains thousands of words of analysis of the evidence, and it is upon this partisan interpretation that most subsequent accounts have been based and from which the orthodox view has arisen. This view has, however, been challenged, and the evidence presented to the court martial has been sifted by critical minds who have, perhaps, come to more balanced conclusions. For example, as one has pointed out, of the seventeen commanders of individual vessels present at the scene only six, including Cochrane, were of the view that Gambier was wrong in not sending heavy ships into the restricted waters of Aix Roads. Thus: 'the majority of senior British professionals who were on the spot [. . .] backed Gambier's refusal to take risks.'[33] Another authority has argued that had Gambier allowed himself to be 'stampeded by his subordinate into a precipitate fleet movement into the strongly tidal waters' the results could have been disastrous.[34]

Certainly Gambier was cautious, and whether or not he was correct in his conduct on 12 April 1809 is certainly debatable. He had been in ultimate command during an operation that eliminated the threat from an enemy 'fleet in being', and he had preserved his own fleet and freedom of action. He was then unquestionably the victor, but it was not a smashing victory such as Nelson might have achieved, and which Cochrane wanted. Indeed, parallels might be drawn, though not in terms of scale, between Gambier's situation and that of Jellicoe during the Great War.

During that conflict Jellicoe's blockade of Germany and the High Seas Fleet was largely monotonous, monotony relieved to any great extent only by the Battle of Jutland of 1 June 1916, after which he was also criticised for being over-cautious. However, Jellicoe was able to inform the British government on 2 June that the Grand Fleet, virtually undiminished in superiority over its adversary, was ready for further action, while the High Seas Fleet skulked in harbour and was obviously unwilling and unable to contest control of the North Sea with the Grand Fleet. It was victory, but, as with the Battle of Aix/Basque Roads, an annihilation, a 'New

Trafalgar' had been expected and anything less was inevitably a disappointment to some. In fact naval victory is seldom Nelsonian in character or outcome, and given this the orthodox viewpoint of Gambier and the battle, based as it is almost totally on Cochrane's opinion, may not thus necessarily be the only legitimate one.

Gambier's court martial, despite being intimately related to the battle seems however less susceptible to revision. The weight of witness opinion, as expressed in numbers holding 'for' and 'against' views, at the court martial did not of itself make a decision inevitable one way or the other. However, given that there were 'undercurrents' at the trial because 'the idea that a commander-in-chief could be court-martialled because a junior officer disagreed with his actions was anathema',[35] it seems probable that there was a predisposition among the panel towards upholding the authority of Gambier, and thus established authority in general.

This was, it may be recalled, a time when criticism of the political and social status quo resulted in prosecution and imprisonment. Victims of this sensitivity included, for example, Thomas Paine who, in 1791, had published his most influential work, *The Rights of Man*, in which he attacked the hereditary monarchical principle and argued for equal political rights. The British government banned the work and charged the author with seditious libel (publishing writings that subverted the authority of the monarch).

It is therefore surely legitimate to conclude that established authority, in pronouncing judgement on a matter of authority, would have been most unlikely to come to a decision, whatever the evidence, that would support subversion to authority; Cochrane would never have been allowed to discredit Gambier. He wasn't to the delight of many, such as Hannah More, who seem to have lain awake at night trembling at the blasphemies contained in the *Rights of Man*. More, considered to have been a leading player in the conservative reaction to the French Revolution, had this to say:

> Terrible as Bonaparte is [. . .] I do not fear him as much as those domestic mischiefs – Burdett, Cochrane, Wardle and Cobbett. I hope, however, that the mortification Cochrane etc. have lately experienced in their base and impotent endeavours to pull down reputations which they found unassailable, will keep them down a little.[36]

Cochrane was indeed mortified, and the end result of the twin affairs, of battle and court martial, were to increase his sense of alienation and near paranoia vis-à-vis his superiors in particular and authority in general. Such feelings became a *leitmotif* for the rest of his days, and of course were reciprocated somewhat – at least for a time.

Immediately following the affairs Cochrane underwent a period of unemployment, during the course of which he reflected, among other things, on the ways and means by which the war against Napoleonic France was being conducted. As already related, following Nelson's decisive victory at Trafalgar in 1805, what remained of the French fleet was stranded in port by the British blockade. The Royal Navy was thus forced into a passive role, forced to wait for a French move against which it could react. The strategy pursued by the Admiralty consisted of keeping the isolated parts of the enemy fleet from combining, and destroying these isolated portions as and when circumstances allowed. The Aix/Basque Roads attack had been such an operation.

The difficulty with this strategy was that the huge naval strength of Britain was being used inefficiently. According to Cochrane's analysis:

> The French Squadrons [. . .] are not yet formidable [. . .] however [. . .] they [. . .] require a force to blockade them [. . .] on so many, and on such distant stations [. . .] [that] this apparently endless, and harassing, and at certain seasons impracticable, mode of warfare, [is] destructive of the spirit of the British Navy.[37]

This semi-passive role, this reaction to a 'fleet in being' – albeit a somewhat dispersed one – was forced on to the British by the difficulties of overcoming the maritime fortifications behind which the enemy protected their dispersed strength, and not all were as ineffectual as those encountered at Aix/Basque Roads. The fundamentals of the problem were tactical: how to overcome stone built land-based works with wooden ships, or, as Lord Nelson himself had styled it, how to 'lay wood before walls'.[38] It was to these questions that Cochrane addressed himself, but the discovery of, as he was to claim, the definitive answer relied upon serendipity, for he was in pursuit of quite a different object when he sailed for the Mediterranean in the first quarter of 1811.

2

The Stink Ships

Had the Spaniards understood the principle [. . .] the Fortifications of Gibraltar [. . .] must have given way to the stink ships; for the volumes of noxious effluvia, evolved from masses of sulphur and charcoal burning close to the lines and driven by the wind into the interior of the place, would have destroyed every animal function.

Thomas Cochrane, 1811

D URING the period of the wars against Revolutionary and Napoleonic France, the island of Sicily was allied to Britain, although the Royal Navy, firmly based in Gibraltar and Malta, only had a few ships spare to protect that ally; British control was far from complete, and the Mediterranean Sea could in no way be considered a British 'lake'. It was this factor, the dangers inherent in sailing alone, combined with what can only be termed a caprice of fortune that led Cochrane to the island. He had visited Malta with the object of providing himself with proof that the Admiralty Prize Court based there was a corrupt institution, and that the officials, by enriching themselves at the expense of British mariners, were inhibiting the prosecution of the Napoleonic War. As he put it:

> The most important object of war [. . .] was suspended by the peculations of a colonial Admiralty Court. Foiled in procuring redress in the House of Commons, where my statements were pooh-poohed by the representatives of the High Court of Admiralty as rash and without proof, I determined on procuring, by any means whatever, such proof as should not easily be set aside.[1]

Accordingly, at the beginning of the year 1811, Cochrane had set off in his private yacht *Julie* for the Mediterranean, and, in the interests of security, changed to a Royal Naval vessel at Gibraltar, arriving at Valletta during the first two weeks of February. Cochrane does not tell us the exact date of his debarkation, and it can only be roughly calculated from the information in his autobiography. Having visited the Admiralty Prize Court and discovered the 'proof' that he had been seeking – a table of fees, which should have been openly exhibited, but was instead secreted within the Judge's chambers – he gave this to a ' brother-officer who was going over to Sicily, and [who] promised to take charge of it till my arrival at Girgenti', now Agrigento.[2]

Cochrane later boarded, after a series of surreal adventures, a ship 'bound to Girgenti, to pick up passengers and letters from Naples',[3] where he presumably retrieved the table from his brother-officer. He records himself as being back at Gibraltar some two months after leaving it, which means around the beginning of April.[4] This visit to Girgenti occurred in March and was the occasion that he witnessed the collateral effects of sulphur manufacture, one of the principal industries of Sicily at the time. As he described it later:

I examined the process of extracting the sulphur from the crude substances with which it is combined; the wasteful method of performing this operation gave me some surprise; but I was indeed astonished to find that the open air, to leeward of the kilns, was so impregnated with deadly fumes, that the country people are prohibited by law from residing within several miles of the mountain during the melting season, whilst nature, by the absence of vegetable production around, seemed to warn the animal creation from the bounds of its productive range. When I thus learnt the effect of these ignited masses of sulphurous ore, a gentle breeze blew from the westward, and the vapour rolled slowly towards the east.[5]

The methodology he saw being employed in order to produce a useable product was a process known as liquation. After its extraction the sulphur had to be separated from the contaminants with which it was mixed using a *calcarella*. This was a small circular brick furnace, set on a slope, into which the sulphur was added and ignited. The resulting heat melted the ore, which was run off through a hole, the *morte*, and captured in damp wooden moulds, or *gaviti*. The fumes thus generated – when burned sulphur produces sulphur dioxide, an extremely poisonous gas – caused the toxic fallout that he witnessed. He also observed that the fumes 'though first elevated by heat, soon fell to the ground, destroying all vegetation, and endangering animal life to a great distance'.[6] He noted one further property of these fumes when viewing a kiln situated upon a hill: 'the fumes of the burning sulphur descended the sides of the hill instead of being carried away vertically as might have been expected'.[7][8]

Here, he was quick to perceive, was a method of attacking an enemy no matter where and how he might shield himself from conventional forms of attack.

My mind being awake to impressions of a professional nature, made at once an application of what I saw, for it occurred to me that, if the open air could be thus deprived of its vital principle, the defenders of all marine fortifications, whether bombproof or not, might be expelled, by means quite irresistible. In order, therefore, to accomplish enterprises, hitherto deemed impracticable, nothing more is requisite than, during a steady favourable breeze, to bring ignited sulphur mixed with charcoal or gas coke (under the shield of obscurity) near to windward of fortifications or batteries, and there consume the mass, by smothered combustion, so that heat shall not raise the current of vapour above the object of attack. Then, whatever object may be contemplated may be safely carried into execution.[9]

Here was a method that would, a century or so later, become known as chemical warfare: 'chemicals do not strike a physical target – they pervade the atmosphere over an area'.[10] It was thus one of the fundamental principles of chemical warfare that Cochrane had discovered and formulated, and this he conveyed in a 'Memorial' on the subject to His Royal Highness the Prince Regent, dated 2 March 1812.[11] This 'Memorial' is much more than an exposition of the effects of sulphur fumes; it is a blueprint for the complete incapacitating of France as a naval power, or 'the destruction of the Marine of France', as he put it.[12] He continued:

As however, the means proposed for the accomplishment of these objects, differ from such as have hitherto been pursued, it may not be irrelevant, first, to take a rapid military view of the existing state of affairs; secondly, to notice the principles which war might be conducted with most probable advantage, by a maritime state, and the application of these principles to particular objects; and lastly, to show that the greater part of the sea lines of defence, fortifications, batteries, moles, basins, anchorage's, and all they protect, and contain, is at the disposal of your Royal Highness.[13]

Cochrane is arguing that his plans for the destruction of France's maritime power are of a different nature from those methods hitherto resorted to, which by implication he regards as unsuccessful. He also proposes to review the current situation and to propose methods by which the application of his plan may be put into force, and the likely results of such an application. In assessing the present state of affairs, Cochrane laments that the blockade of French ports – the policy of the Royal Navy with the object of preventing the various portions of the French fleet from combining – is an 'apparently endless, and harassing, and at certain seasons impracticable mode of warfare' the pursuit of which is 'destructive of the spirit of the British Navy'.[14] Though he does not state it explicitly, he conveys the impression that merely blockading the French navy is a defensive mode of warfare; what he proposes is taking the offensive to the enemy, and rather than being content to 'bottle up' the various flotillas, to seek them out and destroy them. He wants offensive warfare. He also wants offensive combined operations, and names a group of islands – 'Ushant, the Isle Grou, Isle Dieu, the island off Marseilles, one of the Hieres, and Elba' – the British possession of which would 'effectively cut off all intercourse by sea' and, with an eye to extending British influence and trade,

advocates using Elba as a 'depot for the supply of all Italy with British Manufac-
turers, when those of France could no longer be obtained'. He estimates the force
required to carry out this plan to be small, with an occupying detachment 'not
exceeding 3,000 men'.[15]

Cochrane further argues that with a force of 300 men, the 'Semaphoric Tele-
graphs' stationed strategically along the enemy coast and inland – the use of which
by the French to rapidly transmit information of the Royal Navy's movements was
negating their freedom of navigation; 'thus blockades are rendered of very trifling
moment' – could be disrupted. By destroying these devices 'alternately in various
positions' communication may be permanently cut off, and the expense and time
required to repair them would allow 'intermediate mischief's to be effected', which
might be of 'incalculable injury, and lead to consequences of infinitely greater
importance'.[16] While the enemy communications system was disrupted, the
British could undertake operations with a degree of secrecy.

Cochrane goes on to describe the benefits that would accrue if commando-style
operations – as they would later be called – were carried out in Spain: 'Taking the
province of Catalonia as an example, it is to be observed that the only practicable
military road winds along the margin of the sea.'[17] He describes how small garri-
sons are maintained in the towns and villages along this road, and how if they were
'carried off' by a small force of a thousand men the local inhabitants would 'fall on
the enemy', especially if a British force were to maintain a presence.[18]

The above proposals, Cochrane submits, 'are on a very confined scale, intended
only in aid of those pursuing a totally different system'.[19] This 'system' is, of
course, using the navy as a blockading force. Only if the ships can be freed from
this necessity can major harassing operations be put into practice. He therefore
goes on to 'proceed to the chief object, [. . .] the means of destroying the whole
navy and flotilla of France'.[20]

The, what may be termed, unconventional aspects of the plan fall under two
headings, and are concerned with actual weapons and their use, rather than higher
tactics and strategy themselves. The first of these weapons are what Cochrane
dubbed 'Temporary Mortars'.[21] A Temporary Mortar was a ship whose hold had
been specially adapted – the bottoms and sides strengthened with extra timbers
and lined with clay in order to project explosive force upwards – to hold a large
quantity of powder, over the top of which was laid 'carcasses, shells and
grenades'.[22] The idea behind the weapon was

> of the simplest kind; and founded on the known principle that the expansion
> of ignited powder; is in the line of least resistance; and that bodies will receive
> an impulse therefrom, in proportion to the quantity of powder used, and the
> opposition given to its efforts in other directions.[23]

It would be unnecessary to say more on the effect of Temporary Mortars, or Explosion Ships, did not the understanding naturally revolt at Plans which violate preconceived opinions, and search for difficulties to embarrass rather than facilities that are to surmount them; and thus whilst the mind admits, as if by instinct, the prodigious violence exerted by ignited powder on surrounding objects, it may involuntarily withhold assent from the application of the principle to Carcasses and Shells. Therefore let,

ABC	be the segment of ship's hold,
DEF	old cannon and pigs of iron, bedded in clay,
GHIK	transverse logs of old ships timber
LMN	another tier crossing these, and bolted,
OPQR	upright beams of ditto
STUW	old mooring chains, cables and hawsers, surrounding and binding the upright logs,
XY	stones, clay and other tenacious and ponderous matter.

The Mortar thus chambered and bound together, is ready to be charged for service; then let,

pp	represent the powder
w	junk wadding
cvg	carcasses, shells, grenades

It is demonstrable that the expansive effort of the powder (being a ratio to the quantity) will be exerted equally on the bed, and on the shells, and that these aggregate masses will recede from the impulse in an inverse ratio of the matter they contain, and of the opposition made by water to instantaneous motion, to that of air.

Hence the Carcasses, Shells and Grenades will be impelled by a force nearly equal to the whole power of the powder inflamed, and the flight of such will be in the line of least resistance, or between the angle of 45 degrees and the zenith.

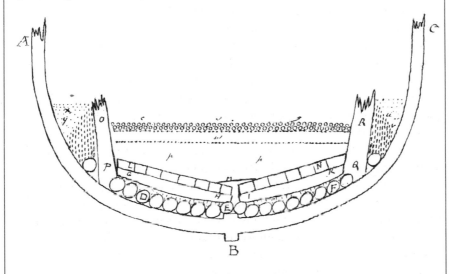

Source: 'Memorial' from Cochrane to the Prince Regent dated 2nd March 1812. The 'Melville Papers'. The Papers of Henry Dundas, 1st Viscount Melville, British Library Add. MSS. 41083 (2nd series) Vol. V. Section 2. Transcribed and computer enhanced by Charles Stephenson.

3 Temporary Mortars: From Appendix A to Cochrane's Memorial of 1812

The similarity between these devices and those he had actually constructed and used at Basque/Aix Roads is immediately apparent. Another feature of his proposed methods, the genesis of which can be ascertained in his earlier methods, was the attack under cover of darkness:

> The explosion vessels would be invisible in the obscurity of night, until the shells and carcasses, rising in the air and spreading as they fly, should scatter devastation on all around to a distance regulated by means already mentioned, so as to give the largest carcasses and shells a sufficient, but not more, than a sufficient momentum to plunge through the decks of large ships and lodge [in] the holds of those of a smaller class; thus imparting to the greatest destructive powers; all the advantages of levity possessed by rockets without abridging the purposes to which they are applicable, or interfering with the regular mode of bombardment.[24]

Cochrane intended to modify 'three old hulks' per target to be attacked; these would in effect be huge, as he states it, mortars, which, when fired, would hurl in an instant in the region of '6000 carcasses and shells' over the protective moles and ramparts and destroy any ships within.[25] He states the result of a trial carried out in Sicily during February 1811, when a wine pipe[26] 'converted into one of these mortars, threw 28 eight inch shells over a wider space than the principle fortifications of Corfu (230 yards) although there were only three pounds of powder to each shell'.[27]

Temporary Mortars were not for the purposes of distant bombardment, and in order for them to 'hurl destructive missiles into naval depots; and lift them over moles, and basins, amidst the vessels they contain' they would need to operate in close proximity to land-based defences.[28] For the purposes of neutralising these defensive works and fortifications Cochrane had devised another weapon – 'sulphur ships, placed during night on the windward side of such fortifications'. He attached a generic plan, though the explanation above hardly needed much expansion, for the mode of attack. He also included a drawing of such a craft, with the notation:

> It is unnecessary to suggest that the vapour will pervade the innermost recesses of bomb-proofs, fill batteries or cones, and that it will roll along under the lee of walls and parapets to a great distance.

Cochrane expounded on the likely efficacy of his plan by using the example of Gibraltar:

> Had the Spaniards understood the principle, on which their intercourse with Sicily might have taught them as they must have witnessed the abandonment

The plan proposed for neutralising Marine Batteries, Bastions, and Works, by means of vessels containing large quantities of sulphur and charcoal, is not liable to some of the objections in Appendix A [Temporary Mortars]; for instance they cannot be blown up, and therefore if conducted at a proper time to a fit situation, their effect is inevitable.

Let BCD be the works of Flushing or the Cones of Cherbourg,
E, a stink vessel
W, the direction of the wind
SUL, Sulphur and Charcoal on a Bed of Clay on the Main Deck

It is unnecessary to suggest that the vapour will pervade the innermost recesses of Bomb-Proofs, fill Batteries or Cones, and that it will roll along under the lee of Walls and Parapets to a great distance. The effect when compared to the Stink Ball now in use will probably be in the ratio of the ignited masses.

<u>Note</u> The intention of placing Charcoal and Sulphur on the Upper Deck and on a bed of clay, is to admit air beneath and to prevent the vessel from consuming soon. The melted sulphur, if any falls, will drop into the sand and water admitted into the hold.

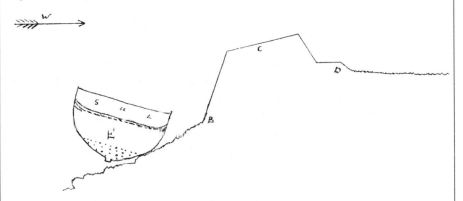

Source: 'Memorial' from Cochrane to the Prince Regent dated 2nd March 1812. The 'Melville Papers'. The Papers of Henry Dundas, 1st Viscount Melville, British Library Add. MSS. 41083 (2nd series) Vol. V. Section 2. Transcribed and computer enhanced by Charles Stephenson.

4 Sulphur Ships: From Appendix B to Cochrane's Memorial of 1812

of the country around the sulphur mines in the melting season [. . .] the Fortifications of Gibraltar even with out the aid of Explosion Vessels,[29] must have given way to the stink ships; for the volumes of noxious effluvia, evolved from masses of sulphur and charcoal burning close to the lines and driven by the wind into the interior of the place, would have destroyed every animal function.[30]

Other examples of where his methods would have been of great utility in producing excellent results – Cochrane was not a man assailed by self doubt – were also set out:

Had Lord Nelson understood the principles now submitted to Your Royal Highness, he could have destroyed the Danish Fleet without the loss of a man; and Sir Sidney Smith would not have had to regret, in his attack on Boulogne, that 'although our people rowed gallantly in night after night and

If the powers of Temporary Mortars be admitted, and that they will not be disputed by those who have witnessed the tremendous explosion of the magazines of large ships, the flash of which darts in an instant many hundred feet in the air, carrying masts, yards, and all impedimenta before it, it becomes unnecessary to enter into detail respecting the means to be employed to ensure effect; yet a few words may not be improper as to the mode of guiding the vessels, with the least possible danger to those employed.

W   *Wind*

S   *a Spar*

E   *Explosion Ships*

F   *French Ships*

F   *French Ships*

For instance, if the attack is to be made with the wind but a little free, all the sails of the headmost vessel should be full, and the min topsails of the ships in tow ought to be braced aback, when sufficiently near to the enemy as in **Figure 1**.

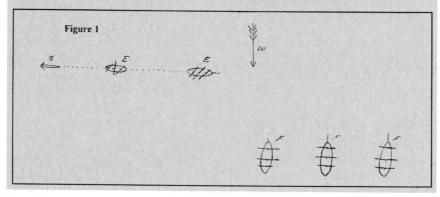

Figure 1

5 Of the means of Conducting Explosion Ships: From Appendix C to Cochrane's Memorial of 1812

On the contrary, should the wind be quite fair, the headsails of the headmost ships only should be set, so as to ensure her going before it, and the vessel in tow ought to have all her sails furled, as in **Figure 2**.

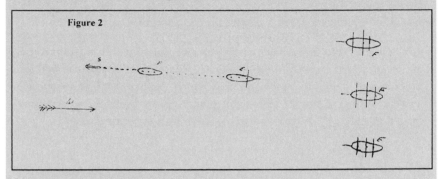

Figure 2

Or, ships may be used singly, by towing large spars thus **Figure 3**. The fuses for exploding must be regulated according to the distance, or grenades placed to let go the anchors, and bring up the explosion vessels, until they explode.

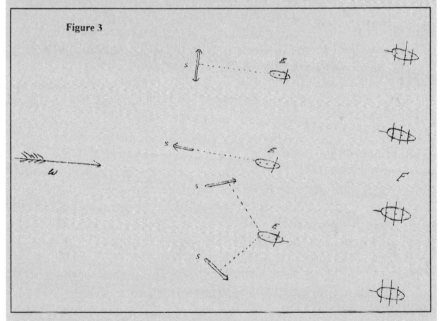

Figure 3

Source: 'Memorial' from Cochrane to the Prince Regent dated 2nd March 1812. The 'Melville Papers'. The Papers of Henry Dundas, 1st Viscount Melville, British Library Add. MSS. 41083 (2nd series) Vol. V. Section 2. Transcribed and computer enhanced by Charles Stephenson.

broke through the line in various places, running right under the bows of the vessels to throw the carcasses, the misfortune was, that, not a vessel was destroyed.[31]

He was also remarkably prescient about future scenes of attack:

If it shall be Your Royal Highness's pleasure to command a detail of the means proposed for accomplishing the [. . .] destruction of the Russian Fleet at Kronstadt, it will be immediately laid before you, together with the means of neutralising Marine Batteries, and Lines of Defence by Sulphur Vessels placed during night on the windward side of such Fortifications.[32]

There were three appendices to the Memorial, containing details of the construction of Temporary Mortars; Sulphur Ships; and of the means of conducting Explosion Ships.[33] It is clear that Cochrane had worked out in detail the methods he was proposing to use and that he had, at least to his own satisfaction, overcome one of the greatest problems in attacking defended fortifications at the time – of pitting 'wood against walls'. The relative vulnerability of wooden ships when matched against stone fortifications and red-hot shot could, he had calculated, be overcome by adopting his methods. His solution to the problem was saturation bombardment and gas warfare.

Cochrane, as has already been related, was not a popular figure within what may be conveniently termed 'the establishment'. His physical courage was equally matched by his moral courage, and he had no hesitation or compunction in attacking graft, corruption, and incompetence wherever he thought he saw it, which did not endear him to those in authority. The fact that his 'Memorial' was addressed to the Prince Regent rather than to his naval superiors at the Admiralty perhaps gives some indication of where he thought he was likely to be listened to most. However, if by addressing the monarch he at least ensured that his plan would receive consideration, it would have to be, in the final analysis, consideration by those naval, and military, superiors least likely to consider anything that had the name 'Cochrane' attached to it.

It must be considered a tribute to his record as a practitioner of the art of war that he was at least considered seriously. The Prince Regent indeed 'was graciously pleased to lay it [the plan] before a commission, consisting of Lord Keith, Lord Exmouth, and General and Colonel Congreve'.[34] Acting as President of this 'secret committee' was the Prince's brother, the Duke of York.[35] There was to be a further paper from Cochrane on 2 May 1812:

Those who would doubt the powers of explosion vessels may be convinced by experiments; therefore holding the theory laid down in Appendix A to be correct, until it is practically disproved it will not be considered as magnifying their utility to state that obstacles which have hitherto delayed besieging armies, and co-operating fleets, may by these means be overcome without loss of time, consequently enormous expense saved, and what is of more importance, the ultimate effects of maritime expeditions may be thus attained before the enemy can prepare for resistance. The evidence taken before the mouth of cannons relative to the failure of the attempt on the fleet, and arsenals in the Scheldt, exemplify this fact.[36]

He is here referring to the disastrous Walcheren expedition of July–December 1809, an attempt to land troops and destroy the French fleet lying between the island of Walcheren and Antwerp. This joint military/naval venture necessitated the assembly of the largest fleet that had ever left Britain: thirty-seven line-of-battle ships, twenty-three frigates, and nearly four hundred transports to convey the army of 40,000 men of the expeditionary force. Formidable on paper perhaps, it nevertheless managed to violate every principle of military strategy. Secrecy and surprise were sacrificed – the purpose and objective of the force had been discussed in the press for months; and the army had a split command – the fleet was commanded by Admiral Sir Richard Strachan, and the army by Lieuten-ant-General the Earl of Chatham. The attempt, predictably with hindsight and perhaps also with foresight, failed and some 14,000 soldiers were felled by disease after occupying the Dutch islands and doing nothing further. A popular lampoon perhaps summed it all up:

> Lord Chatham, with his sword half drawn, Stood waiting for Sir Richard Strachan.
> Sir Richard, longing to be at 'em, Stood waiting for the Earl of Chatham.

The operation was exactly the kind that Cochrane foresaw his methods super-seding. Instead of ponderous, slow, resource- and manpower-intensive ventures like it, he wanted lightning attacks on unsuspecting enemy strongholds with his new devices. Cochrane actually states in his *Autobiography* that, at the time of the expedition, he had proposed using a version of his plans:

> I laid before the Admiralty a plan for destroying the French fleet and the Flemish dockyards, somewhat analogous to that which would have proved completely effectual in Basque Roads [. . .] My new plan had, moreover, received an important addition from the experience there gained, and was now as formidable against fortifications as against fleets.[37]

This passage presents something of a puzzle, and unfortunately Cochrane does not tell us what this addition was. In the Dundonald Papers there is reference to a document dated 1810 entitled 'Lord Cochran's outline of a plan for the capture of islands and forts on the coast of France with drawings'.[38] There is also mention of the operation being aided with the use of 'stink-balls'. However, the document itself is not present.

Stink-balls, or shells, were hollow containers containing sulphur and other inflammable, and smelly, ingredients. They were principally designed, as their name suggests, to produce a suffocating atmosphere in confined spaces, the gun-decks of ships, for example, in order to discomfit those inhabiting them. Such devices have their origins in ancient warfare – discussed more fully in Chapter 6 – but they would seem, though accounts seldom mention them and information is somewhat sketchy, to have formed a part of the available ordnance of naval warships up until the middle of the nineteenth century. Their effect, if they were ever used as intended, was negligible, and given the amount of smoke and fumes generated by the discharge of black-powder charged weapons – a feature often remarked upon – this is hardly surprising. There is a reference to such weapons in the writings of a Dr Cottman, an American of Anglophobe tendency, who lived in Russia at the time of the Crimean War. He stated, referring to the Allied bombardment of Odessa on 22 April 1854:

> They had no intention of injuring the city by the 2000 asphyxiant bombs thrown into it. The officers well knew that the asphyxiating principle contained in the bomb would decompose the explosive principle in the capsule, and prevent the bursting of the shell, and, as they were useless, they concluded to rid the fleet of them.[39]

Cochrane, however, in Appendix B of his Memorial, highlights the greater effect of his sulphur vessels in comparison to the 'Stink Ball now in use'. So, though in the absence of solid evidence it cannot be much more than speculation, it might be the case that Cochrane had formulated an idea for firing such missiles at fortifications with the object of 'smoking-out' the personnel manning them. If so, since the first portion of the Walcheren expedition, as it became known, started out in the summer of 1809, this would mean that Cochrane had thought of a scheme for utilising 'gas warfare' on a small scale some eighteen months before he saw the Sicilian sulphur industry in 1811. It may be that what impressed itself upon his mind in Sicily was not the *principle*, but the *scale* upon which this would be possible. But, as stated, in the absence of documentary evidence, this cannot be much above the level of speculation. There is one further caveat: the *Autobiography* appeared some fifty years after the above events occurred and is not always reliable in minor details. It remains quite possible therefore that the passage in question was no more than a retrospective conflation of events.

Whatever the case, the failure of the venture, of which Cochrane offered no opinion – 'these matters being already well known' – merely reinforced his view that the strategy and methods being used were wasteful and ineffective. Using his methods the French navy would be destroyed quickly and effectively, and thus free the blockaders for more important work.

Following the destruction of the enemy ships Cochrane would then use these British vessels, formerly engaged on blockading duties, to wage his commando operations upon the enemy communications and outlying posts. In a paper entitled Additional Observations of 11 May 1812, he expanded on the strategic advantages, as he saw them, of pursuing his policy:

> This species of warfare is certainly that in which this country can engage with the greatest prospect of advantage; for whatever may be the state of affairs in the peninsula, it may be fairly asked, whether it is to be expected, that the number of men which England is capable of sparing, will be competent to contend against the succession of troops, which the government of France have it in their power to employ.
>
> Granting the military power of England to be equal to that of France, which probably is placing it in the most advantageous point of view, that the warmest advocates for continental co-operation could reasonably desire, it may be asked, can the most sanguine look to decisive victory, without numerous and hard fought battles?
>
> It is not necessary to state the consequences that might attend a reverse of fortune in the centre of Spain, but admitting the greatest evils which can befall our armies, to indecisive contests, and no-one will assert, that even on a supposition of equality, the British can drive the French armies before them without variety of fortune, more men would perish in these conflicts, than Britain now maintains in the peninsula. A rapid [. . .] mode of warfare therefore ought to be pursued, as possessing innumerable advantages over the limited operations and known movements of continental armies; and, as it is obvious, that the population of Great Britain, cannot contend in the open field, with a probability of ultimate success against France, and her dependant states, some plan of operation differing from that hitherto presented, can alone terminate the contest with success.[40]

The strategic outline described above demonstrates that while Cochrane undoubtedly possessed genius in the tactical sphere, in the larger realm of strategy his touch was less sure. He was certainly not the last person to take the view that the best way to defeat a continental land power was by *not* confronting it head-on in the field. To move forward a century or so, the strategic problems presented in the effort to defeat Imperial Germany have remarkable parallels with those necessary to defeat Napoleonic France. The Germany of Wilhelm II was primarily a land power that could only be defeated by the breaking of its armies on land. However, accepting this fact condemned the allies in the Great War to the horrors of the

Western Front, while in the Second World War it was amid the even greater horrors of the Eastern Front that Hitler's army was broken. Accepting it during the earlier conflict meant that Wellington's Peninsula campaign and the other, much greater, battles fought to bring down the armies of Napoleon Bonaparte could not be avoided. Sea power could assist in this, and was of significant, indeed vital, importance in so doing, but ultimately it could not secure *of itself* the victory required. The corollary of this, of course, is that the destruction of Napoleon's 'Navy and Marine' would have had an impact, but would not have proved decisive in securing the Emperor's defeat in itself, and neither would Cochrane's campaign of, necessarily peripheral, harassment.

As in the Great War of the following century, Britain and her allies eventually triumphed, after long and costly land campaigns had used up the enemy armies. The aspects of the struggle concerning sea power, and the lessons learned, were distilled into two hugely influential works by the American seaman and scholar Captain Alfred Thayer Mahan; *The Influence of Sea Power on History* (1890) and *The Influence of Sea Power upon the French Revolution and Empire* (1892). The latter work contains Mahan's most famous, and quoted, phrase: 'those far distant, storm-beaten ships upon which the Grand Army never looked, stood between it and the dominion of the world'.[41] It was by the use of the close blockade, and 'other storm beaten ships [. . .] on which the French generals and admirals frequently looked'[42] that Britain prevented that army from ever being able to make use of the shipping to enable it to win the 'dominion of the world'. Napoleon had, on paper, a powerful fleet to the end, but it was the Royal Navy's blockading strategy that prevented it ever becoming a unified fleet and thus realising its potential.

However unsound Cochrane's strategic conceptions might have been, or to put it another way, what he wanted done *after* the destruction of the French Navy in its dispersed and protected harbours, this in no way invalidates his proposed methods for destroying that fleet on a tactical level. Whatever use was made of the Royal Navy following its release from blockading duties is relatively unimportant, for this 'apparently endless, and harassing, and at certain seasons impracticable mode of warfare' was being conducted for a purpose. That purpose was an end in itself, and Cochrane's plan contained an alternative, certainly faster, and definitely cheaper, means of attaining that end than the strategy of blockade – 'which no sailing navy before had ever attempted'.[43]

However, despite the various signs of approval and endorsements, the plan was not to be wholeheartedly supported. Unlike the investigations of some future committees into his Secret Plans, the deliberations of the Duke of York's committee have not yet come to light. However, their favourable opinion of at least a portion of them can be inferred from contemporary correspondence. Lord

Keith observed, in a paper of 9 March that with respect to what he termed 'the combustible weapon' he was unable to form a judgement, but conceded that:

There is, no doubt, valuable matter in the plan for consideration, and, if put into skilful management, tempered with prudence, may be attempted with good effect. To obtain information respecting the situation of places intended to be attacked is of the first importance, and of the number of men that can be speedily collected. In the Channel and Bay of Biscay the tides must be well understood or the boats might be left dry. In short, to render such a plan effectual a considerable nautical and military science must be combined.[44]

A letter from Cochrane to Lord Keith of 23 March 1812 also contains second-hand information as to the opinion of the committee:

His Royal Highness the Duke of York has expressed himself satisfied with the military part of the plan submitted to the Regent; and His Royal Highness also informed me that Mr. Congreve, after some days consideration, gave a favourable opinion as to the practicability of using Explosion and Sulphur vessels as pointed out.[45]

In his autobiography Cochrane quoted from 'a private letter from Lord Keith', stating that the officers:

Gave it as their opinion that under the circumstances detailed in my explanatory paper, such a mode of attack would be irresistible, and the effect of the power and means proposed, infallible.

The Prince Regent and the Duke of York fully concurred with the committee in the destructive character of the plans submitted.[46]

Cochrane was summoned to Carlton House and commanded to 'secrecy' on his part, and he explained that only himself, Sir Alexander Cochrane, and his uncle, Mr Cochrane Johnstone, knew his plans, the latter having actually penned the 'Memorial'. 'Not long' after that interview Lord Melville informed him that it was intended to put into action a portion of the war-plan, requesting his [Cochrane's] attendance at the Admiralty 'for the purpose of conferring on the subject'. To this he demurred on the grounds that 'development of a portion might give the enemy such an insight of the whole as would enable him to turn it against ourselves on a large scale'.[47] However, he was prevailed upon by Lord Keith, and accordingly formulated a plan to destroy the enemy ships in the outer roads of Toulon. Part of his reasoning here was the assurance that 'a success once achieved, the popular voice would place it in my power to enforce the execution of the more destructive portion of the invention within the enemy's inner harbours'.[48] On 12 May 1812 Cochrane wrote to Lord Melville stating what force he considered necessary for executing the plan for the destruction of the Toulon fleet: 'One seventy-four [line-of-battle ship armed with that many cannon]; Two 38-gun frigates; Two 18-gun brigs; Two cutters or schooners; [. . .] requisite as an escort and to protect the boats.'[49]

It is clear from the above, since the fleet was situated in the *outer* roads of Toulon, that the portion of the plan the Admiralty was interested in utilising concerned the explosion vessels or Temporary Mortars. In his original Memorial Cochrane had enunciated his belief that with three such vessels 'the French fleet may be burnt at their anchors or driven onto the rocks in the outer roads, where they anchor during the summer months' Even the reduced plan was not put into effect, which Cochrane was to blame on

> ill feeling against me at the Admiralty [. . .] [as it] would have placed me in command of a squadron, with my flag flying in a line-of-battle ship [. . .] and the project after long fruitless expectation was dropped.[50]

It was not to be resurrected during the course of the rest of the conflict, and the Royal Navy continued its blockading strategy, with ultimate success. Cochrane, however, played no further part in the rest of the struggle. Burning with indignation at his perceived treatment by the Admiralty and government, he continued his crusade against corruption in high places, in his position as MP for Westminster, and busied himself with various scientific work. The chance to return to a theatre of war came in 1814 when his uncle, Admiral Sir Alexander Cochrane, was appointed to command the North American station. Britain and the United States had been at war since 1812 – 'another of the British government's monumental blunders'[51] – and this addition to her foes had been somewhat embarrassing to the Royal Navy. According to an American historian: 'The causes of the war of 1812 are among the more complex in our history, being in fact a gradual escalation of incidents none of which [. . .] triggered war of itself.'[52]

War when it came, however, proved that the navy of the fledgling republic was more than a match for that of its more senior opponent, and in a series of single-ship actions 'they inflicted greater damage on the morale of the British Navy than it had suffered in 20 years of war against the great powers of Europe'.[53] The US frigates were bigger, faster, better-armed, and, it has to be said, better handled by their volunteer crews than were their opponent's. Thomas Cochrane was undoubtedly one of the greatest living exponents of single-ship warfare, and it was as his uncle's flag captain that he was to be employed. According to his son and biographer, there was a proposal to try the Secret Plan against the Americans.[54] Sir Alexander was of course familiar with them, but perhaps the Plans, and certainly Thomas Cochrane himself, were prevented from being employed on the other side of the Atlantic by the Stock Exchange Trial. The aftermath of this was to see Cochrane officially disgraced and, expelled from Parliament and deprived of his Order of the Bath, forced to earn his living abroad as, in effect, a mercenary.

He accepted an invitation from the fledgling Chilean government, in 1817, to take command of their navy, and remained in this service until 1822. During this period they succeeded in their revolt against their Spanish colonial masters, and Cochrane was held to have distinguished himself in his position. In 1823 he transferred his allegiance to the Brazilians, who were in revolt against Portugal, and remained in their service until 1825, when he returned to Europe and undertook the leadership of the Greek navy in another anti-colonial struggle, against the Turks. This rebellion was unsuccessful and he returned home to Britain in 1828 where he succeeded his father, as 10th Earl, in 1831. Reinstatement into the navy followed in 1832. Having given a pledge of secrecy concerning his Secret Plans to the Prince Regent, he refrained from utilising them during his service in South America and Greece. He had not forgotten them, though, and following his return to Britain, and rehabilitation, he was to press them upon the authorities of the day with his accustomed vigour.

3

'Lord Dundonald Thought Otherwise'

The fact that England was at peace [was] a sufficient reason for not discussing the value of a new instrument of war. Lord Dundonald, however thought otherwise.

Thomas Barnes Cochrane and H.R. Fox Bourne, 1869

THOMAS Cochrane returned home to Britain in 1828, and despite succeeding to the earldom of Dundonald, as 10th Earl, some three years later, still remained in a state of semi-official disgrace. Having a conviction for fraud meant that he was socially disreputable, and, through his mercenary activities in South America and Greece, potentially in legal peril through being liable to further prosecution for contravening the Foreign Enlistment Act. In characteristic manner he prepared to lobby or litigate in order to right these wrongs, as he perceived them; restoration to the Naval List and to the Order of the Bath were his other two aims. He was spared this particular battle, in an arena ill suited to him, however, when the slate was wiped clean, as it were. Adopting less formal means, his wife, the Countess of Dundonald, petitioned King William IV. This had the happy result of a royal pardon, which was granted on 2 May 1832. William IV had himself served in the Royal Navy and must have been at least tolerably familiar with both Dundonald's reputation and his War Plans. We can deduce the latter because 'soon after his accession' in 1830 the secret was 'explained [. . .] to his Majesty, who acknowledged its value, and paid a tribute to Lord Dundonald's honourable conduct in keeping his secret so long and under such strong inducements to an opposite course'.[1]

Lord Dundonald resumed his naval career, which in the long period of peace following the final defeat of Napoleonic France was, by comparison with his former standards, undisturbed and unexciting. Eventually, through the system of Buggin's Turn, he rose to flag rank and, on 7 March 1848, was appointed to the command of the North American and West Indian Stations – a position once held by his uncle. An interesting vignette of how he was perceived from the lower deck at that time comes down to us courtesy of Seaman Thomas Branton, who served aboard his flagship *Wellesley*:

I was one of the crew of the Admiral's galley and was never tired of hearing of the fine old fellow's exploits when, as young Lord Cochrane, he fought the French and Spaniards in Nelson's day. He was a fine old man with typical Scotch features. He was an ideal officer, and was so beloved by the men that his name on the lower deck was 'Dad'. He would not allow flogging, greatly to the disgust of some of the other officers, who considered that such leniency was bad for discipline. When he was in the galley he would talk to his coxswain and the crew as though we were his equals.[2]

Despite the benevolent nature Cochrane displayed to the men of his command his warrior instincts had not abated, and he had neither forgotten his War Plans, nor was he to abandon efforts to have them adopted by the British government. For example, he pressed them upon the government in 1834, 1838, and yet again in 1840. On 3 August of the latter year he had written to the incumbent political head of the Navy, Lord Minto, in reference to an opinion of the Plans passed by no less a figure than the Duke of Wellington:

> If the people of France shall force their Government to war with England, I hope you will do me the favour and justice to reflect on the nature of the opinion you have received from the Duke of Wellington in regard to my plans, which is the same as that given to the Prince Regent by Lords Keith and Exmouth and the two Congreves in the year 1811, and that your Lordship will perceive, that 'although two can play at the game'[3] the one who first understands it alone can be successful. In the event of war, I beg to offer my endeavours to place the navy of France under your control, or at once effectually to annihilate it. Were my plans known to the world, I should not be accused of over-rating their powers by the above otherwise extraordinary assertion.[4]

'Lord Minto's answer', as his first biographers laconically noted, 'was very brief': 'I shall bear your offer in mind; but there is not the slightest chance of war.'[5] This, characteristically, did not deter Lord Dundonald. The direct parliamentary route was now closed to him; as a Scottish peer he had no automatic right to sit in the House of Lords, and his earldom barred him from standing for the Commons. This was so because the 1707 Act of Union between England and Scotland specified that the peers of Scotland could elect sixteen of their number to sit in the British House of Lords. Holders of a Scottish peerage, however, were also, unlike their Irish equivalents, barred from sitting in the House of Commons. This exclusion from direct involvement did not prevent him from raising the issue, and on 2 August 1844 his petition was heard in the House of Lords, with perhaps disappointing results as far as he was concerned:

> Upon reading the Petition of Thomas Earl of Dundonald; taking notice of a Discovery recently made for the Purpose of destroying Vessels, and

accomplishing other warlike assailing and destroying hostile fleets, and applicable also to other Purposes of War, and praying their Lordships 'to take the Circumstances into Consideration, and that an Inquiry may be instituted as to the relative Qualities of the Two Inventions:' It is ordered that the said Petition do lie on the Table.[6]

Despite 'lie on the table' merely being a parliamentary expression meaning that the petition was to be made available for reference by their Lordships, and that it had been accepted for consideration,[7] Dundonald, correctly as it turned out, perhaps concluded that it meant it would indeed 'lie on the table' – and be ignored. Some fifteen months later, on 29 November 1845, he returned to the fray by publishing an acerbic, and very long, letter in *The Times* – at the time, and indeed for many decades, an assured conduit to the eyes, and hopefully minds, of the British ruling elite. His missive commenced by lambasting, in no uncertain terms, what we might today call the conservative and bureaucratic mindset of those in positions of power, which was, characteristically, perhaps not the best tactic to bend them to his modes of thought:

> Had gunpowder and its adaptation to artillery been discovered and perfected by an individual, and had its wonderful power been privately tested, indisputably proved, and reported to a government, or to a council of military men, at the period when the battering-ram and cross-bow were chief implements in war, it is probable that the civilians would have treated the author as a wild visionary, and that the professional council [. . .] would have spurned the supposed insult to their superior understanding.[8]

He went on to argue that the advent of steam-powered warships need not be countered by the construction of the large works then in development, as his method had made such techniques obsolete. Dundonald made absolutely no bones about the identity of the 'enemy' that he foresaw being the recipient of his Secret War Plan: France, or rather the navy of France, was the target. The period in question was one of naval rivalry between that country and Britain, and was also a time of much technological change, both in general terms and in the area of naval warfare; steam power and shell-firing rifled ordnance were the premier items in the latter category. The development of the explosive shell, and, perhaps more significantly, the ability to deliver it accurately at long range through the use of rifled artillery, spelt death to wooden ships. It was a case of materials and techniques offensive in nature having outstripped their defensive opposites, and the balance in the matter was only to be restored by constructing vessels of non-penetrable and non-combustible material: armoured iron, and later steel, warships. These of course lay a little in the future, though much experimentation with cladding wooden walls with iron was undertaken. The clear implication was that a nation with a large wooden navy, such as Britain, was, potentially at least, in possession of merely so much firewood if faced with an enemy who could incinerate that navy. France had equipped many of its batteries and fortifications with rifled shell-firing artillery and was therefore in a position to neutralise, at least in coastal waters, any attacking or blockading fleet that came into range. It was believed to be equipping its fleet with such weaponry, which would make it a formidable instrument in any attack on a harbour or port containing wooden ships – hence Dundonald's preoccupation with the threat. To be precise, it was only a potential threat as Britain and France were at peace. As his son and co-biographer rather succinctly put it: 'the fact that England was at peace [was] a sufficient reason for not discussing the value of a new instrument of war'.[9] He did however make the percipient observation that 'Lord Dundonald, however [. . .] thought otherwise.'[10]

Lord Dundonald did indeed think otherwise; his *Times* letter continued:

I am desirous of showing that the use of steam-ships of war, though at present available by rival nations [. . .] need not necessarily endanger our national existence, which appears to be apprehended by those who allege the necessity of devoting millions of money to the defence of our coasts. I contend that there is nothing in the expected new system of naval warfare, through the employment of steam-vessels, that can justify such expensive and derogatory precautions, because there are equally new, and yet secret, means of conquest, which no devices hitherto used in maritime warfare could resist or evade.

[. . .] with this all powerful auxiliary invasion may be rendered impossible [. . .] by the speedy and effectual destruction of all assemblages of steam-ships, and, if necessary, of all the navies of the whole world [. . .] Away with the projected plans of 'protective forts and ports' [. . .] ports on the margin of the Channel cannot be better protected than those which exist, respecting which I pledge any professional credit I may possess, that whatever hostile forces might therein be assembled could be destroyed within the first twenty-four hours favourable for effective operations, in defiance of forts and batteries, mounted with the most powerful ordnance now in use.

Protective harbours [. . .] may be likened to nets, wherein fishes seeking to escape, find themselves inextricably entangled [. . .] No effective protection could be afforded in such ports against a superior naval force equipped for purposes of destruction [. . .] The hasty adoption of such measures, and the voting of the vast sums required to carry them into execution, are evils seriously to be deprecated. It is therefore greatly to be desired that those in power should pause before proceeding further in such a course. It behoves them to consider [. . .] the overwhelming influence of the secret plan which I placed in their hands, similar to that which I presented in 1812 [. . .] to the Prince Regent.[11]

The conclusion of this missive contained a scarcely veiled threat that he would, unless his methods were given serious consideration by the government, and unless that government reversed its policy on maritime defence, reveal all:

> Thirty-three years is a long time to retain an important secret, especially as I could have used it with effect in defence of my character when cruelly assailed [. . .] and could have practically employed it on various occasions to my private advantage. I have now, however, determined to solicit its well merited consideration, in the hope, privately, if possible, to prove the comparative inexpedience of an expenditure [. . .] for the construction of forts and harbours, instead of applying ample funds at once to remodel and renovate the navy [. . .]
>
> However injudicious it might be thought to divulge my plan [. . .] if its disclosure is indispensable to enable a just and general estimate to be formed of the mongrel terraqueous scheme of defence now in contemplation, as compared with the mighty power and protective ubiquity of the floating bulwarks of Britain, I am satisfied that the balance would be greatly in favour of publicity.[12]

Again one wonders at the effectiveness of such tactics: was abusing (virtually) and threatening the political and ruling elite of the nation the most likely method of gaining their support, and getting them to change government policy? Not on this occasion at least, it seems, for the threat, and surely it can only be judged as such, was revealed as hollow when it was not made good.

With the remarkable persistence that was an enduring, if not always endearing to those in authority, feature of his character Cochrane again, on 3 August 1846, managed to get the matter raised in Parliament. As the *House of Lords Journal* records:

> Upon reading the petition of Thomas Earl of Dundonald, Vice Admiral of the Blue; praying, 'That their Lordships will be pleased to adopt Measures for securing to the Petitioner an Investigation of the Merits of his Plan for speedily and effectually dismantling or destroying Forts and Fleets' It is ordered that the said petition do lie on the Table.[13]

This time, however, the petition was taken off the table, the interest of the government was engaged, and an investigation was undertaken. Cochrane's first biographers attributed this to the fact that 'his friend' Lord Auckland was now the political head of the Admiralty as First Lord, and exerted some influence.[14] In truth we simply do not know, but what can be ascertained is that, for whatever reason, on 10 September 1846, Lord Dundonald presented the latest version of his Secret War Plan to the Admiralty:

> I have the <u>honour</u> to enclose a brief, but I hope sufficient explanation of my War Plans; which, if they are worth the paper on which they are written, I am satisfied are worth an hundred millions sterling to the country.
>
> I have only to add that I am ready, if required, to afford any explanation, either generally, or in detail to whomsoever their Lordships shall be pleased confidentially to refer their consideration.[15]

The Plan, now in two parts, was under autograph inscription, with the words that were later taken, with justification, as exemplifying Dundonald's philosophy:[16]

> To the Imperial mind one sentence will suffice: All fortifications, especially marine fortifications, can under cover of dense smoke be irresistibly subdued by fumes of sulphur kindled in masses to windward of their ramparts.[17]

Secret Plan Number 1, 'For ensuring at one blow the maritime superiority of England',[18] contained details concerning the use of smoke screens, and exemplified the dangers that were apprehended by the adoption of the latest ordnance by the French:

> The new ordnance for projecting horizontal shells, for the defence of ports or naval equipment, is described by the Committee of scientific and practical men, appointed by the French Government to ascertain its effect, to be so formidable, that it 'would render impossible the success of any enterprise attempted against their vessels in harbour, by a squadron whatever might be its force.'
>
> There is no doubt but that the opinion so expressed of the power of the new ordnance, as a means of defence, against every mode of attack hitherto practiced is correct – for the damage to which an attacking force would be exposed, from such method of resistance, would be greater in proportion to the number and size of the attacking vessels; and, consequently, in the event of war the fleets and squadrons of France might ride in security in their Ports and Harbours, in defiance of any attack that could be made by <u>combustible</u> ships: but, the like missiles, being proposed to be used in their steam vessels and gunboats, would also prevent their ports from being blockaded.
>
> As the introduction of so formidable a mode of attack or defence, by such a power as France, might prove injurious (perhaps destructive) to the

interests and preponderance of England, I am desirous again, most respectfully, to offer my Secret Plans, to counteract these evils, to the deliberate
consideration of government.

It is obvious that the 'marvellous and infallible' effect anticipated from the
use of mortar cannon, projecting horizontal shells, carcasses, or hollow red
hot shot, as a defence for Roadsteads and Anchorages, must depend on the
attacking force being visible from the Batteries and Fortifications, whence
the resistance is to proceed – in a dense fog, such cannon and missiles could
be of no utility, and, of very little use in a dark night; but, naval operations,
on a great scale, cannot be safely conducted under such circumstances. If
however the enemy can be involved in obscurity, whilst the attacking force
acts in broad daylight, operations may be conducted with as much security as
if such mortar batteries did not in reality exist.

Coal, soaked with refuse gas tar, embarked in old and useless vessels, being
kindled to windward of such fortifications, will produce dense clouds of
smoke, impervious to sight, during a period sufficient for the achievement of
any ordinary enterprise – but if embarked in iron vessels it will burn for a
week. Thus, not only an attacking force might be concealed from the
Batteries on shore, but half, or any portion of an enemy's fleet at anchor,
might be prevented from seeing, or giving aid to the portion attacked.

If any doubt shall exist as to the dense obscurity to be thus produced,
nothing can be more easy than to test the fact, even without divulging the
secret – for a government coal vessel might be kindled, as if by accident to
windward of the batteries protecting Spithead, the Downs, Sheerness, or to
windward of any other fort or battery, and the inefficiency even of the
vaunted mortar cannon, for the protection of Roadsteads and Harbours,
would be fully demonstrated.

Under the shield of such obscurity, there is no port used by the Naval
Force of France, that might not be thus invaded, and its shipping destroyed.
Had this plan occurred to the gallant Nelson, the Pile and other batteries of
Boulogne, would have been rendered harmless; whilst, by bombardment, he
assailed (on a known bearing) the flotilla and town in despite of Napoleon
and the Grand Army. A single smoke vessel would have rendered the 150
cannon, placed in one night by Sebastiane on the point of the Seraglio, ineffectual as a protection to Constantinople.

Under the guidance of discretion, I know of no case of Naval enterprise, in
which the judicious use of smoke vessels might not be rendered highly bene-
ficial. There is no doubt but that a steady favourable breeze will occur, at
some period, during war. The foreknowledge of weather, acquired by
seamen, is nearly as correct as a barometer.[19]

Plan Number 2 contained, after a brief outline of how Dundonald had arrived at his conclusions regarding the use of sulphur, an overview of how poisonous fumes might be applied to overcoming specific targets. If the obscuring properties of smoke were a feature not expounded in the 1811 version of his methods, and if the Temporary Mortars had vanished for the moment, then the Stink Ships had moved to become the very core of the Plan. He claimed vast potential for them:

> New York, Brest, Toulon, Rochefort, Cherbourg, Algiers, Flushing, and Cadiz could impose no effectual resistance. [Admiral] Sir Alexander Cochrane assured me that Lord Exmouth, who was one of the original committee appointed by the Prince Regent to report on my Plans, informed him, that if he had been at liberty to have used them, not a single shot could have been fired at his fleet from the ramparts or mole of Algiers.
>
> These Secret Plans would enable the American Squadron easily to seize on San Juan de Ulloa, the Gibraltar of Mexico, and so at once place their Army, artillery, stores, and baggage on the high road to the Capital.
>
> It is scarcely necessary to observe that the garrisons of Blockhouses, Martello towers, or such like strongholds, may be expelled, and lines, like those of Paris, may be broken through between the redoubts.
>
> I shall be most happy if called on to explain any doubtful point or to shew in detail the application of these plans of attack to places deemed impregnable.[20]

The receipt of these documents was followed, two days later, by a request from one of Auckland's colleagues, the Marquis of Anglesey, that Captain Sir Thomas Hastings, Storekeeper of the Ordnance, form a committee to investigate the Dundonald Plans.

> I am commanded by my Lords Commissioners of the Admiralty to request you will, in conjunction with Lt. General Sir John Burgoyne, select an artillery officer to join you, the Master General of the Ordnance having given his sanction to your being so employed, and having so done, that you will enter into an enquiry as prayed by the Earl of Dundonald, in his petition to the House of Lords of the 3rd of August last, into the merits of his plan, for speedily and effectually dismantling and destroying forts and fleets, and you are further requested to enter into this enquiry in such manner as may fully put to the test the merits of the said plan, and so as to provide that the secret of the Earl of Dundonald shall not be divulged.[21]

The minutes of the deliberations of the committee, consisting of Hastings, Burgoyne, and Lt-Col. J.S. Colquhoun, have not yet been discovered, but the direction of their investigations can be ascertained by scrutinising the available correspondence. On 26 November, Dundonald, in an obvious reply to a document containing a succession of queries, addressed to them an enumerated series of points, simply entitled 'Answers'/ Many of these merely reiterated, and where necessary illuminated, the points that had already been put forward. For example, point number 4:

> The sulphur vessels would be screened from view by smoke vessels, which ought to be kindled when the enemy's shot becomes inconvenient – thus under the shield of obscurity, they may approach to any distance which the nature of the beach, or the state of the weather, will permit – of course, the nearer the more concentrated will be the vapour, but I hold that no animal could sustain, for five minutes, the effect of two hundred tons of charcoal or coke, and fifty tons of sulphur, at a mile, or even double that distance, to leeward.

Further answers were in response, it may be inferred, to queries concerning his practical knowledge of the properties of the fumes he proposed generating:

> The vapour from the kilns of Girgentum, certainly rolled down the mountain like waves, the fumes however are not <u>so ponderous</u> that the impelling force of the atmosphere, in motion, will not drive it up the side of the hill, or over any impediment which wind will surmount; no doubt it would lap over the summit of the Rock of Gibraltar with a westerly breeze, leaving neither a living rat nor monkey in its course.
> The dispersion, horizontally, of the fumes of sulphur, may be inferred from that which is manifested by smoke. It will follow the same course, and will undoubtedly go as fast as the wind. As to the period during which their effect would remain in operation, it would be (in old wooden vessels until they were consumed) in iron vessels, until the coal and sulphur were exhausted – perhaps a week.[22]

As stated, perusal of these answers readily indicates the nature of the queries that gave rise to them. It is evident that, as had been the case previously, Lord Dundonald harboured no doubts as to the efficacy of his methods, or if he did then this was not at all reflected in his written submissions. Considering he had never actually carried out any practical experiments, and had extrapolated all his claims from the phenomenon he had observed in Sicily in 1811, this seems somewhat presumptuous. However, it could also be argued that his categorical mode of thought was, in the circumstances, permissible; he was making a case for his methods and it was the committee's function to pronounce on their likely effectiveness, after experimentation if they saw fit. No doubt owing to the fact that the committee members had no specialised knowledge themselves, they sought advice on the physiological effects of sulphur dioxide, and this was obtained from a manufacturer of sulphur products. Again, only the reply to the query has been unearthed (the signature of the author is, alas, illegible) but as with the 'answers' referred to above, the nature of that request can be discerned from the reply dated 12 December 1846. This was addressed personally to Hastings:

> It is quite certain that no animal could exist in the vapour produced by the combustion of sulphur – [which is] sulphurous acid gas, which is always formed when sulphur, at a temperature of 560° – and upwards, combines with dry atmospheric air. I am therefore of opinion that the danger to animal life by the combustion of [masses of] sulphur in the open air, would be in direct proportion to the distance from its influence.
>
> The specific gravity of sulphurous acid gas being greater than that of atmospheric air, it has a constant tendency to displace the latter, and therefore every place in its neighbourhood becomes dangerous more or less in proportion as these places are confined or not.
>
> In the process of obtaining the Flowers of Sulphur by distillation (carried on here daily) if the small plug hole in the boiler is left open, the escape of this vapour would render it impossible to exist in the place for any length of time, particularly if the doors and windows were closed I have questioned the foreman, who states, that but for the means of constantly maintaining fresh air, it would prove prejudicial to his health, though at times when he has been obliged to expose himself to the influence of the gas in even a very diluted state, he has suffered considerably from its effects. If the vapour produced by ignited sulphur is allowed to pass too quickly into any room, an explosion will take place, and its effects will be in proportion to its line of least resistance.
>
> I have written this rather in a hurry but I think you will find it embraces both the open air and closed places.
>
> If there is any explanation [required?] of what I have written, or any question arising out of it, I shall feel great pleasure in doing any tests to afford every information in my power – and I shall have equal pleasure in carrying out any experiments you may like to entrust to me, with the means I have at this establishment.[23]

There was a further paper from Dundonald to the Committee on 1 January 1847, again provided at the request of that committee. This paper, detailing an attack on the French port of Cherbourg, is important in forming an understanding of the tactical plan Lord Dundonald had evolved for utilising his inventions in practice at a particular place:

> In conformity with the desire of the commission to arrive at a complete and

distinct view of the mode of executing the 'secret war plans', together with the measures I would adopt, were I commander in chief of the Channel Fleet, in the event of war, and threatened invasion of this Kingdom from the port of Cherbourg.

I would recommend to the Government, and to the Admiralty, that no preparation which could attract public attention to these plans, should be made in our ports. Old and useless small vessels however might be collected at Portsmouth, and converted to coal and coke depots for the supply of steam ships on service.

Of course the enemy, in order to unite their ships of war and transports, whether steam or sailing ships, must run them from various ports to the general rendezvous.

To this operation I would make such resistance only as would induce a belief that it was deemed important to prevent their junction; but I would give positive orders that NO British chasing steam ships should be exposed to the fire of coast batteries – which would be considered by the enemy, and promulgated through their journals, as arising from a dread of the 'marvellous effects' of their new artillery, which they believe 'renders impossible the success of any enterprise (within their range) whatever might be the attacking force.'

I would, as commander in chief, apply for one fourth more blockading power than that suffered to be collected at Cherbourg, which, with the exception of the necessary look out vessels, I would keep together, in the inactivity of former blockades – having transports bring necessaries, [and etc.], so as to familiarise the enemy to such ordinary intercourse. The English newspapers would publish articles from their correspondents, clamouring for a young admiral – to adopt energetic measures – which would confirm the enemy in their security.

It matters not how many sailing ships and steam vessels may be collected in Cherbourg; let good information be obtained, when the fifty thousand, or any other number of troops are prepared to embark, or are actually onboard – then the time will have arrived to execute the smoke and sulphur plans on the first favourable steady breeze. To ensure which, patience, only, is necessary – for, vessels having troops onboard will never dare to put to sea, in presence of a superior hostile force.[24]

Cherbourg, a naval station, fortified town, and seaport, is situated at the mouth of the Divette River, and is located in the extreme west of Normandy, between the Cap de la Hague and The Pointe de Barfleur, on the north shore of the Cotentin peninsula. Its major drawback as a harbour was the lack of any natural shelter to the north, thus rendering it exposed to the prevalent severe weather conditions. It

6 'View of a Cone constructed in the year 1785 being conducted to its place in the Road of Cherbourg in order to be sunk'
In 1776 work began on modernising and enlarging the port of Cherbourg, masterminded by Captain de la Bretonnière. To protect the port a series of enormous cones in two lines, the 1st and 2nd *Digue*, were constructed of wood filled with stones, and sunk to form a break water between the west end of St Anne's Bay and Pelee Island. Intended to serve as fortifications as well as sea defences, the project was doomed to failure as the cones swiftly began to disintegrate after their emplacement. By 1789 it had become obvious that they were not working, and the decision was taken to construct a masonry breakwater.
Graphic from a 1794 engraving by Thomas Pratten in the National Maritime Museum

was in an attempt to counter this problem that Louis XIV first conceived of constructing a breakwater in 1750. In 1783, civil engineer Alexandre De Cessart, hit upon the idea of creating such a device out of ninety truncated cone-shaped timber structures, approximately 45.5 m diameter at the base and 19.5 m diameter at the top with a height of 19.5 m. It was proposed that each cone would be filled, after being sunk in place, with loose stone and then capped with a 2 m thick layer of concrete, but in a cost-cutting measure, the concrete cap was only completed for the first two cones. By 1789 approximately 4,000 m of breakwater had been completed but with only 18 cones, which were between 59 m and 390 m apart. This arrangement was unsuccessful and the cones themselves were unable to withstand the effects of weather. By 1788 the concept was abandoned and attempts made to fill the gaps with stone; between 1788 and 1790 over 2,665,400 m^3 of stone were used. Work was halted during the Revolution and did not resume until 1802, when the design was changed to employ a masonry parapet,

7 Cherbourg

Cherbourg, a naval station, fortified town, and seaport, is situated at the mouth of the Divette River, and is located in the extreme west of Normandy, between the Cap de la Hague and the Pointe de Barfleur, on the north shore of the Cotentin peninsula. This sketch-map shows the principal defences and the detached breakwater.
Graphic from an 1863 map in the author's collection

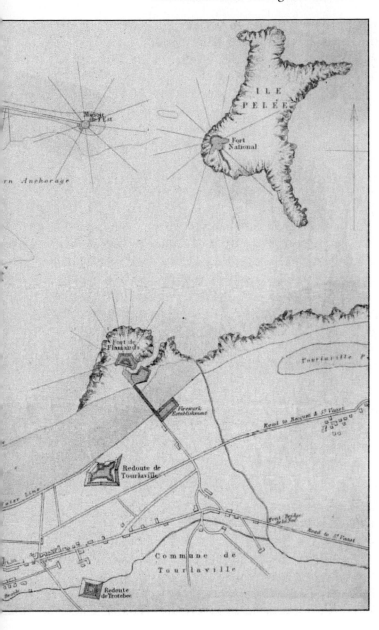

a road along the crest of the breakwater, which was detached from land at either end. This design was not completed until 1853, and the conclusion of the project was not celebrated until 1858 when Emperor Napoleon III visited the site.[25]

The 'Cones of Cherbourg' are mentioned by Dundonald in Appendix B of his 1811 'Memorial', and their ineffectuality as fortifications must not have been obvious to outsiders, as otherwise he would not have thought them worthy of attack. By 1847 the breakwater was nearly complete, though the state of readiness with respects to the fortifications is unknown, and, potentially at least, constituted a formidable obstacle to an attack from the sea.

The preliminaries having been disposed of, as it were, Dundonald then moved on to describe in detail his 'Mode of Attack'.

The wind being, as suggested by the commission, in the most favourable point, or North West, – though it might be at any point from WNW to ENE – I would, when the time arrived, make the signal for all commanding officers to open and peruse their secret sealed instructions – which would contain a general outline of the intended proceedings – each, such officer to denote, subsequently, that he had complied with the order and understood their purport – of course for particular or separate service, its nature, extent, and mode of performance would be indicated.

{Tar would be contained in barrels onboard the coal vessels, and sulphur in barrels or cases onboard the coke vessels (the nature of the latter article being concealed and unknown) yet, both, or either might be poured out, or scattered at a moments notice}

All being ready, I would display the preparations to execute instructions, and the signal for the three smoke vessels – laden with coals soaked with tar, and the three sulphur vessels – <u>each</u> charged with as much coke as they could contain, and with fifty tons of sulphur – to proceed, as instructed, to within long range, directly to windward of the forts of Querqueville, the Fort Central, and the Fort Royal on the Isle Pelee, attended by the boats, and an adequate escort.

The preliminary smoke vessels, having arrived at long range, as before mentioned, should <u>there</u> be kindled – in the lower part of the combustible materials – in order to evolve, and send before them, that dense obscurity, which would render an approach to the most formidable batteries subject to little risk, either to the tugs or to the smoke vessels in tow. A bow and quarter hawser, with the helm of an abandoned vessel wedged to port or starboard, are well known means to keep the vessel towed on a broad angle. The sulphur vessels, <u>still unkindled</u>, and their protecting escorts, would be equally secure, involved in clouds of vapour, as regards the vision of the enemy.

I would direct that, in the obscurity of the smoke, to windward, two or three [cannoches] well charged with gun powder, should be exploded, in order, by the dread of such explosions, to deter the enemy from attempting to tow off the smoke and sulphur vessels, either when proceeding to, or when anchored at[,] their stations.

Beside the three specified services before mentioned, I would place a vessel, which might have smoke and sulphur combined, near to the eastern end of the breakwater, in order that the fumes and smoke, extending across the passage between the Isle Pelee, might prevent any successful attempt to escape by the eastern channel.

Almost simultaneously, or soon after these preliminary arrangements were on the point of being fully executed, I would make the signal that six of the smoke and sulphur vessels – indicated by their instructions – should approach the western or great entrance to the roads of Cherbourg, each attended by a tug – and I would accompany this division by all the force I deemed necessary to overcome whatever resistance could (under the circumstances of the three outer forts being effectually marked, and two of them probably in our possession[26]) be presented by the enemy vessels; the whole of which I would expect to drive (from their haste to avoid instant peril) on the banks and shoals between the 'Roches des Flamands' and the Isle Pelee. There they might be destroyed, but I would prefer, for appearance sake, deliberately to heave them all off, and bring them to England. To enable this additional service to be executed quickly, and with facility, the attack should be <u>after</u> high water – and the reserved smoke and sulphur vessels should be held in readiness near to the scene of action, to protect or obscure such operations from view.

With the wind at NW, proceedings would differ in no degree, were smoke vessels alone to be employed – but the chance of complete success would thereby be diminished, and a probable loss of lives and vessels might be the result – which I am sure ought not to be incurred in a contest where explosive and incendiary projectiles are used against shipping.

Should the attack be made with the wind to the eastward of north, the chief difference would be that the smoke and sulphur vessels, destined to dislodge the enemy would enter at the eastern instead of the western passage – and the latter, instead of the former, would be blocked up by a <u>stream</u> of sublimated sulphur, blown across the passage.

It does not appear that the success of this enterprise could in any degree be affected by the number of troops, whether onshore or onboard. I would prefer the latter, by reason of the confusion they would occasion, especially when the fumes of sulphur reached them.

Regarding the extent to which such fumes would reach, it is probable that no man in Britain, except myself, ever witnessed the sublimation of fifty ounces, whereby he could guess, even in the remotest degree, at the effect to be produced by fifty tons. I repeat my conviction, that, with a gentle westerly breeze, a dozen of such vessels would annihilate every living thing on the Rock of Gibraltar – even were they kindled a league from the works;[27] but at a place like Cherbourg, such vessels might be placed close to the chief defences of the port. It is therefore submitted, that such harbours as that of Cherbourg can afford no efficient protection to shipping against a competent attack – consequently the vast sums proposed to be expended on ports <u>for refuge in wars</u> (save as places of retreat in storms) may be more usefully employed. The new mole of Algiers, now constructed as a place of naval security, is even more exposed than the extended anchorage, and scattered forts of Cherbourg.

I feel assured that I have overstated the means actually necessary to destroy all the vessels which the roads of Cherbourg could contain – nevertheless, the importance of the object to be achieved, would warrant the number of smoke vessels being doubled on all the points enumerated, and the placing of two more on the northern lines extending westward from 'Fort Momet' – as well as that, all these vessels, instead of being old and useless craft, should be iron transports. Even admitting such additional expense to be incurred, the whole cost would not exceed two per cent of the value of the vessels thereby captured or destroyed. I deem this kind of enterprise far less liable to contingencies than ordinary operations.

Although I have thus given to the commission a <u>rude</u> mode of performing the service, in order, in the first instance, to ensure extensive success, yet it is obvious that iron smoke and sulphur vessels may be <u>permanently</u> fitted, with cavities surrounded by water, which would enable a repetition of their respective duties; in like manner as is performed by bombs and other vessels. That however is unworthy of consideration, compared to effecting the <u>first</u> blow in secrecy.

As my attention has been directed solely to the application of such means to <u>naval</u> purposes, with which I am acquainted, I wholly withdraw any collateral observations I may have made regarding their probable effect in military operations[28] leaving the consideration thereof to officers who are better acquainted with such subjects. I however [verily, really] believe that a knowledge of my plans would enable even the Moors of Algeria, by bundles of straw or brushwood dipped in sulphur, to take and destroy every blockhouse or barrack established in the interior of their country by its invaders.

It is obvious however that the secret plans are more applicable to naval purposes, at least in the ratio of ships loads to cart loads of materials; even smoke alone would enable ships,[29] presenting the most formidable batteries, to approach maritime fortifications (the depth of water permitting) within range of grape shot, uninjured; which thus would prove decisive of the fate of all dependent on their protection.[30]

This document clearly reveals the detailed tactical plan formulated by Lord Dundonald for use at an actual location. Again it will be noticed that as far as the author was concerned there were absolutely no doubts relating to the efficacy of the scheme. Neither did the report that the committee submitted to the Marquis of Anglesey on 16 January. This report recommended that the smoke-screen aspect of the plans be investigated, but it did not embrace the sulphur; for reasons of humanity rather than practicability:

> In conformity with your Lordship's instructions, we the undersigned have met to consider and report on the Secret War Plans of Vice Admiral the Lord of Dundonald, transmitted to us, by the First Lord of the Admiralty, the Earl of Auckland.
>
> These plans may be classed under three heads, 1st, one on which an opinion may be formed without experiment, for concealing or masking offensive warlike operations, and we consider that, under many particular circumstances, this method of his Lordship might be made available, as well by land as by sea, and we therefore suggest that a record of this part of Lord Dundonald's plans should be deposited with the Admiralty, to be made use of, whenever, in the judgement of their Lordships, the opportunity for employment may occur.
>
> 2nd, One on which experiment would be required before a satisfactory conclusion could be arrived at.
>
> 3rd No 1 and 2 combined for the purpose of hostile operations.
>
> After mature consideration we have resolved, that it is not desirable, that any experiments should be made.
>
> We assume it to be possible that the plan No 2 contains power for producing the sweeping destruction the inventor ascribes to it, but it is clear, this power could not be retained, exclusively, by this country, because its first employment would develop both its principle and application; this last observation applies equally to plan No 1.
>
> We considered in the next place, how far the adoption of the proposed secret plans, would accord with the feelings and principles of civilised warfare, we are unanimously of the opinion that plans numbers 2 and 3 would not do so.
>
> We therefore recommend that as hitherto, plans No 2 and 3 should remain concealed.
>
> We feel that great credit is due to Lord Dundonald for the right feeling, which prompted him, not to disclose his secret plans, when serving in war, as

Naval Commanders in Chief of the forces of other nations, under many trying circumstances, in the conviction, that these plans, might eventually be of the highest importance to his own country. We have only to add, that we have sealed up, under one cover, all the papers, which have been submitted to our consideration, by the First Lord of the Admiralty and the Earl of Dundonald, and our correspondence with the latter, in another, which we have marked secret.

With regard to the disposal and future custody of all these papers, we await instructions from your Lordship, or the Earl of Auckland, to whom we propose this letter should, after your Lordship has [listed?] it, be transmitted.[31]

Auckland informed Dundonald of the committee's findings in a letter of 22 January that was virtually a duplicate of the report he had received, though it did, apparently for the first time, inform Dundonald who the members of the committee were:

Major General Sir John Burgoyne RE Lieut Col Colquhoun RA and Captain Sir Thomas Hastings, the officers to whom, at my request, the secret war Plans, as invented by you, were referred by the Master General of the Ordnance, have concluded their enquiry and delivered their report.[32]

Dundonald's response, given the tone of his letter to *The Times*, was, initially at least, curiously muted. Writing to Auckland on 27 January, he asked to be permitted to express his 'deep sense of obligation to your Lordship in causing my Plans of War to be thoroughly investigated by the most competent authorities'.[33] He continued, however, in a vein that reflected his bitterness at what he perceived had been the way 'authority' had treated him, and even harked back to the Stock Exchange Trial of several decades before:

While I am highly satisfied by your Lordships approbation of my conduct, in so long possessing important secrets for which, had my purposes been selfish, I might long ago have derived great advancement, I trust that I may be permitted to draw your [...] attention to the consideration, [of] how far it is possible that a person capable of such self denial, should have degraded himself by the commission of a contemptible fraud for a trifling advantage – of which I have been accused, and under the stigma of which I am still suffering. Surely my innocence of that disgraceful transaction is much more probable than that which is now proved to be a fact, that prior to its perpetration I had discovered the adaption of an Agent (I may say Agents) so incomparably more powerful than gun-powder, that no fortification theretofore useful as a protection to shipping, could resist its attack.[34]

Comparison of this statement with the view as evinced by Seaman Thomas Branton quoted earlier gives an excellent insight into the dichotomy of views that prevailed about Dundonald. As a leader of men he probably had few peers; as a subordinate he was dreadful. Given his tenacious character and continuing sense of injustice it comes as little surprise to note that he did not long accept the decision of the 'competent authorities' referred to; the following year, on 18 April 1848, the issue was again before the House of Lords:

Upon reading the Petition of *Thomas* Earl of *Dundonald;* setting forth, 'That in the Year 1811, long before it was dreamt of adopting stationary Means of Defence for the Safety of these Kingdoms, the Petitioner presented secret Plans for the Conduct of offensive Operations, which were referred by His then Royal Highness The Prince Regent to a scientific and professional Committee, by whom the said Plans were declared to be practicable, and, under the Circumstances of the Memorial of the Petitioner, irresistible: That the Petitioner again, in 1847, submitted his said Plans to a similar official Secret Commission, by whom, after Six Months Deliberation, the First Plan was reported to be applicable on shore and afloat, but the Second and Third Plans, being Means of 'Sweeping Destruction,' were deemed 'not to accord with the Principles and Feelings of civilized Warfare:' That the Petitioner respectfully submits to this House that such Objection can apply only to the Adoption of his Plans in opposition to Enemies by whom clod Shot is exclusively used, and not as opposed to Forts, Batteries, or Vessels throwing horizontal Shells, Carcasses, or other Missiles, to blow up, burn or exterminate the Crews of our Ships of War, which Devices, though differing in Degree of destructive Power, are equally inconsistent with the Principles of Civilization: That the Petitioner believes that the Expenditure of Hundreds of Millions of Sterling in War could be avoided by the Adoption of his said Plans, whereby hostile Fleets and Armaments can speedily and effectually be destroyed, and aggressive States for ever afterwards precluded from possessing the Means of Maritime Invasion: That the Petitioner (judging from a recent Occurrence, feels assured that these Facts, so important to the Interests of the Country, are to this Day discredited by high Authorities,) most respectfully offers his said Plans to the Judgement of such Committee or Commission as their Lordships shall, in their Wisdom and Prudence, appoint to investigate the aforesaid Question of Defence; humbly stipulating, that if the Decision of the said Committee or Commission shall prove adverse to the Opinion long entertained and deliberately given by the Petitioner, he may, without Reproach, publicly explain the Grounds of his firm Belief that the Execution of his Plans would also spare the unavailing Cost of contemplated Forts and Ports of Refuge, prevent future Wars, and promote

Civilization: That it appears to the Petitioner that these Facts can be ascertained by Examination of his Plans, deposited, under Seal, at the Admiralty;' and therefore praying their Lordships, 'That they will vouchsafe (before sanctioning any Substitute for Naval Protection) to cause an Examination of the said Documents, demonstrative that our Country can be in no Peril from any aggregate Force collected for Invasion, provided that the Plans of Defence to which the Petitioner hath alluded shall not be erroneously pre-judged, or injuriously set aside, from mistaken Principles or Feelings, when the Stability of the Throne and the Independence of our Country shall be in danger.'

Perhaps predictably, and despite the elaboration that differentiated this approach from the previous efforts, the result was nevertheless similar: 'It is *Ordered,* That the said Petition do lie on the Table.'[35] Lord Dundonald's Secret War Plans were indeed to lie unheeded for the next six years; perhaps the fact that 'England was at peace' was indeed a sufficient reason for not investigating or developing 'a new instrument of war'.

However, if such was indeed the case then the state of war that Britain found itself in on 28 March 1854 effectively negated this reason. The enemy on this occasion was of course Russia, and one of the allies that Britain fought in concert with was France, the 'enemy' against which Dundonald had conceived, and consistently pressed, his Plan. Though there is no evidence that he suffered from the same type of mental ossification as Lord Raglan, C-in-C of the British forces in the Crimean peninsula, who is reported as having habitually referred to the Russian opposition as 'the French', he nevertheless appeared to have harboured, if not necessarily a degree of animus then surely, something approaching dislike towards that country and its inhabitants. This can be adduced from the tone of one of his comments to the Hastings Committee:

> When a boy, I have used sulphur to [destroy] wasps and hornets [. . .] and, deeming the French forces, at least, in Algiers, of the like description [. . .] I consider it would produce the same effect.[36]

These, no doubt long-held, sentiments by no means prevented him from recasting and refocusing his methods so that their recipient was the new enemy, for in any event the problems he had identified as requiring his methodology to overcome were more or less universal and by no means confined to the coasts of France or that of French territory. Thus it was that once again Lord Dundonald set about proposing the usage of his Secret War Plan, utterly convinced, as he was, that in his methods Britain possessed an irresistible weapon with which to smite her enemies whomsoever they might be.

4

Laying Wood before Walls

I took the liberty of observing that the business of laying wood before walls
was much altered of late, and that even if they had no hot shot, which I
believe they had, that the quantity of powder and shot which would be fired
away on such an attack could be much better directed from a battery on
shore.

Horatio Nelson to Lord Hood, 29 July 1794

ON 28 March 1854 Britain declared war on Russia. The resulting conflict
became known as the Crimean War from the location of its main theatre of
operations, and was the only occasion between 1815 and 1914 when British forces
engaged with those of another European state. The causes of this conflict, waged
by an *ad hoc* alliance of Britain, France, Turkey, and Piedmont-Sardinia on the one
hand, and Russia on the other, need not detain us here; suffice to say that as
regards French involvement, the compilers of the Fourteenth Edition of the
Encyclopaedia Britannica placed the responsibility at the feet of the newly crowned
Emperor Napoleon III. According to them, he was:

> Too good a son of the Catholic Church to acquiesce in the Russian claims to
> special treatment for Orthodox Christianity in the Ottoman Empire; too
> much a Bonaparte not to wish to revenge 1812 and the occupation of Paris;
> and too uncertain of his new throne not to welcome a successful war, that
> first and last thought of an insecure dynasty.[1]

The Crimean peninsula only became the main theatre by default. Russia had
invaded Turkish territory and the other powers despatched naval and military
forces in support. These initially landed at Varna, on the western shore of the Black
Sea, upon which the Russians withdraw, thus leaving the Allies searching for
somewhere to bring their power to bear. Eventually it was decided to attack the
port of Sevastopol.

In popular memory the resulting war is probably epitomised by the activities of
the Lady with the Lamp and the Light Brigade. To the student of matters naval it is
not generally considered, apart from the armoured floating batteries sometimes
deemed to have been the first armoured ships, to have offered much in the way of

pointers to the future. Likewise, only in the demonstration of the potential of extempore earthworks can the military scholar usually discern any portents. However, had the 10th Earl of Dundonald had his way, and utilised the methodology inherent in his Secret War Plan, the course of the conflict might have been very different indeed.

The political head of the navy, First Sea Lord Sir James Graham, became the latest British politician to encounter Lord Dundonald and his Secret War Plans; their author wrote to him on 22 July 1854 in respect of the ongoing naval operations in the Baltic where it had been ascertained that operations might be conducted profitably. To that end a fleet under Vice-Admiral Sir Charles Napier had been despatched. Dundonald had been considered for the command of this fleet, but, in a backhanded tribute to his abilities, Sir James Graham had vetoed the appointment. His letter of 9 February 1854 to Queen Victoria put it thus:

> Lord Dundonald is seventy nine years of age; and though his energies and faculties are unbroken, and though, with his accustomed courage, he volunteers for the service, yet, on the whole, there is reason to apprehend that he might deeply commit the force under his command in some desperate enterprise, where the chance of success would not countervail the risk of failure and of the fatal consequences, which might ensue. Age has not abated the adventurous spirit of this gallant officer, which no authority could restrain; and being uncontrollable it might lead to most unfortunate results. The Cabinet, on the most careful review of the entire question, decided that the appointment of Lord Dundonald was not expedient.[2]

Russian naval strength in the region consisted of some twenty-seven ships of the line and a host of smaller vessels, a fleet superior to the force commanded by Napier who could initially muster only six ships of the line, an equal number of steam frigates and several other vessels. Moreover, the British fleet was undermanned with crews largely untrained. The Admiralty ordered Napier to prevent the Russian fleet from leaving the Gulf of Finland and to report on the possibilities of offensive action against the enemy bases. The Russian defences in the region were based on four strong points: Kronstadt, Sveaborg, Revel, and Bomarsund. The supreme prize was the Russian Baltic fleet, which had withdrawn to the naval fortress of Kronstadt. Situated on the island of Kotlin, guarding the approaches to St Petersburg, the Russian capital, it was a position of immense strength. Napier studied the island and attendant fortifications for several days before despatching a signal to the Admiralty, to the effect that the position was impregnable with the forces at his disposal; accordingly the Allied fleet left the waters around Kronstadt on 4 July 1854 without a shot being fired.

Disappointing as this news may have been to an expectant British public, it was undoubtedly the correct decision for Napier to make. The technology of naval

8 The Baltic Theatre: 1854–55

The Russian maritime defences in the Baltic were based on four strong points: Kronstadt, Sveaborg (now Finnish), Revel (now Tallinn, Estonia), and Bomarsund (now also Finnish). The supreme prize for the British and French was the Russian Baltic Fleet, which had withdrawn to the naval fortress of Kronstadt. Situated on the island of Kotlin, guarding the approaches to St Petersburg, the Russian capital, it was a position of immense strength.

Map courtesy of Michael Collins

warfare had hardly undergone any basic change since Nelson's day, with several important exceptions, and, as Nelson had observed, when before Calvi some fifty-eight years before and requested by General Hood to attack from the sea:

> I took the liberty of observing that the business of laying wood before walls was much altered of late, and that even if they had no hot shot, which I believe they had, that the quantity of powder and shot which would be fired away on such an attack could be much better directed from a battery on shore.[3]

The difficulties of attacking shore-based works from the sea, of laying 'wood before walls', was not totally resolved even when steel had replaced wood. Writing some years later, Sir George Sydenham Clarke RE, secretary to the Committee of

Imperial Defence, noted: 'Warships are not built to attack defences on shore, and can rarely be spared for the purpose, while the progress of military science has turned the balance heavily against them.'[4] He had examined the results of the 1882 naval bombardment of the Egyptian positions at Alexandria after the action, and though it had been successful in silencing the batteries, he concluded that it had demonstrated the inherent inaccuracy of naval gunfire in such situations. He had studied the Egyptian positions after the action and discovered that:

> out of 1650 rounds fired (seven inch and upwards) only eleven hits at and near the crests (by near the crest is meant near enough to blow it in upon the emplacement) of the Egyptian batteries were obtained; but as many of them did not occur in front or nearly in front of a gun, they would in a traversed battery have been quite ineffective.[5]

Incendiary projectiles were one of the things that the sailors of wooden ships feared the most. It was rare for such vessels to be sunk in engagements where solid shot was the only ordnance, but projectiles such as hot shot, iron cannonballs heated to incandescence, caused fires, and fire on a wooden ship meant almost certain destruction. Two vital changes in the technology of naval warfare were the invention of the explosive shell, which posed an even greater danger than hot shot, and the rifled gun. Though adopted by military forces some years before, it was not until the 1830s that explosive shell was taken aboard ships. The detonation of such a missile in a wooden structure caused a primary fire at the site of the explosion, and secondary conflagrations where the red hot splinters landed. The development of the rifled gun meant that such missiles could be delivered with greater accuracy over longer ranges than had been possible with smooth bore cannon.

Off Sinope in 1853, an event that was, in all probability, fresh in Napier's mind, the Russian Black Sea fleet surprised a part of the Turkish fleet and completely destroyed it by using explosive shell, against which the Turks could only reply with the traditional solid shot. Not only did the Russian shell incinerate the fleet, but the town itself was set ablaze and a good part reduced to ashes. Dundonald, it may be remembered, had been a good deal concerned about the effects, as he had perceived them, of shell firing guns and the relative helplessness of wooden vessels before their fire. His Plan, as proposed against France following his rehabilitation, was his contribution to restoring the balance between ships and ordnance.

Needless to say, the defences of Kronstadt were well equipped with shell and incendiary missiles and against them the Allied vessels would have been at a severe disadvantage; for although the French navy had adopted shell in 1837, with the Royal Navy following suit in 1839, neither had evolved any protective measures for their wooden ships. Had the [wooden] Russian fleet given battle the outcome may have been uncertain; against the stone forts guarding Kronstadt the Allied fleet would have been committing suicide. The conventional way to deal with such matters was to land a military force and assault or lay siege to the works. This is what happened at Sevastopol, though a purely naval attack was attempted on 17 October 1854, which achieved nothing beyond the loss of six ships and some five hundred men.

A glance at the map showing the defences of Kronstadt will indicate that this type of operation would have been fraught with danger; many of the forts were situated on islands with interlocking fields of fire commanding the approaches. It would also, even if successful, have been a time-consuming and expensive business. Lord Dundonald, however, had his methods of accomplishing such objects rapidly and efficiently, as he would have it, and informed Sir James Graham of this in his letter of 22 July:

> I am desirous through you to offer for the consideration of Her Majesty's cabinet ministers a simple yet effective plan of operations, showing that the maritime defences of Kronstadt (however strong against ordinary means) may be captured and their red hot and incendiary missiles prepared for the destruction of our ships turned on those they protect.
>
> Permit me therefore, in the event of my plans being approved, unreservedly to offer my services (under the passive protection of the fleet) to put them in execution, without command or authority, except over the very limited means of attack, the success of which cannot fail in its consequences to free and ensure (perhaps forever) all minor states from Russian domination.
>
> Personal acquaintance with Vice Admiral Sir Chas. Napier [. . .] assures me that no feeling of rivalry would exist, save in the zealous performance of the service.[6]

It requires little in the way of imagination to conclude that Sir James was decidedly interested in such a plan, and evidence for this may include the fact that he rapidly replied to Dundonald on 26 July:

> You offer for the consideration of H.M. Government a plan of operations, by which the maritime defences of Kronstadt in your opinion may be captured; and in the most handsome manner you disclose your readiness to assist and superintend the execution of your plan should it be adopted.
>
> When the great interests at stake are considered, and when the fatal effects of a possible failure are duly regarded, it is apparent that the merits of your plan and the chances of success must be fully investigated and weighed by competent authority.
>
> The Cabinet unaided can form no judgement in this matter and the tender of your services is most properly made by you dependant on the previous approval of your plan.
>
> The question is a naval one, into which professional considerations must

enter largely. Naval officers of experience and high character are the judges, to whom in the first instance the question ought to be submitted.[7]

Sir James then proposed that Dundonald laid his plan before a 'committee' of four senior officers, three naval and one military. Under the chairmanship of Admiral-of-the-Fleet Sir Byam Martin, the comptroller of the navy, he nominated: Admiral Sir William Parker, C-in-C Plymouth, Admiral Berkeley, the First Sea Lord, and General Sir John Burgoyne, the Inspector-General of Fortifications. His letter continued:

I am sure that you will not regard this mode of treating your proposal as inconsistent with the respect which I sincerely entertain for your high professional character, resting on past services of no ordinary merit, which I have never failed to recognise, but my duty on this occasion prescribes caution and deliberate care, and you will do justice to the motives by which this answer to your request is guided.[8]

Sir James wrote to Sir Thomas Byam Martin on 29 July informing him that Lord Dundonald accepted 'the proposed reference' and on 2 August, with Sir Thomas taking notes, they:

Assembled at the Admiralty [. . .] and entered into a discussion with Lord Dundonald respecting his plans, but it was, in the first instance, indicated to his Lordship that we thought he might be desirous to have the assurance of perfect secrecy regarding his plans, and that we would at once set him at ease on that point, by an unqualified declaration that nothing relating to his plan would be mentioned by any member of the committee, except in their report to Sir James Graham, we therefore urge his lordship to enter unreservedly into an explanation of his plans, and his mode of carrying them out.[9]

The notes go on to explain that 'after much conversation', sadly unrecorded, the committee put several questions to Dundonald, and he delivered several memoranda. The questions and answers were recorded, apparently verbatim, and they go on at some length. In order to carry out his plan, Lord Dundonald explained he would require twenty-four old iron colliers or iron lighters; sixteen of these would be fitted out as 'smokers' and eight as sulphur craft. They would require to be crewed by 210 officers and men. The smoke craft would be filled with bituminous coal and other smoke-producing substances; the sulphur vessels would be filled with coke charcoal and sulphur – some two hundred tons of 'common, crude sulphur'. The boats from the fleet, 'at least one from each ship', would be required to support the attack but the fleet itself would not be required to join in.[10]

Dundonald was asked if he was 'aware of the enemy having a vast number of gun boats and so many boats standing guard[,] and under such circumstances do you expect to get undiscovered and unopposed to within a distance of one mile?' His reply was that 'I should expect to go undiscovered, but should expect the certainty of final discovery', and made the point that he would 'ignite the matter which is to effect the great purpose' when the enemy's shot commence to tell'.[11] He was then asked, 'Suppose you are discovered before you get within one mile and you still push on[.] [H]ow long will it take to ignite the noxious matter when you think you are within reach of the object [of attack]?' The reply was 'instantaneous – the whole mass in a minute'.[12]

The committee were concerned about the composition of the fumes generated by the sulphur vessels: 'Do you wish to withhold from us a knowledge of the component parts of this noxious matter?' They were reassured: 'No, sulphur, charcoal and coke will completely decompose all the atmospheric air that comes in contact during combustion.'[13] They also sought clarification on some of the wording contained in the original letter to Sir James Graham, relating to his statement that the defences may be captured. They enquired whether military forces would have to be landed to effect this capture. Dundonald replied: 'If you want to capture it there must be men provided, but if the destruction of the fleet be the only object it may be affected without landing.'[14]

What he proposed was the obscuring or disabling of two or three of the outlying works to facilitate the passage of the ships boats. The crews of these would occupy the defences along the sea wall, the garrison of which would have previously been disabled by sulphur fumes; and, using the weapons of these works, the crews would destroy the Russian fleet: 'their red hot shot and incendiary projectiles [. . .] turned on those they protect'. The committee expressed concern that this implied a large landing force would be required, and were also worried about the effectiveness of the methods advocated: 'What practical proof have you ever had, on a large scale that the smoke will have a sufficient spread to conceal your operations?'[15] Lord Dundonald replied that he had only experienced such phenomena on a small scale while he was near sulphur works in Sicily – confirmation, if any were needed, that the author of the Plans had no real idea of how effective his methods would be in reality, though, as on previous occasions, he appeared to harbour not the slightest shred of doubt as to their efficacy.

This comes through quite clearly in a paper he then delivered to the committee for their consideration:

> Red hot shot and carcasses being now generally used in maritime fortifications, it is manifest that attacking ships are infinitely more endangered than formerly when cold shot were the only missiles – especially during their approach, when elaborate aim can safely be taken from casemates and embrasures before the guns of the ships can bear.

To avert this peril it is proposed that iron vessels containing large masses of combustible materials (bituminous coal or other matter) shall be kindled at a proper distance to windward of the fortifications or batteries to be attacked so that dense vapours – more obscure than the darkest night – shall conceal the ships from the batteries, until they arrive at a position to attack in earnest.

If the assailing force, as there is great reason to believe, is still endangered by incendiary missiles, sulphur vessels may be conducted to appropriate positions, the fumes from which will expel artillery men from the strongest casemates, and drive them from their guns, wherever situated, within a mile of the burning sulphur carried down the breeze.

The works at Kronstadt are particularly exposed to this mode of attack - being partly isolated and partly situated on a long sea wall running in the usual course of the prevailing wind, whereby one or two smoke and sulphur vessels would clear the whole range.[16]

The committee once again raised doubts about the effectiveness of the smoke:

As your opinion of the spread of the smoke is founded only on what you have witnessed when passing near sulphur works, it seems evidently a matter of conjecture as to the degree to which you may be capable of spreading over a large space 'a dense vapour more obscure than night' so as to conceal your operation from the enemy. The smoke will naturally take a lateral direction when sent forth from each smoke vessel [. . .] but it is difficult to envisage its density continuing for any length of time, over a space so great as to shut out the garrison and the fleet from discovery of your position and proceedings – even if other smokers contribute an additional supply is it not probable that the smoke would pass off in a narrow current, or at best provide only a transient eclipse of the light, you have already stated that the operation must not be undertaken in a calm.[17]

Lord Dundonald could only reply that he did not expect the smoke to behave in the way the committee expected, even though he had no empirical knowledge upon which to draw. They again returned to the subject of the need for men to land and take possession of the defensive works:

What additional force of men do you consider necessary to attack and take possession of Fort Alexander and other isolated forts in the event of their garrison being temporarily paralysed by the fumes of the sulphur craft.'[18]

Dundonald replied:

If the fleet is the object there is no occasion to take possession of the isolated forts, paralysing the garrison of fort Alexander and obscuring the others would suffice. It is obvious however that if animation is suspended a boats crew would suffice, if not, an army would not accomplish the storming of such structures.[19]

The committee also asked for a complete list of all the requirements for mounting an attack as proposed, and requested that it be delivered within two days. Dundonald replied that he would comply, but pointed out that the questions he had answered left little more to say. Nevertheless, the next day his memorandum entitled 'Preliminary Requisites' was delivered:

> In order to enable a full explanation to be drawn up, showing the practicability of successfully attacking Kronstadt, a large outline chart of the island and anchorage is essential – say on a scale three times greater than those sold in the shops.
>
> Enquiry ought to be made as to the number of old iron vessels and large Thames lighters that can be procured. Also as to the practicability of procuring two or three hundred tons of sulphur [common crude sulphur].
>
> Coals, coke, gas tar and such like articles can be had in abundance at a moments warning, and these consist of the chief requisites.
>
> The whole except the old vessels being of trifling value.[20]

He had already informed the committee that he estimated the total cost of the operation to be £200,000.[21] This concluded the interview with Dundonald, and the committee set out to deliberate. It drew up a list of seven questions which were transmitted to him, and also communicated details of the scheme, presumably with his concurrence, to the most eminent scientist of the day, Professor Michael Faraday, together with the same set of questions. It may be inferred from the tone of the verbal questioning that the committee viewed the plan in a somewhat less than favourable light; this tone was reflected in the written questions:

> 1. Can it be shown by any proof the different requirements for vessels, the quantity of matter to be ignited, the distance at which it will be of avail, and the amount of wind to render it effective; must these be nicely adjusted or do each of them admit of considerable latitude?
>
> 2. What is the amount of effect in intensity anticipated on the individuals, and if not totally destructive, to what period of time would it paralyse them?
>
> 3. What proof is there that supposing the vapours to be intolerable along the surface over which the wind carries them, that under cover of the parapets or by closing the windows or shutters, which probably exist at the embrasures of the casemates, the same vapour would penetrate and extend with sufficient intensity?

4. If the smoke is to conceal the ships from the view of the batteries how are the ships and smoke vessels themselves to approach, by <u>probably an intricate passage</u>, through the same smoke?

5. Where the batteries are dispersed as at Kronstadt, there must be separate smoke vessel sufficient for each, and as the bearing of their guns are in complicated lines and distances mutually flanking each other, would it not be a matter of difficulty to obtain a simultaneous effect on each, which would be very necessary?

6. The extent laterally that would be covered <u>with effect</u> by the vapours from each vessel – would need proof?

7. How are the smoke and vapour vessels to be brought into position with sufficient rapidity? (Once on) the position are they to lay to, or to anchor, or to move on; if the first two how are our own boats to pass through the smoke; and if the last how are these vapour vessels to direct their course?[22]

Lord Dundonald's reply to this series of questions was dated 5 August:

1. No practical proof exists of the different requirements for vessels, though inferences may be drawn as to the quantity of matter to be ignited, by the effects on a small scale. The more combustible matter ignited the greater will be the effect. No nice adjustment is necessary, the wind should not be too strong so as to alleviate the smoke or dilute the emanation of sulphurous fumes.

2. We breath about a dozen of times in a minute so that even by holding the breath it is probable that one minute would suspend animal life.

3. No embrasures are so closely fitted as to exclude <u>atmospheric air</u>, which in point of stability is in no degree different from <u>decomposed air</u>.

4. The smoke vessels are guided by vessels placed in a line with the fort to be attacked, and cross bearings may in like manner denote when the attacking force has arrived at a proper distance to anchor.

5. One or more forts may be attacked at a time, provided that the view of the others is intercepted by dense fumes – which, in that case, may prevent intervention without actually embracing the objects.

6. The vapour that issues from the funnel of a steam vessel when fresh fuel is thrown on, being produced by a few shovels of bituminous coal, may afford some idea what would be the amount occasioned by the ignition of hundreds of tons – soaked, if necessary, with tar.

7. The smoke vessels will burn for many hours, perhaps for days, in iron vessels. They need not however be counted on in this latter period. In certain cases such as an attack on fort Alexander they might be anchored, but if on a dead wall or rampart such as commanding the docks at Kronstadt they may be left to drift alongside that which they cannot but encounter.[23]

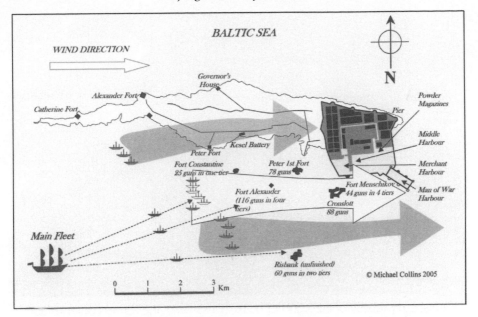

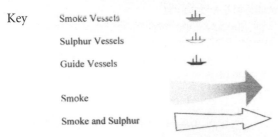

9 Lord Dundonald's proposed attack on Kronstadt, 1854
Map courtesy of Michael Collins

On 7 August he submitted two more papers for consideration, one entitled
'Brief Outline Of A Proposed Means Of Attacking Kronstadt In Reference To The
Accompanying Chart' (see Fig. 9):

> The British fleet may be anchored at four or five miles distant from the
> enemies isolated fortifications. The small steam vessels and regularly fitted
> smoke vessels may be brought up anywhere contiguous.
>
> Coasters, or captured coasting vessels, may be fitted as explosion vessels,
> and placed at a greater distance from the fleet. Some of these may be
> prepared as sulphur vessels by filling them with compressed straw, reeds,
> shavings or chips of wood, or other combustible materials soaked with tar.
> Which equipment will have the advantage of enabling them to float though

10 Artistic impression of the Island of Kotlin in 1854 with the Fortress of Kronstadt and St Petersburg, the Russian capital, in the distance
The naval base of Kronstadt lies on Kotlin Island near the head of the Gulf of Finland. Peter the Great captured the island from the Swedes in 1703 and built it into a naval fortress to protect his new capital of St Petersburg. This impression gives an idea of the difficulties an attacking fleet would have had in attacking the Russian Fleet, ensconced in the 'Man-of-War' harbour, using conventional methods. Author's collection

pierced by shot. Indeed it seems probable that this mode of fitting – aided by a ground tier of empty casks – might be substituted for <u>iron</u> vessels containing bituminous coal.

Guide vessels must be placed [at three or four miles distant from the enemy] so that a line drawn through these vessels shall bisect the fort to be attacked. The wind being Westerly and steady, and all in readiness for the attack, small craft crammed with the tarred materials may be sent down along shore and anchored off certain points in order that when kindled the smoke shall obscure the operations, about to take place, from the enemy.

Several modes of attack may be adopted, but it seems indispensable that the lofty fort called 'Alexander' should be taken or silenced, lest the mast heads of the attacking force should be seen from its summit.

To capture this fort it is essential that the other isolated forts shall be obscured – or simultaneously assailed, but to avoid detail, let the former be exemplified, and let the assailing force proceed along the line direct towards Fort Alexander – each tug vessel having two smokers in tow by quarter hawsers of such length that the towing vessel shall not be involved in the smoke during the two mile run after the smokers are kindled.

Astern of the smoke vessels the sulphur craft – towed in like manner – must keep the guide vessels 'on with each other' so as not only to follow in the direct course themselves but to be able to indicate to the smoke tug when 'my cross bearing is on' in order so the smokers being 'brought up' by an anchor attached to their tow lines in the tug. The sulphurous craft are to be anchored to leeward of these.

It is obvious that a second and third dose of sulphur may be administered if required, which in the case of the lofty castle called 'Alexander' may be necessary – a circumstance which doubtless may be ascertained if the top of the castle is visible from the fleet above the smoke.

The hundred gun tower being taken or silenced, Fort Constantine, Fort Peter and Fort Risbank may simply be obscured, so that the grand attack might at once take place against the Western and Southern ramparts, and against Fort Kronstadt, which forcibly protect the anchorage of the hostile fleet.

The effect to be produced by numerous small smoke vessels [to deter the enemy boats] and by sulphur craft sent adrift before the wind against that broad space indicating the channel between Kronstadt and Fort Menshekof is so obvious that detail seem unnecessary.[24]

His other paper was entitled simply 'Preliminary Observations'.

Before enlarging on the explanation of arrangements necessary to mask, silence or capture the detached forts, and assail the long line of ramparts that protect the fleet at Kronstadt, it may be well to refer to a more simple case (now in progress of execution at Bomarsund) where the British ships of war – with good reason – have been restrained from acting until the arrival of an army to co-operate on land.

The chief battery, is said to have seventy guns in casemates, supported by two towers on the heights – the former being close to the waters edge, where there is sufficient depth to permit the near approach of ships of any size.

Now, it is submitted that neither prudent hesitation on the part of the naval force, nor the presence of an army would have been necessary, had it occurred, that half a dozen of captured coasting vessels – crammed with reeds, compressed hay, straw, shavings, or chips of wood soaked with tar, on being kindled and run on the weather side of the battery – would have produced obscurity more intense than night – and had as many more sulphur vessels [or had the tar in the smoke vessels been imbued with sulphur] would have enabled the British ships to approach with without risk, and to have pounded the walls without opposition.

Whether afloat or onshore these means must supersede all tedious modes of attack. Narrow channels may be passed or 'ground may be opened'

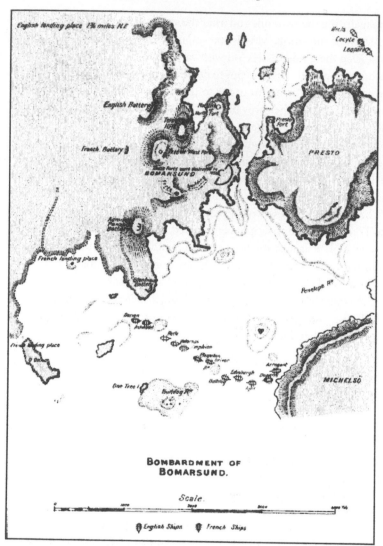

11 Bombardment and capture of Bomarsund, 9–16 August 1854
Having declined to attack Kronstadt and Sveaborg ('un-attackable by sea or land'),
the Allied commanders, Vice-Admiral Sir Charles Napier and Admiral Ferdinand de
Parseval-Deschênes, decided to attack one of the two remaining Baltic strong
points: Bomarsund. This was assailed and taken during 9–16 August 1854. Though
dubbed the 'Gibraltar of the Aaland Islands', the fortress was in fact incomplete and
weakly defended; some sources state around 2,500 men and 66 guns. The naval
forces, apart from carrying and landing the troops, played a secondary part,
providing support through the use of gunfire from the sea.
Map taken from: Vice-Admiral P.H. Colomb, *Naval Warfare: Its Ruling Principles and
Practice Historically Treated*, 3rd edn (London: W.H. Allen, 1899)

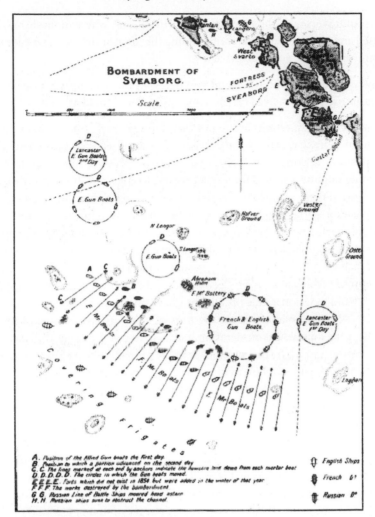

12 Bombardment of Sveaborg, 9–11 August 1855

Following the capture of Bomarsund in 1854 the forces in the Baltic had achieved little that was noteworthy. Kronstadt remained untouched, but Sveaborg, the second largest fortress in the Baltic theatre, which guarded the approaches to Helsingvors (Helsinki), was thought a potential target for bombardment. The Baltic Fleet, under the command of Rear-Admiral Richard Dundas and Rear-Admiral Charles Pénaud, was now equipped with a number of gunboats and mortar vessels designed for such operations. The level of damage caused to the fortress was significant, although the effort rendered many of the mortars unserviceable and the fleet was compelled to withdraw. The bombardment was the last significant operation in the Baltic. Map taken from: Vice-Admiral P.H. Colomb, *Naval Warfare: Its Ruling Principles and Practice Historically Treated*, 3rd edn (London: W.H. Allen, 1899) without traverses on the very glacis of fortifications, where mounds may be raised and batteries situated commanding the interior defences, whence the enemy inevitably would be driven.[25]

Professor Faraday's reply, 'I send you herewith the best answer I can make to your enquiries', was received on the same day as Dundonald's two papers:

Very few of the questions are so put that I, in reference to their chemical or physical character, can give any consistent or distinct answer to them. The proposition is correct in theory, i.e. dense smoke will hide objects, and burning sulphur will yield fumes that are intolerable, and able to render men involved in them incapable of action, or even to kill them. But whether this proposition is <u>practicable</u> on the scale proposed and required, is a point so little illustrated by any experience, or by facts that can be made to bear upon it, that for my own part I am unable to form a judgement . . . I should hesitate in concluding that ten or twenty vessels could give a body of smoke, the columns of which at a mile to leeward, would coincide and form an impervious band to vision a mile broad; but I have no means of judging [. . .]

[. . .] I may remark, that as 400 tons of sulphur have been spoken of, perhaps the following consideration may help to give some general ideas, in the present state of the proposition, as to the probable effect of its fumes. If a ship charged with sulphur were burning in a current of air, a continuous stream of sulphuric acid fumes, mingled with air, would pass off from it. This stream, being heavier than air, would descend and move along over the surface of the water; and, I suppose, would sink perpendicularly and expand laterally, so as to form a low broad stream. The noxious height would probably soon be less than 15, or perhaps even 10 feet (but I cannot pretend to more than a guess) and its width by degrees more and more. The water [. . .] would tend continually to take part of the noxious vapour out of it. Now 400 tons of sulphur would require 400 tons of oxygen; and that it would find in about 1740 tons of air. Supposing that this product were mixed with ten times its bulk of unaltered air, it would make nigh upon 20,000 tons of a very bad mixture; and one, which if a man were to be immersed in it for a short time, would cause death [. . .]

In respect of the seven questions, there is hardly a point in them to which I am able to give an answer of any value.

1. I suspect much larger quantities of matter will be required than is supposed. – I do not imagine that if burnt in heaps coals would burn fast enough to give the smoke required.

2. The data is wanting.

3. I suspect the upper part of high buildings would frequently be free from

the sulphurous vapours; and that jets or eddies of fresh air from above would occur behind.

4. [Left unanswered]

5. [Left unanswered]

6. The lateral extent at the distance of a mile very doubtful - would need proof.

7. [Left unanswered]

> The proposition is [. . .] correct in theory, but in its result must depend entirely on practical points. These are of so untried a character [. . .] that I have the utmost difficulty in speaking at all on the matter [. . .] All I need add is, that if the project were known or anticipated, it would not be difficult for the attacked party to provide respirators, which would enable the men, in a very great degree or even altogether, to resist a temporary invasion of an atmosphere such as that described.[26]

Sir John Burgoyne had also put pen to paper and delivered his view of the plan to Sir Byam Martin and the committee. He outlined his doubts as to whether the smoke produced to mask the movements of the attackers would be effective:

> It is extremely doubtful that it would be obtained to the amount of preventing occasional glimpses [. . .] of what was proceeding behind it, the forts being generally lofty . . . and the smoke alone would not prevent the service of the guns [and] their fire would as soon as the process began be directed at the front of the smokers and whatever might be behind them [. . .] probably with damaging effects [. . .] At the same time it would be extremely difficult to regulate the movements of the assailants [. . .] behind this great cloud of smoke, nor is it comprehended how any great advantage is to be obtained [. . .] against works that are enclosed all round, or against any considerable strength of garrison.

He was equally dismissive of the sulphur ships:

> As regards the application of the sulphurous vapour, independent of the barbarous and uncivilised character that would be given to it, there are very great doubts of its efficacy which are itemised by Mr. Faraday who has been consulted as one of the highest authorities on such subjects.
>
> There is no proof, nor should I think [. . .] that any trials should be recommended.[27]

He also related his belief that the complement of the works to be 'sulphured' would escape from the worst effects of the fumes owing to the expected properties of the cloud of vapour, 'its weight being greater than atmospheric air would tend to keep it low'. And of the physical characteristics of the defences:

> Now as the lowest tier of batteries are probably not less than fifteen feet above the water and the rest twenty four and upwards, this quality would be conclusive against the efficacy of the undertaking.

With these various negative pieces of advice, and taking into account the sceptical tone of the verbal questioning, it comes as little surprise to note that the committee advised Sir James Graham against adopting the plan. In their written submission to him they reiterated Michael Faraday's observations and alluded to Sir John Burgoyne's paper in handsome terms: 'we can with much satisfaction refer to a paper delivered to the committee [. . .] in which everything is said that <u>can be said on the subject</u>'.[28] Sir John added his own rider to the letter sent to Sir James: 'I am quite of the opinion that the project is very little likely to be successful on any great scale, and if not so the attempt would be attended with considerable odium.'[29] It fell to Sir James Graham to write to Dundonald explaining that his plan was not to be adopted at that time, but making an attempt to mollify him by paraphrasing the committee's conclusion that:

> If such an enterprise were to be undertaken we are certain it could not be in better hands than Lord Dundonald's whose professional career has been distinguished by remarkable instances of skill and courage in all of which he has been the foremost to lead the way and by his personal heroism has gained an unfading celebrity in the naval history of the country.[30]

Dundonald dismissed the committee's findings and continued to press the government for his scheme to be given a chance, alluding in letters to the press that he had powerful methods that would equalise the disparity between wooden ships and stone forts: 'There is but one means to place these parties on an equal footing, and that I confidentially laid before the Government.'[31] He again wrote to Sir James Graham in November stating that: 'I will undertake to subdue every insular fortification at Kronstadt within four hours from the commencement of the attack.'[32] He offered to apply his methods to the capture of Sevastopol, and repeated this offer in a letter to the Prime Minister, Lord Aberdeen. Sir James was obliged to reply stating that as his proposals had been rejected by the committee then: 'Neither Lord Aberdeen nor I can venture to place our individual opinions in opposition to a recorded judgement of the highest authority.'[33]

In one of his earlier replies to Dundonald's canvassing he had expressed the hope that Sevastopol would fall without recourse to unconventional methods. The failure of this to happen was to cause a change of ministry, replacement for Sir James and a new opportunity for Dundonald to press his schemes.

Kronstadt and the Russian Baltic fleet were to remain unmolested, by conventional or other methods, and the Allies concentrated on the Southern Theatre, landing their armies on the Crimean peninsula and moving on Sevastopol. Unfortunately, after winning the battles of the Alma, Inkerman, and Balaclava, Lord Raglan's expeditionary force failed to move quickly enough and gave the defenders time to fortify. Sevastopol was somewhat analogous to Singapore in the next century; it had minimal permanent defences against a land approach but was heavily fortified against attack from the sea. The south and east sides of the city were the only realistic approaches open to the attackers, the north being bounded by the harbour and dominated by a modern fortification, 'Star Fort' as it was nicknamed by the British, while the permanent southern defences consisted only of the Malakoff Tower, a two-storey masonry affair. Thanks to the breathing space allowed them, however, the Russians constructed an earthworks system to augment their defence, which grew to a size and complexity previously unknown. That this was done was primarily owing to Colonel Franz Todleben, an engineer of some genius, and Admiral Kornilov, the chief-of-staff of the garrison, who mobilised all available resources to aid Todleben. They had three weeks of uninterrupted peace to complete their preparations while the Allies brought up siege guns; this time they used well. Todleben's opposite number on the British side, the chief engineering officer, was Sir John Burgoyne.

Orthodox military opinion held that only permanent defensive works were of use and that earthworks were of limited utility. Orthodox opinion was wrong and the siege was to last for 349 days, testament not merely to the static component but also to Todleben's dynamic direction of the defence. The Allied cause was also hampered by the fact that for a large portion of the operations they were inferior in artillery. The Russians had augmented their military guns with naval ones, removed from the ships of the Black Sea fleet, which lay sunk; this was not through enemy action but done on the orders of Todleben, who had scuttled them in the harbour mouth to deny access to Allied vessels.

The failure to destroy the Russian Baltic Fleet and the bogging down of the Crimean campaign before Sevastopol caused the crisis in the British government that led to the Aberdeen ministry falling in February 1855, and a new ministry under Lord Palmerston taking its place. With the new government came a new ministerial position, Secretary of State for War, within which office were combined the two posts formerly responsible for army affairs. The first holder of this important post was Fox Maule, second Baron Panmure, known generally as Lord Panmure. The scandal caused by reports of the conditions under which the British army served during the winter of 1854–55, combined with the apparent failure of the Allies to progress their siege successfully, made Panmure and Palmerston receptive to any idea that promised an end to the venture. It was in this light, the harsh light of national embarrassment, that Lord Dundonald next proposed his Plan for scrutiny and operational usage.

5

Expelling the Russians from Sevastopol

I agree with you that if Dundonald will go out himself to superintend and direct the execution of his scheme, we ought to accept his offer and try his plan. If it succeeds, it will, as you say, save a great number of English and French lives; if it fails in his hands, we shall be exempt from blame [. . .]

Lord Palmerston to Lord Panmure. 7 August 1855

THERE is something of a minor mystery about the behaviour of both Dundonald and the new government in the context of the Plans during 1855. In public, or semi-public anyway, for the details of what was being argued about remained a mystery to all but a few, there were the appearances of an argument over the matter with letters to newspapers and articles in journals. For example, there were no fewer than five articles calling for the adoption of the Plan in *Punch* during 1855, the first, in May, being an 'Ode to Lord Dundonald' that called for his plan, whether it be 'poison fumes, or liquid fire' to be put into effect.[1] The pressure was kept up by two pieces in the July edition, 'A Proposal to Lord Dundonald'[2] and 'It Will Never Answer',[3] both urging the adoption of his Plans by the government, and an article in August, 'The Chemistry of the Cannon'.[4] The final article, 'The Peace Projectile Company', continued the theme.[5]

There was also hostile questioning in the House of Commons, as is evidenced by the columns of *Hansard*. Colonel the Rt Hon. Fitzstephen French was the Liberal Member for Roscommon County from 1832 until his death in 1873. His rank derived from him being appointed colonel of the Roscommon Militia in 1854.[6] His connection with Dundonald is unclear, but it is apparent from the content of his parliamentary questions that he was relatively *au fait* with the Plans and the proposals to have them adopted. The MP raised the matter with Palmerston on four different occasions between 4 May and 29 June 1855. On the earlier date the following exchange took place:

Mr. FRENCH. The Government might . . . have safely availed themselves of the plans which he [Lord Dundonald] had submitted to them; but they had forced him to divulge these plans to seven or eight persons, and it might possibly be that the first experiment they heard of them would be in the destruction of their own forces. [. . .]

74

Viscount PALMERSTON. [. . .] The plan which Lord Dundonald proposed last year was [. . .] necessarily submitted to the consideration of [. . .] professional and scientific persons; and the effect of their . . . consideration was that there appeared to be such difficulties of execution and such doubtful expectations as to the result that nothing was then done upon it. The plan has recently been again pressed on the consideration of the Government by Lord Dundonald. [. . .] all I can say is that it is under consideration [. . .] and I think [. . .] there can be no great advantage in publicly discussing it, or pointing it out to the enemy.[7]

Colonel French raised the issue again on 10 May, asking Palmerston:

If he had any objection to inform the House who the persons are to whom Lord Dundonald's plan for the destruction of the Russian fortresses have been submitted [. . .]?

Viscount PALMERSTON: . . . I have no objection to state that the invention in question has been referred to several eminent scientific men, amongst whom are Professors Faraday, Playfair, and Graham.[8]

Palmerston again deprecated the public airing of such matters, but his answers did not satisfy Colonel French, who was clearly in possession of a good deal of knowledge concerning the current status of the Secret Plans. If the source of his knowledge is unknown, both the content and tone of his next effort, on 18 May, to interrogate the Prime Minister give as clear a hint as to the guiding hand behind Col. French as we are likely to get:

Mr. FRENCH said [. . .] he had twice already put questions [. . .] and although the replies were courteous they were certainly not [. . .] satisfactory. [Palmerston] had stated that a commission of scientific gentlemen had been appointed, consisting of Professors Faraday, Playfair and Graham. He believed he might assert [. . .] that no meeting of those gentlemen had taken place [. . .] He could state, on authority, that no call had yet been made on the Earl of Dundonald to explain the alleged or supposed difficulty of carrying his plans into execution. Now he wished to state to the House and the country what the proposal of the noble Earl was. [. . .] the period during which operations could take place in the Baltic was very short; it was certainly not more than three months. The noble Earl was prepared by the end of June, if his plans were adopted and his services were accepted, without fee or reward for the carrying [of] them into execution, to demolish every Russian fortress in the Baltic – and that too, at an expense to the country of less than £200,000. The question [. . .] was [. . .] whether his [Dundonald's] plans and his personal services [. . .] would be accepted by the Government.

Viscount PALMERSON: Sir, the hon. Member has misunderstood what I stated on a former occasion. I did not say that the Commission of scientific men had been appointed since the present Government was formed. In point of fact the plan of Lord Dundonald was referred in the course of last summer and autumn to a Commission of military and scientific persons; and since that period I have consulted others other persons on the subject. Really, as far as I have been able to form an opinion, I must say the difficulties of the plan appear to increase in proportion as the details are considered; and I am not prepared to tell my hon. Friend when I shall be able to give him an answer.[9]

Colonel French did however get his answer on 29 June when he addressed a question to the new First Lord of the Admiralty, Sir Charles Wood, asking if the government was prepared to offer Lord Dundonald 'any practical means of testing that discovery', which he had revealed in a letter to the press, the use of which would 'strike a blow at the military power of Russia more fatal than the capture of Sevastopol'. He was bluntly informed 'The Government were not prepared to carry into execution the scheme proposed by Lord Dundonald.'[10]

As pointed out, both the tone and content of the questioning bear the hallmark of Dundonald inspiration, and there is clear evidence that Palmerston was being disingenuous in his replies. His Secretary of State for War, Lord Panmure, communicated with Sir James Simpson, whom he had appointed as Chief of Staff to the British C-in-C Lord Raglan, on 20 July, asking him 'What would you say to try Dundonald's scheme on the Malakoff? It might answer. Let me know by telegraphic message what Jones thinks of it.'[11] On 7 August, a little over five weeks after the government had denied point blank in the House of Commons that it was considering the scheme, the Prime Minister was writing to Panmure:

I agree with you that if Dundonald will go out himself to superintend and direct the execution of his scheme, we ought to accept his offer and try his plan. If it succeeds, it will, as you say, save a great number of English and French lives; if it fails in his hands, we shall be exempt from blame, and if we come in for a small share of the ridicule we can bear it, and the greater part will fall on him. You had best, therefore, make arrangements with him without delay, and with as much secrecy as the nature of things will admit of.[12]

Palmerston enclosed with this letter a paper by Dundonald, entitled 'Brief Preliminary Observations', which set out the background to his scheme.

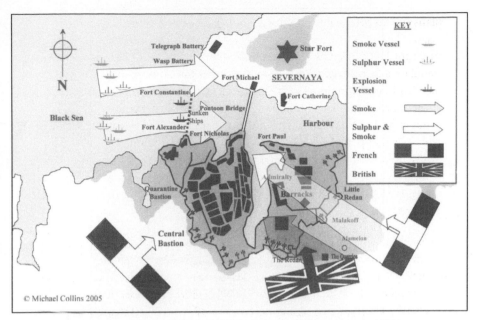

13 Lord Dundonald's proposed methods of attacking Sevastopol, 1855
Map courtesy of Michael Collins

It was observed when viewing the Sulphur Kilns, in July in 1811, that the fumes which escaped in the rude process of extracting the material, though first elevated by heat, soon fell to the ground, destroying all vegetation, and endangering animal life to a great distance, as it was asserted that an ordinance existed prohibiting persons from sleeping within the distance of three miles during the melting season.

An application of these facts was immediately made to Military and Naval purposes, and after mature consideration, a Memorial was presented on the subject to His Royal Highness the Prince Regent on the 12th of April 1812, who was graciously pleased to lay it before a Commission consisting of Lord Keith, Lord Exmouth, and General and Colonel Congreve (afterwards Sir William), by whom a favourable report having been given, His Royal Highness was pleased to order that secrecy should be maintained by all parties.[13]

As well as getting the date of his 'Memorial' wrong – it was actually dated 2 March 1812[14] – Dundonald might be accused of somewhat skating over the conclusions of the 'Commission'. Having outlived all of its members, however, there was no one to contradict him should Palmerston have sought clarification. Also included was a document setting out the *materiel* requirements for expelling the 'Russians from Sevastopol':

13a 'Observation' and 'Mode of Proceeding' together with a sketch showing the method of attacking a specific fort or position at Sevastopol

Observation: In order to conduct the smoke vessels, Brigs, or guide vessels must be placed on a line, which shall intersect <u>them</u> and the fort, or object to be attacked – so that, when the fort shall be obscured, the steam tug conducting them may be steered in a direct course A, B, C.

Mode of Proceeding: The wind being settled and favourable let two smoke vessels be taken in tow by the tug steam boat <u>D</u> – each vessel, on a broad sheer, on opposite quarters – and, when within range of shot, let one or both vessels be kindled – which will prevent direct aim from the batteries. When the vessels are near enough to the fort, which may be ascertained by a cross bearing, the tug boat is to 'cast off' the tow lines, each of which must have an anchor attached 'to bring the smoke vessels up'.

From an Undated Memorandum ['An Outline of Irresistible Means of Attacking Sevastopol', GD233/874/82] by Lord Dundonald

Experimental trials have shown that about five parts of coke effectively vapourise one part of sulphur. Mixtures for land service, where weight is of importance, may, however, probably be suggested by Professor Faraday, as to operations on shore I have paid little attention.

Four or five hundred tons of sulphur and two thousand tons of coke would be sufficient.

Besides these materials, it would be necessary to have, say, as much bituminous coal, and a couple of thousand barrels of gas or other tar, for the purpose of masking fortifications to be attacked, or others that flank the assailing positions.

A quantity of dry firewood, chips, shavings, straw, hay or other such combustible materials, would also be requisite quickly to kindle the fires, which ought to be kept in readiness for the first favourable and steady breeze.

The objects to be accomplished being specially stated, the responsibility of their accomplishment ought to rest on those who direct their execution. [An oblique reference to the fact that Dundonald had been asked to delegate responsibility for carrying out the project to others; a request he brusquely denied.]

Suppose that the Malakoff and Redan are the objects to be assailed, it might be judicious merely to <u>obscure</u> the Redan [by the smoke of coal and tar kindled in 'The Quarries'] so that it could not annoy the Mamelon, where the sulphur fire would be placed to expel the garrison from the Malakoff, which ought to have all the cannon that can be turned towards its ramparts employed in overthrowing its <u>undefended</u> ramparts.

There is no doubt but that the fumes will envelop all the defences from the Malakoff to the barracks, and even to the line-of-battle ship, the *Twelve Apostles*, at anchor in the harbour.

The two outer batteries, on each side of the port, ought to be smoked, sulphured, and blown down by explosion vessels and their destruction completed by a few ships of war anchored under <u>cover</u> of the smoke.[15]

Dundonald, though a sailor of distinction, had, in a somewhat superficial manner, envisaged the use of smoke and noxious fumes to aid military operations previously, as per his paper 'Preliminary Observations' of 7 August 1854, delivered to the Martin Committee. However, what had certainly changed since his submissions to that committee was his revealing that 'experimental trials' had taken place. It may be recalled that he had informed Martin and the others that he had 'only experienced such phenomena on a small scale whilst he was near sulphur works in Sicily'. In fact there had been further investigations, and small-scale experimentation had occurred in the intervening period. These tests had taken place under the auspices of Professor Lyon Playfair, head of the chemistry

14 Lord Panmure (l) and Lord Palmerston (r)
Photographs from the author's collection

department at Edinburgh University, who had himself proposed the use of a shell filled with a chemical agent for use against Russian ships (see Chapter 6).

Dundonald supplied him with a memorandum, annoyingly undated, detailing his plan for attacking Sevastopol from the sea, and Playfair had consulted with Professor Thomas Graham of University College, London, and Michael Faraday, and produced a report. It is clear that the Palmerston ministry was actively considering the adoption of Dundonald's Plan as early as April 1855. A letter from Playfair to Earl Granville dated the 20th of that month mentions that 'Lord Panmure is to bring Lord Dundonald's Plans before the cabinet tomorrow.'[16] The letter continued:

Lord Dundonald has confided his Plans to me. Should my name be mentioned in connection with them I ask Your Lordship to understand exactly what I think of them. There are two essential points connected with the scheme one being chemical, the other being the engineering process of carrying the chemical part into execution. Of the first part I may be a judge – of the second I am absolutely unqualified to express an opinion. With regard to the chemical point, I think the proposed agents properly applied may be made a formidable means of attack and that their proper mode of

15 Michael Faraday (l) and Lyon Playfair (r)
Engraving and photograph from the author's collection

application is susceptible of useful consideration by chemists and might be made [. . .] harassing to an enemy and drive him from positions, although generally I think he would have ample time to escape with life.[17]

Playfair's words are further evidence that Palmerston was playing a double game when informing the House of Commons of the 'difficulties of execution' and 'doubtful expectations as to the result'. Clearly these statements were not based on the scientific advice his government was receiving. That such advice was being received from Playfair *et al.*, and that Palmerston's memory had played him false when he had referred to them undertaking their investigation under the auspices of the previous government, can be deduced from the available evidence. Frustratingly, however, and in a like manner to Dundonald's Sevastopol proposals that were its subject, the report of the 'Playfair' investigation, as it might usefully be termed, carries no date. This though can be roughly calculated, from correspondence vis-à-vis it. For example, on 1 May 1855 Dundonald had written to Playfair:

In answer to your question 'at what distance I propose that the sulphur vessels shall act' I propose to place them as near the object of attack a possible. There is no obstacle to running them alongside other than [that the] water is deep enough; this I should propose to do in regard to the insular fortifications at Kronstadt.[18]

Clearly he still considered the Baltic as an area of future operations, and another missive the day following expanded on the scale he considered necessary to accomplish his objectives; considered a point clearly communicated to him by

Playfair; and also, tellingly, reiterated Dundonald's suspicion of those in high places, his life's *leitmotif,* and their determination, as he saw it, to deny him justice.

> Pray do not run your calculation short of the <u>material</u>. If there is any doubt as to the efficiency of 59 tons, say 118, so that the effect may be certain.
>
> I have reflected on the consequences of the angle of elevation which you assigned and it seems to me greatly to depend on the strength of the breeze, as is manifested by the angle shown even close to the chimney of a steam vessel – whence the smoke forms a stratum for miles nearly parallel to the horizon.
>
> Where it otherwise three vessels instead of one, or more vessels instead of three, would exclude the possibility of a lower space being free from <u>vapour</u>.
>
> Pray consider well before you suggest any doubt <u>that is possible to over-</u><u>come</u> – for it will be sure to be laid hold of and magnified into an insur-mountable obstacle. Then 'murder will out', and the plan will supersede all other modes of affecting the objects in [question] as [well as] objects of similar nature, at a future time.[19]

Despite the mention of Kronstadt in the earlier communication, Dundonald's memorandum had, as stated, Sevastopol as its target, with a fairly detailed outline plan setting out his mode of attack. It is interesting to note that explosion vessels, which had not figured in his proposals vis-à-vis Kronstadt, reappear here. First he set out his material requirements:

> Twenty, thirty or more old vessels, procured at Constantinople or elsewhere, are required, also – A thousand tons of coal. A thousand barrels of gas tar. Two thousand tons of sulphur, and a quantity of fire wood, shavings, straw, reeds or other such materials, <u>compressed</u>, which are to be soaked with tar.
>
> Half the vessels may be fitted as smoke vessels. One fourth as sulphur vessels, and the remainder as explosion vessels. Note. The coal vessels must be kindled from rude galleries made of fire wood below the coal; all the materials being soaked with tar.
>
> Sulphur mixed with carbonaceous matters may be placed in the same vessel abaft the fire, in order to produce evaporation of its fumes. Sulphur vessels, fitted separately, must have wood coke or charcoal intermixed, and should be kindled from the fore part of the materials.
>
> The explosion vessels may be packed with masonry, especially on the side opposite to that on which the effect is to be produced.[20]

Perhaps mindful of one of the criticisms directed at his Plan by Sir John Burgoyne in his critique of the previous year, arguing that 'it would be extremely difficult to regulate the movements of the assailants', he attached a sketch and details of exactly how such navigation might be accomplished. In fact he had informed Burgoyne, and the other committee members, of his navigational methods: 'The smoke vessels are guided by vessels placed in a line with the fort to be attacked, and cross bearings may in like manner denote when the attacking force has arrived at a proper distance to anchor.'[21] Perhaps Burgoyne had forgotten this. In any event the 'Mode of Proceeding' as he termed it on this occasion was as follows:

> The wind being settled and favourable let two smoke vessels be taken in tow by the tug steam boat D – each vessel, on a broad sheer, on opposite quarters – and, when within range of shot, let one or both vessels be kindled – which will prevent direct aim from the batteries. When the vessels are near enough to the fort, which may be ascertained by a cross bearing, the tug boat is to 'cast off' the tow lines, each of which must have an anchor attached 'to bring the smoke vessels up'.
>
> A sulphur, or sulphurous vessels, must follow, ready matched, and anchor abreast, between, or to leeward of the smoke vessels; and another may be towed backward and forward opposite to the fortification, so that the fumes shall pervade every part.
>
> The batteries being silenced, explosion vessels may then be run along side of the ramparts to shatter the buildings or destroy the works; and ships of war may, in safety, take up positions and complete the ruin. In the latter case the smoke and sulphur vessels should be of iron.[22]

Tagged on to the end, a 'reflection', as he termed it, was a brief note concerning the applicability of his methods to military, as opposed to naval, operations. It is fairly clear that he had not, at this stage, given a high degree of thought to such matters, as a comparison with his 7 August memorandum to Lord Panmure will readily indicate:

> Tar barrels, matched with oakum, shavings, or other carbonaceous wicks, may be kindled to obscure an attacking force – and fascines, imbued with sulphur, may be set fire to and carried on poles towards the ramparts to be assailed – whence the defenders will infallibly be driven.[23]

The report from Playfair and his colleagues is of crucial importance as it is the first scientific appreciation of the ideas contained in the Plan, and is written in precise and scientific language that deals in the main with the facts of the matter rather than opinions. The opening paragraph is a succinct précis of the scheme:

> The Plan embraces two devices, the rendering of the air to windward of the place attacked irrespirable and asphyxiating by means of the fumes of

burning sulphur and the application of opaque smoke produced by the burning of tar and other combustibles to precede and conceal the sulphur vessels and thus facilitate their near approach to the point attacked.[24]

It moves on to deal with the assumptions, as they might be termed, that Lord Dundonald had concerning the effectiveness of his methods, and touches on an area of possible weakness hardly considered by him. It may be recalled that despite having no evidence that such was the case, Dundonald had consistently believed and stated that his methods were infallible. The Playfair report was not so sanguine:

Lord Dundonald rests the efficacy of his plan a good deal upon testimony of ordinary experience as to the suffocating effects of sulphurous fumes. He further has observed that from certain sulphur kilns in Sicily visited by him and which were situated upon a hill, the fumes of the burning sulphur descended the sides of the hill instead of being carried away vertically as might have been expected. It does not however follow that the direction taken by the fumes in such circumstances was due to their weight, as a descending current of air which is often observed on the flank of mountains might readily evolve and carry them with it.[25]

With the exception of Michael Faraday's contribution to the Martin Committee – which had been perhaps circumscribed by the nature of the enquiries put to him – those pronouncing previously on the plans had effectively no scientific knowledge to guide them as to the actual effects of sulphur dioxide. It is the case that Sir Thomas Hastings had sought advice from a manufacturer of sulphur on the properties of the fumes – fumes necessarily confined – but other than this there had been more conjecture than fact. For example, the Hastings committee report in 1847 had stated 'we assume it to be possible that the plan No 2 contains power for producing the sweeping destruction the inventor ascribes to it', but it had rejected plan No 2 on other grounds without ascertaining whether or not its assumption was correct. The Playfair report rectified this omission – an omission, it may be noted, of nearly fifty years' standing:

The current information on the asphyxiating powers of sulphurous fumes being in our opinion vague and imperfect we have found it necessary in order to obtain data for forming a judgement on Lord Dundonald's plans, to make some experiments on the subject and also to consider the mode in which the heat of the same fumes would affect their passage in a horizontal direction under the influence of wind.

Our experiments prove that the combustion of 1lb of sulphur which in burning produces in round numbers 12 cubic feet of sulphurous acid renders 15,000 cubic feet of [normal] air wholly irrespirable, in fact one fourth of this quantity of sulphur burned in the same volume of air rendered the air intolerable to some individuals but not to all, some could respire in it certainly for several minutes and all by making use as a respirator of a folded towel frequently moistened in water – any exertion causing deep and full inspirations would however have been impossible in the room charged with this lesser quantity and it may be supposed therefore that even this amount would incapacitate an enemy from working his guns.

Considering these two experiments together we may safely reckon that six pounds of sulphur would render 100,000 cubic feet of air wholly intolerable even for a few seconds, while 2lbs of sulphur in the same volume of air would produce an atmosphere unfit for active exertion although life might be preserved in it.

Supposing that it was decided to render fully asphyxiating a [quantity] of air having a square mile at base and a height of 100 feet. 75 tons of sulphur would require to be burned in it and if we suppose this quantity to be burned in a line of fires one mile in length in the course of 20 minutes and in a breeze which travelled a mile during the same time (in other words in a three mile per hour breeze) we should have the square mile charged with sulphurous acid to the degree required. If the same quantity [...] were burned in twenty minutes as before but with a wind of six miles per hour the air would be charged with sulphurous vapours only to the extent of one half, and with a wind of 12 miles per hour, at one fourth [...] the sulphurous vapours being diluted in proportion to the velocity of the wind sweeping over a given quantity of burning sulphur.[26]

Having moved that question on to a scientific basis, however, in establishing what the fumes generated by the burning of sulphur would probably achieve from given quantities, the report proceeded to specify the problems concerning the production of the sulphur dioxide, due to the heat produced in so doing. Faraday had more or less addressed this question in his earlier deposition and stated:

If a ship charged with sulphur were burning in a current of air, a continuous stream of sulphuric acid fumes, mingled with air, would pass off from it. This stream, being heavier than air, would descend and move along over the surface of the water; and, I suppose, would sink perpendicularly and expand laterally, so as to form a low broad stream.

There is no evidence, however, and it certainly would seem improbable, that he had actually carried out any physical experimentation to validate his opinion on that first occasion. The Playfair committee had, at least on a minor scale, rectified that omission, and the findings were somewhat discouraging to the author of the Plans:

In burning sulphur a considerable quantity of heat is generated and this by heating the air into which its fumes pass renders it lighter and gives to it an ascenscional direction which removes it from the surface of the earth.

The amount of sulphur burned in the air to the extent of 6lb to 100,000 cubic feet, the proportion necessary to render it highly asphyxiating, would, supposing there were no cooling agencies at work, raise the heat of that air 14° [F] and give it an ascenscional velocity of 3 feet a second or rather less than 9 miles an hour. In actual practice from the cooling agencies of the sea or land, the heating and consequently the ascenscional velocity would be less considerable. This ascenscional velocity produced by the lightness of the heated air would be compensated to a small extent by the increased weight of the sulphurous acid gas which is twice as heavy as common air, but the amount of [this] deduction [. . .] is only one thirty fourth part of the amount of the ascenscional power.

Both in the case of the heating of the air by the sulphur and by the burning of the smoke materials the ascending air would produce as a secondary result currents of air tending from all sides to the focus of heat and this might produce in the case of a slight breeze an alteration or even stoppage of its effects in that particular place. [. . .] The eddies thus produced and the usual subordinate movements of the wind would no doubt tend to bring down some of the asphyxiating air which had ascended and in this way the sulphurous fumes might be [sensible?] in the direction of the wind to a great distance from the burning sulphur although greatly under the asphyxiating strength. The irregular movements of the air referred to are entirely beyond calculation and to depend upon them would be to leave the issue to chance.

From what has preceded it will be obvious that the ascenscional movement of the heated air charged with sulphurous fumes withdraws all certainty from its asphyxiating effects at considerable distances, that is such distances as several hundred yards, as the only result that can be calculated upon is that the fumes will have ascended so high by that time as to prevent their enveloping the object to be attacked when drifted over it by the wind.[27]

The problems associated with combustion having been identified as a major, but not necessarily fatal, flaw in the Plan, the report goes on to put the above information in context with regard to the limitations it imposed:

Lord Dundonald states that his intention is in all cases where there is sufficient depth of water to run the sulphur vessels under the cover of the smoke close to the forts to be attacked and that 100 yards he would generally consider to be a maximum distance for their position. This is in fact the limit which we are inclined to assign for probable success against a fort of small elevation and the nearer to which the fort can be approached within this maximum the more certain will the action of the fumes become.

In conclusion then we consider that Lord Dundonald's plans as submitted to us offer a reasonable prospect of success when sulphur vessels can be brought within a distance of 100 yards which his lordship considers attainable but that beyond this distance the presumption is against success.[28]

The report sets out the clearest indication so far of what degree of success in action might be achieved, and thus falls on Lord Dundonald's side of the fence as it were. It can be viewed therefore as a partial, if not total, vindication of Lord Dundonald's long-laid Plan. This judgement stands in curious contrast then to Palmerston's 4 May utterances in the House of Commons; clearly 'a reasonable prospect of success' on the one hand and 'such difficulties of execution and such doubtful expectations as to the result' on the other are statements difficult to reconcile. Perhaps, though, these difficulties are only true for the non-politician, and that Palmerston was a masterful practitioner of the political arts is hardly a proposition open to question. Certainly he was concerned with keeping the matter as quiet as possible, and if his prevarications were indeed in the interests of national security then he is entitled to the benefit of any doubt. Clearly his statement to Panmure of 7 August suggests that he had been 'economical with the truth' in the House of Commons, but whatever political machinations were involved, approval had effectively been given for active use of the Secret War Plans of Lord Dundonald, directed by their author in person. Indeed, directing them in person was what he insisted upon according to his autobiography:

> In the late war with Russia, I twice offered these plans to the Government. [. . .] As regarded [sic] Sevastopol, the question was put to me whether I would instruct two engineer officers in applying them? My answer was, 'No, I have offered to risk my own life and reputation on their efficacy, but will not impart my mode of applying them to others, who may not, either from preconceived notions or professional jealousy of naval inventions, comprehend them.'[29]

Sadly, at least from Lord Dundonald's point of view, it was not to be. That the scheme was never put into operation, and that Sevastopol fell following conventional and, in terms of casualties, expensive operations are matters of historical fact. On this occasion, rather than obstructive bureaucrats or those whom he always reckoned to have secretly conspired against him, the enemy had been time. The same enemy was to catch up with the Plans' author some five years later, when the long and eventful life of the 10th Earl of Dundonald finally ended.

16 The 10th Earl of Dundonald (1775–1860) in
his last years
Photograph courtesy of the 15th Earl of Dundonald

Lyon Playfair met his own end on the 29 May 1898, and the following year a biography of his life was published using correspondence collated by his widow, as well as an unpublished autobiographical essay.[30] There is a brief account of his involvement with the Dundonald Plans during the Crimean War:

> The Government appointed my former teacher [Professor Thomas] Graham, then Master of the Mint, and myself, to receive the secret communications from Lord Dundonald and to report on their probable efficacy. [. . .] Lord Dundonald was then to me a new acquaintance, but our intercourse speedily ripened into a friendship, although he knew perfectly well that I reported unfavourably as to the chief part of his invention, while I thought that the minor part, to which he did not attach much importance, was susceptible of extensive application. [. . .] The Master of the Mint and I did not feel justified in recommending the Government to adopt them [the Plans], and Lord Palmerston coincided with our views.[31]

It is difficult to reconcile the above account with the documentation produced

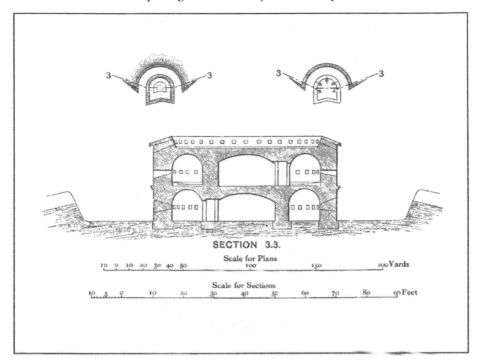

SECTION 3.3.

Scale for Plans

10 0   10   20   30   40   50   100   150   200 Yards

Scale for Sections

10   5   0   10   20   30   40   50   60   70   80   90 Feet

17 The Malakoff Tower

On 8 September 1855, the French stormed the Malakoff using traditional methods and, after desperate fighting, took and held the place, albeit the Tower had been reduced to rubble. The fall of the Malakoff position was the end of the siege; the Russians evacuated Sevastopol after sinking their ships and blowing up all the defences.

Drawing taken from Sir George Sydenham Clarke, *Fortification: Its Past Achievements, Recent Developments, and Future Progress*, 2nd edn (London: John Murray, 1907.)

contemporaneously, and the reference to the 'chief' and 'minor' parts of the invention is equally tricky to settle. For example, it is clear from the documents quoted that the use of sulphur fumes formed the main or 'chief' part of the plan, and the use of smoke the 'minor', and indeed Playfair suggested ways in which the use of sulphur dioxide might be enhanced, and one moreover that would have approximated the gas warfare of a later century more closely. This is so because while identifying the limitations inherent with the heat generated during the *in situ* process of generating sulphur dioxide, he had also suggested means of overcoming them:

> No such limitation as we have made for forts at low elevation need be assigned if the sulphurous fumes were cold and if methods of cooling the vapours were devised a powerful means of attack at very considerable distances would in our opinion be attained.

Without further enquiries we are not prepared to recommend such methods, but we would at the same time point out that it is quite within the range of chemical knowledge to evolve large volumes of cold sulphurous acid. [. . .] It would even be easy by mechanical means to fill strong iron boilers with liquid sulphurous acid made by condensing sulphur fumes under pressure and this liquid acid on the removal of the pressure would assume the form of a gas producing much cold on doing so. Whether such devices might be used alone or in combination with the cheaper mode of burning sulphur in order to cool the air when it is decided to act upon works at a considerable distance from the besiegers is rather a subject for future enquiries than for an opinion on the one method submitted by Lord Dundonald.[32]

Substitute 'iron cylinders' for 'iron boilers' and what one has, to all intents and purposes, is the same equipment as was used during the Great War, by all sides, to deliver cloud gas attacks.

The difficulty in reconciling Playfair's words in his memoirs, the relevant portion of which was taken from his autobiographical notes, with the documents he produced is rendered all the greater because he makes plain that he had the documents in his possession until he returned them to the Dundonald family:

> In the year 1886 I gave to his grandson, the present Lord Dundonald [the 12th Earl], all the papers relating to his grandfather's inventions, so that they are not likely to be lost to the world by my death, if my estimate of their value was not a correct one.[33]

The 12th Earl says that the papers he received from Playfair concerning the Plans were given to him only 'shortly before his [Playfair's] death', and that they consisted of more than just the documents authored by Playfair:

> When Lord Dundonald died he left his Plans with his friend Professor (afterwards Lord) Playfair, [. . .] [who] entrusted them to me under a pledge of secrecy, to divulge them only in case of national emergency.[34]

Perhaps Playfair's dating of 1886 as the year he returned the Plans to the Dundonald family is mistaken and he meant 1896, which would be more in accord with the 12th Earl recalling being given them shortly before Playfair's death in 1898. Unfortunately, only speculation is possible, as it is with regard to the discrepancies between Playfair's autobiographical writings and his contemporaneously produced documents. Perhaps conceiving them as having potential he wished to divert any attention from them by, in public, asserting their uselessness. Regrettably, we shall never know.

What does seem more certain is that had Sevastopol not fallen when it did, it is probable that Dundonald would have proceeded along the lines he had outlined at assorted times over the years. He had, utilising contemporary technology, conceived a method of generating an effective chemical weapon, and one in substantial quantities at that. If the success he always claimed would attend his endeavours eluded him, however, it would have been entirely possible to have developed the technique along the lines suggested by Playfair – if indeed any such development was required. Had Dundonald been able to stage the attacks he wanted, it is legitimate to conclude that such a full-scale usage would have ushered in the age of chemical and poison gas warfare somewhere between sixty and one hundred and four years before such 'modern' methods were introduced to a shocked world. Whether or not this would have been a praiseworthy achievement is, of course, a matter of judgement, but it was in the year 1914 that such a period of 'national emergency' as the 10th Earl could hardly have envisaged transpired. Accordingly it fell to his grandson, the 12th Earl, to offer the Plans to the government of the day.

6

Different Lines of Thought?

When difficulties and dangers perplex all minds, it has often happened in history that many men by different lines of thought arrive at the same conclusions.

Winston S. Churchill, 1899

S OME accounts of the origins of chemical warfare claim that Thucydides chronicled the first use of burning sulphur as a weapon in *The History of the Peloponnesian War*, therefore the technique was evolved in antiquity.[1] Thucydides does indeed relate how sulphur was burned at two sieges, but upon reading the relevant accounts it is difficult to conclude that it was burned with the same intention that Dundonald had. The first account deals with the siege of Plataea in 429 B.C. It tells how the Peloponnesians decided to try the effect of fire to destroy the city as they did not relish the prospect, or expense, of a long investment. They built up a huge heap of timber between their works and the city and set it alight: 'using sulphur and pitch to make it burn'.[2] This produced a huge fire, which nearly succeeded in its aim, but was extinguished by a rainstorm.

The second incident was in 424 B.C., at the siege of Delium. It details the construction and use of what might have been known in later times as an 'infernal machine':

> They took a great beam, sawed it in two parts, both of which they completely hollowed out, and then fitted the two parts closely together again, as in the joints of a pipe. A cauldron was then attached with chains to one end of the beam, and an iron tube, curving down into the cauldron, was inserted through the hollow part of the beam. Much of the surface of the beam itself was plated with iron. They brought up this machine from some distance on carts to the part of the wall that had been principally constructed of vines and other wood. When it was close to the wall, they inserted into their end of the beam large bellows and blew through them. The blast, confined inside the tube, went straight into the cauldron which was filled with lighted coals, sulphur and pitch. A great flame was produced which set fire to the wall and made it impossible for the defenders to stay at their posts.[3]

According to the *Encyclopaedia Britannica*, sulphur 'has been known from ancient times, and owing to its flammability, was regarded by the alchemists as the principle of combustion'.[4] With this in mind, and without any information as to the proportions of the various substances, it seems probable at least that, in the above examples, the sulphur was added for its flammable properties, rather than for its fumes when ignited.

Fire was as great a danger to the sailors manning wooden ships in the third century B.C. as it was to their descendants in the nineteenth century A.D. (and still is to a certain extent, as per the *Sheffield* during the 1982 Falkland Islands campaign). It also seems that sulphur was one of the constituents of those incendiary substances known as Greek fire, wildfire and sea, or wet, fire. Unfortunately, the secret of the composition of these devices has been lost to the modern world, though many have speculated upon it, including the science-fiction writer Isaac Asimov:

> We *guess* that Greek fire was some combination of sulfur, naphtha, quicklime (calcium oxide) and niter (potassium nitrate). Naphtha is a hydrocarbon mixture found naturally in the Middle East that is not too different from modern gasoline. [...] When water is added to Greek fire, it reacts with the calcium oxide and develops considerable heat in the process – enough heat to ignite the naphtha in the presence of oxygen released from the potassium nitrate. This, in turn, ignites the sulfur, making it burn and produce choking vapors of sulfur dioxide. If the Greek-fire mixture is placed in brass-bound wooden tubes and if a jet of water hits it from behind, it will burst into flame. The push of the water and the expansion of the exhaust gases formed will combine to fling the burning mixture out of the tube for considerable distances. If the burning mixture hits the ocean surface, it will float and it will burn all the more fiercely.[5]

Lord Hankey records that while carrying out research into 'expedients and stratagems of the past' during 1914–15 (see Chapter 7) he investigated Edward Gibbon's prescription for Greek Fire.[6] Gibbon recorded it as follows:

> The principle ingredient of the Greek fire was the naptha, or liquid bitumen, a light, tenacious, and inflammable oil, which springs from the earth, and catches fire as soon as it comes in contact with the air. The naptha was mingled, I know not by what methods or in what proportions, with sulphur and with the pitch that is extracted from evergreen firs. From this mixture, which produced a thick smoke and a loud explosion, proceeded a fierce and obstinate flame [which] instead of being extinguished [...] was nourished and quickened by the element of water; and sand, urine, or vinegar, were the only remedies that could damp the fury of this powerful agent.[7]

Hankey's laconic comment was that the above 'did not provide a satisfactory starting point for our researches'.[8]

The historian Sir Steven Runciman records how during the siege of Constantinople in 1453, the Turkish Admiral, Suleiman Balthoglu, reduced a fortification on the island of Prinkipo, in the Sea of Marmora. With cannon proving ineffective against its defences, he gathered together timber, placed it against the walls and ignited it, adding sulphur and pitch to the flames.[9] This drove the defenders from their position; the ones who survived the fire were put to death for their pains. Again we see the use of sulphur, but probably as an aid to ignition, rather than as a 'chemical weapon'.[10]

The burning of various substances in order to drive miners from their galleries during formal investments has been chronicled. Johann Grant's driving the Turk from their mines under the walls of Constantinople during 1453[11] and the attempts to foil Cromwell's miners at Edinburgh Castle in 1650[12] are examples, though poorly documented, of this technique being utilised in specific circumstances in the pre-industrial age.

Later events have generated rather better sources. For example, upon the outbreak of the Crimean War in 1854, Lyon Playfair 'wrote a letter to the Prince Consort which he forwarded to the Master of the Ordnance, suggesting one or two applications of science to the purposes of war'.[13] The first application he suggested was the development of an incendiary shell, 'a hollow brittle shell containing phosphorous dissolved in bisulphide of carbon for the purpose of producing conflagration of the enemy's stores or property'.[14] The account continued:

> The other proposal in my letter was to have a hollow brittle shell containing cyanide of cacodyl. This is an intensely poisonous substance, a few drops of which in a room would poison the occupants. Such a shell going between decks of a ship would render the atmosphere irrespirable, and poison the men if they remained at the guns. This suggestion was considered inadmissible by the military authorities, who stated that it would be as bad a mode of warfare as poisoning the wells of the enemy. There was no sense in this objection. It is considered a legitimate mode of warfare to fill shells with molten metal which scatters among the enemy, and produces the most frightful modes of death. Why a poisonous vapour which would kill men without suffering is to be considered illegitimate warfare is incomprehensible.[15]

Playfair was thus among the first of many to discover that methodology considered 'humane' by those who shared his scientific outlook nonetheless instilled something close to revulsion in the minds of those not so endowed. This was to become a recurring theme vis-à-vis the use of chemical weapons. A more pertinent point, in the utilitarian sense, was made by Wyndham D. Miles when he noted that, had the idea been taken up, the British government would have had to put 'half the chemists in the British Isles at work in order to get sufficient material for the bombardment of one Russian warship'.[16]

The practical difficulties with ordnance of an unconventional kind became apparent on several occasions during the American Civil War. One such occurred on 22 August 1863 when an artillery piece of the Union Army emplaced at Morris Island marsh fired its first shot at the Confederate city of Charleston. This weapon, dubbed 'Swamp Angel' by its crew, was an eight-inch 200-pounder Parrott rifle. To emplace it had involved laying a trestle road some two and a half miles through swamp. At the end of this road, piles were hammered into the mud to a depth of twenty feet and upon these a platform constructed, and some 13,000 sandbags, containing 800 tons of sand, were built around it for protection. The Swamp Angel, weighing in at 16,500 pounds, was then hauled into position. General Quincy Adams Gillmore, commanding the Federal forces, had ordered the employment of the rifle as a weapon of terror; its function was to punish the citizens of Charleston for refusing to surrender. To this end the shells employed were of an incendiary nature; the substance they contained was called 'Greek Fire' by its inventors, Berney and Short, but the exact composition, as of the original substance, is unknown.[17]

Twelve Berney shells and four Short shells were fired during the first night of the bombardment, causing the desired terror, but not much damage. General Pierre Beauregard, the Confederate commander, issued a protest at this 'act of inexcusable barbarity' and the British consul at the city tried to see Gillmore in person to remonstrate.[18]

The *Nashville Union* later mocked the protests, and referred to some side effects of the incendiary filling:

> Tis sweet to draw one's dying breath for one's dear land, as Horace saith,
> But dreadful to be stunk to death.[19]

The last laugh was, momentarily, had by the citizens of Charleston, for after firing its thirty-sixth round the 'Swamp Angel', charged with quadruple weights of powder to achieve the desired range, burst.

Other guns, however, soon came within range of the city and the incendiary bombardment continued, with the same disappointing results. The unfortunate tendency of the Short shells to burst in, or just on leaving, the gun did not endear them to the gun crews. The Berney variation fared no better. Levi Short visited the scene and tried to make *ad hoc* improvements to his weapons, but without success. He proposed the addition of noxious ingredients, of an unspecified nature, to his shells for the purpose of 'stinking out' the rebel garrison of nearby Fort Sumter,[20] but the military's faith in him and his works had evaporated. Conventional shells

95

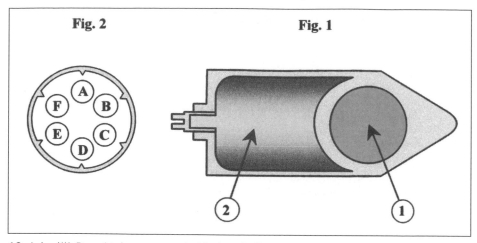

18 John W. Doughty's proposed chlorine shell

On 5 April 1862 John W. Doughty, a schoolteacher from New York, had written a letter to the US Secretary of War, Edwin M. Stanton, urging upon him the employment of 10 inch (254 mm) artillery shells filled with liquid chlorine. The letter included a drawing, reproduced here, with an explanation:

Fig. 1 Longitudinal section.

Fig. 2 Transverse section of chlorine chamber.

The flanges A–F are to strengthen the chamber without much diminishing its capacity.

1. Chamber of common shell.

2. Chlorine chamber.

There is no communication between the two (though) they are both in the same casing.

Graphic courtesy of Michael Collins. From an original reproduced in Scott D. Bennion and Kathy David-Bajar, 'Cutaneous Reactions to Nuclear, Biological, and Chemical Warfare', Chapter 5 in 'Military Dermatology, Part III: Disease and The Environment', in Brigadier-General Russ Zajtchuk (ed.), *Text book of Military Medicine* (Washington, DC: Office of The Surgeon General Department of the Army, 1994)

replaced the incendiary versions and caused great damage to the city and surrounding works, demonstrating that, with the technology available, recourse to 'chemical warfare' was unprofitable.

Levi Short's proposals were not the only ones made during the American Civil War for utilising 'chemical' weaponry. On 5 April 1862 John W. Doughty, a schoolteacher from New York, had written a letter to the US Secretary of War, Edwin M. Stanton, urging upon him the employment of 10 inch artillery shell filled with liquid chlorine. He explained the principle of his proposed device, which he accompanied with a drawing.

The above is a representation of a projectile which I have devised to be used as a means for routing an *entrenched* enemy. Believing it to be new and valuable, I send the War Department a brief description: Chlorine is a gas so irritating in its effects upon the respiratory organs, that a small quantity diffused in the atmosphere, produces incessant & uncontrollably violent coughing. It is [two and one-half] times heavier than the atmosphere, and when subjected to a pressure of 60 pounds to the inch, it is condensed into a liquid, its volume being reduced many hundred times. A shell holding two or three quarts would therefore contain many cubic feet of the gas.

If the shell should explode over the heads of the enemy, the gas would, by its great specific gravity, rapidly fall to the ground: the men could not dodge it, and their first intimation of its presence would be by its inhalation, which would most effectually disqualify every man for service that was within the circle of its influence; rendering the disarming and capturing of them as certain as though both their legs were broken.

To silence an enemy's guns or drive him from his entrenchments, it would be only necessary to explode the shells over his head or on his windward side. If exploded in rapid succession over or within a fort, evacuation or surrender could not be delayed beyond fifteen minutes. Casemates and bomb-proofs would not protect the men.

This kind of shell would, I think, in the present advanced state of military engineering, be a very efficient means for warding off the attacks of iron-clad vessels and *steam rams*; for, as to the steam ram, a ten inch gun that would carry a shell containing a gallon or two of the liquid, would with ordinary accuracy, be able at the distance of ¾ of a mile, to envelop him in an atmosphere that would cause his inmates to be more anxious about their own safety than about the destruction of their enemy.

It may be asked if the gas which drove the enemy from his guns, would not prevent the attacking party who used the gas from taking possession of the abandoned position. I answer it would not: for, this shell does not, like the Chinese stink-pots, deposit a material emitting a deleterious gas *lighter* than the atmosphere, but suddenly projects into the air a *free* gas much *heavier* than the atmosphere, which does its work as it descends to the earth, where it is soon absorbed.

Experiment alone can determine whether this shell has any practical merit. Possibly, I overrate its value; but it must not be forgotten, that while it does the work of an ordinary shell, it also carries with it a force against whose effect the most skilful military engineering can not possibly make any adequate provision.

As to the moral question involved in its introduction, I have, after watching the progress of events during the last eight months with reference to it, arrived at the somewhat paradoxical conclusion, that its introduction would very much lessen the sanguinary character of the battlefield, and at the same time render conflicts more decisive in their results.[21]

Doughty's letter went to General James Wolfe Ripley of the Ordnance Department, who at first took no action, and then, on further enquiry from Doughty, replied that the department was too busy to pursue the matter, a statement that was undoubtedly true. Doughty tried again two years later, but with no more success.[22]

On the Confederate side similar thoughts had occurred. In 1861 Private Isham Walker had written to Lucius Walker, the Secretary of War, proposing a futuristic scheme whereby air-delivered poison gas be used against Fort Pickens and the Federal ships guarding it near Pensacola, Florida. The delivery vehicle was to be a balloon, but the idea was not proceeded with.[23] On 10 June 1864 Brigadier-General Pendleton, Lee's chief gunner, had written to Lt-Col. Baldwin, the Army of Northern Virginia's Chief of Ordnance:

> I saw noticed in a recent paper a stink shell, and it seems to me such missiles might be made useful to some extent at least. We have a few howitzers, chiefly 12-pounders, which can be used somewhat as mortars. They can throw shells occasionally in or near the enemy's trenches. The question is whether the explosion can be combined with suffocating effect of certain offensive gases, or whether apart from explosion such gases may not be emitted from a continuously burning composition as to render the vicinity of each falling shell intolerable. It seems at least worth a trial.[24]

The reply Pendleton received from Lt-Col. W. Le Roy Brown was: 'Stink-balls, none on hand; don;t keep them; will make if ordered.'[25]

The positional warfare waged during the campaigns around Richmond and St Petersburg bears close resemblance to the fighting of the Great War some fifty years later. As during the Crimean War conventional methods were discovered to be, if not inadequate, at least inordinately expensive and time-consuming, and alternative methods of dislodging the defenders of difficult-to-assault positions were bound to be contemplated; hence the consideration of 'chemical' weaponry. Writing much later, in 1937, Lt-Col. A.M. Prentiss of the US Army Chemical Warfare Service stated:

> The value of chemicals as war weapons had attracted the serious speculation of military minds as early as our civil war, but no practical progress was made in this field because of the then undeveloped state of the chemical industry [...] The use of chemicals as warfare agents was not practicable, even though the possibilities may have been recognised, until the chemical industry had attained sizeable proportions.[26]

This comment well illustrates the practical difficulties of introducing new weapons. Where are they to come from and how are they to be manufactured? Something may be fine in theory but will usually prove difficult, as a study of any aspect of military history will demonstrate, to put into practice. As it was, the War Departments and industrial capacity of both sides were taxed to the limit supplying the 'ordinary' requisites of war .

The Franco-Prussian war of 1870–71 was a very different conflict from the American Civil War. Conducted, at least initially, by professional armies consisting of a core of full-time troops brought up to war strength by the mobilisation of trained reserves, it swiftly demonstrated the superiority of the German system over that of the French. The German invasion, following on the French declaration of war on 15 July 1870, was more than ably directed by General Helmuth von Moltke – it was to confirm his reputation as a strategic genius.[27] The French field armies were speedily neutralised during a three-month campaign, which, following the decisive German victory at Sedan, saw Paris invested on 20 September 1870.

The city of Paris was well defended by a ring of fortresses, and the Germans had to decide how best to reduce the place. The military were, in general, against bombardment and assault, preferring investment with starvation and deprivation to do their work for them. They had therefore made no plans for bringing up a siege train. Bismarck wanted the city bombarded without further ado and gained the support of the Prussian King, William I, in this. Despite the inevitable logistical difficulties, Moltke had four armies in France, which all relied on the French rail network, stretched and prone to interdiction as it was, the 250 heavy guns decreed necessary for the effort were brought up. Following the essential preparations, the bombardment commenced on the morning of 27 December 1870.

The inhabitants of Paris, with no hope of relief after the newly formed Republican armies, raised in the provinces, proved utterly incapable of matching the Germans, made several attempts to break the investing lines, but without success. With the failure of 'ordinary' methods, and bearing in mind that there was little in the way of central authority, various committees sprang up and proposed new means of defeating the invader. Dozens of madcap proposals were put forward, but among the more 'rational' were ones for 'decomposing' the air around the Prussians, for manufacturing shells that would emit 'suffocating vapours' and for bombarding the enemy positions with bottles containing smallpox germs.[28] A chemist announced that he had discovered a powerful new explosive called 'fulminate of picrate of potass', which he described as ten times stronger than 'simple picrate of potass'. With this instrument of destruction he undertook to sweep the enemy from the face of the Earth. He also professed to have invented a preparation that would asphyxiate any living creature upon which it was projected.[29]

The composition of these substances remains obscure, and their actual manufacture and use was highly improbable, but the description 'fulminate of picrate of potass' suggests a composition of, or containing, picric acid. Picric acid is a powerful explosive, which was adopted as a filling for high-explosive shell during the latter years of the nineteenth century, until it was superseded by TNT in the early part of the twentieth. Adopted by all major military powers, and known to the British as Lyddite, picric acid gives off extremely toxic fumes following its detonation, and this may have been the effect referred to as regard the 'asphyxiating preparation'. Whatever the chemists of Paris had postulated or created was to be of no avail, for Paris and France eventually conceded to the German forces, an armistice being signed on 28 January 1871. This was not to end the conflict within the city. The 'civil war' between the Commune and the Versailles government was to add to the tribulations of the much-troubled metropolis.

A communard scientist, Dr Parisel, studied 'chemical' methods of warfare and sought information as to the availability of sulphur, phosphorous and the like. An attempt was made to manufacture Greek Fire, but the effort was sabotaged. In one of the revolutionary papers, the *Cri du Peuple,* a threat to the government was printed: 'Not a soldier will enter Paris. If M. Thiers is a chemist, he will understand.'[30] On 16 May 1871 the Commune officially informed the government that its adhesion to the Geneva Convention would not prevent it from employing: 'the new engines of war of which the revolution disposes'.[31]

All this was pure fantasy. There were no 'new engines of war' that could have made any impact on the military situation, and even if there had been chemicals that possessed the properties claimed the quantities required would not have been available. The Germans defeated the French using normal methods. The French resisted in the conventional manner, and the fighting between the Versaillese and the Commune retained a traditional, though bloodthirsty, character.

A military history, published in 1894–95, had this to say on the subject:

> The grand chemical agents of wholesale destruction, like a great many similar inventions, remain untried. Either there is no composition capable of effecting these enormous massacres, or governments shrink from employing such weapons, which, moreover, might at any time be turned against themselves. Yet science is every year entering more and more into the operations of warfare, which increases in deadliness to an equal degree; and it is impossible to say what may not be done in the future.[32]

The British did consider using an asphyxiating gas to protect what was considered in certain quarters to be a scheme that would tear a hole, if not a great gap, in the Island Nation's defences. The concept of a tunnel between Britain and France attracted great opposition from some sections of the British military. It was a Frenchman, Thome de Gamond, who had submitted a plan for such an endeavour to Napoleon III in 1856, and he had gathered the support of several eminent personages on the British side also. Queen Victoria and the Prince Consort were much in favour and such well-known engineers as Brunel, Lock, Stephenson, and Hawkshaw were most enthusiastic. The railway companies on both shores also took the project seriously. The two governments concerned went so far as to sign a convention to regulate the project in 1875.

The possibility of an enemy utilising such a work to invade Britain was what concerned several eminent military, and political, men. The prospect of an enemy landing force capturing the British end and then being reinforced via the tunnel itself exercised their minds to a large degree. Among the generals most opposed was Sir Garnet Wolseley. A committee of military personnel was convened in May 1882 to consider methods of closing the tunnel to an enemy should the occasion arise. Presided over by Major-General Sir Archibald Alison the members were: Major-General Gallwey, Colonel Stokes, Colonel Clarke, Colonel Alderson, Colonel Majendie, Professor Abel, Mr Gregory and Mr Graves. This committee advised, among a host of other proposals, that a mechanism for discharging irrespirable gases should be installed.

However, Wolseley was vehement in his denunciation of the project and swept aside the assurances that the work could be closed off if necessary:

> The various means for blowing up, drowning or asphyxiating people in the tunnel, controlled as such means would be by various agents liable to accidents while testing the plant, would [. . .] prevent passengers from using the tunnel, which would have greater terrors than the sea passage. Public opinion would be sure to cry out for the removal of these mines and other safeguards, and in this event surprise would be facilitated.[33]

It has to be conceded that he had a point. Whatever the merits of the various arguments for or against, the Channel Tunnel project was stopped, only to re-emerge in the 1980s, by which time the technology of warfare had made the idea of utilising it for invasion purposes obsolete.

The asphyxiating effects of the products of combustion or explosion were to give rise to the accusation that gas was being used many decades before its actual employment. During the South African war of 1899–1902 the Lyddite shells used by the British army were considered by some to be contravening the recent Hague Declaration on the use of gas shell. Picric acid was extremely toxic, and many accounts of the campaign refer to the yellow residue left following its detonation.[34] An excellent illustration of its toxic properties can be found, by jumping forward a number of years to 1914, in the eye-witness report of Bert Kiel, the chief petty officer of the British gunboat *Cadmus*, who visited the wreck of the *Emden* at the Cocos Islands, following her destruction at the hands of HMAS *Sydney*:

The Sydney had lobbed Lyddite broadsides into her. Lyddite is poisonous. We saw all those lifeless, poisoned corpses stretched out next to one another on deck, over two hundred of them. Others before us had brought blankets from below deck and tied them around the necks of the bodies. We saw yellow everywhere, the yellow colour of the Lyddite powder.[35]

It would have been cold comfort to the victims to know that what had poisoned them was not, strictly speaking, a gas shell, and was therefore a 'legitimate' weapon. Likewise the Boer victims in South Africa, though they had small reason to complain, being equipped with modern Krupp artillery themselves, which fired a shell containing the German equivalent of Lyddite. The distinction was made explicit in a somewhat self-righteous account by a British surgeon vis-à-vis the Great War:

The fumes emitted by bursting charges of Lyddite, Melinite or Turpenite must not be confused with the poison gases sent out over our men by the Germans. The Lyddite and Melinite are put in the shells for a definite object which is permitted by the Hague Convention, and by the opinion of mankind generally. Their object is to burst the shell at the desired time and distance, and plaster the enemy with the iron or shrapnel. They are not intended to kill, and do not kill by poisonous fumes.[36]

The Japanese name for their high-explosive was Shimose,[37] and it was much in evidence at the epic siege of the Russian fortress of Port Arthur. This investment, an almost isolated campaign of the Russo-Japanese war of 1904–05, saw the Japanese Third Army stalled for a considerable period. The siege lasted for 154 days, after General Nogi's initial failure to take the place by storm, as he had done in 1894 with the loss of only sixteen men. Following this, though the attempt to storm was to be repeated several times with the same result, a formal investiture was begun. Eventually progress was made against tough opposition, and one of the keys to the Russian defences, Fort Chikuan (North fort No. 2), was reached by the Japanese sappers. Mining, and counter-mining, was practised by the protagonists and, ironically, it was the detonation of a Russian counter-mine on 23 October 1904, which, according to B.W. Norregard, one of the 'few foreign correspondents attached to the 3rd Imperial Japanese Army',[38] revealed to the Japanese a portion of the concrete covering of the counterscarp gallery of the fort.

This gallery was built wholly in concrete, with walls more than 6ft. thick. Along the front and western flank it was partitioned off by thick concrete walls into eight chambers communicating with each other by narrow arched doorways.[39]

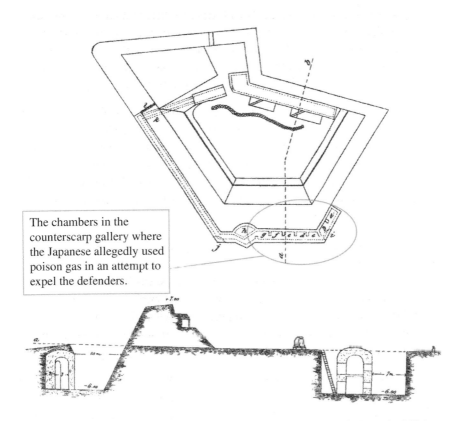

The chambers in the counterscarp gallery where the Japanese allegedly used poison gas in an attempt to expel the defenders.

19 The Japanese use of poison gas during the attack on Fort Chikuan in 1904
On the morning of 30 October 1904 the Japanese sappers had everything ready for an attempt to capture the counterscarp gallery of Fort Chikuan, also known as North Kikuan and North Fort No. 2. They breached the outer wall at 'i' and thus gained access into the chambers that divided up the gallery, eventually taking possession of chambers 'a' through to 'e'. It was during attempts to gain the remaining, Russian-held, chambers 'f' and 'g' that poisonous gas was allegedly used to drive out the defenders.
Drawings taken from B.W. Norregaard, *The Great Siege: The Investment and Fall of Port Arthur* (London: Methuen, 1906)

The Japanese penetrated the concrete wall of the gallery and entered the works, but found themselves confined to one of the chambers mentioned above; the Russians had blocked the communicating doorways with sandbags and were vigorously defending. The attackers managed to gain control over the five western chambers by placing dynamite charges in the loopholes facing the moat, and then rushing into the space before the defenders could reinforce it. The taking of the remaining three chambers proved more difficult. 'For nearly three weeks they fought desperately, day and night, down in these underground dungeons [. . .] to get possession of the next two chambers.'[40]

The chamber in contention had become a subterranean 'no-man's land', made uninhabitable because of 'hand grenades and other devilry'.[41] Given the difficulty of fighting in these awful conditions the Japanese sought to find alternative methods of expelling the Russians. Pumping the works full of water was considered but the difficulty of utilising the only water supply large enough, the sea, which was several miles away, frustrated this scheme. The next effort was a return to the ancient practice of making an underground work uninhabitable by allowing the products of combustion to asphyxiate, or drive out, the defenders. The Japanese:

> next tried to pile up stalks of kaoliang (the Chinese high millet) and set fire to them in order to smoke out the Russians. But the device did not work well; the draught took the smoke the wrong way, through the Japanese chambers, choking them and for a time forcing them out of their part of the gallery. The experiment was too dangerous to try again.[42]

Failing the success of the above scheme, the Russians alleged that the Japanese made another attempt:

> They sent down a man, rigged out in a diver's dress [. . .] provided with an air pump, by which he pumped the galleries full of asphyxiating gases. But, they say, it was a stratagem that cut both ways; for, though it certainly drove out the Russians, it also stopped the Japanese from entering until the air had become pure again, and then they found the Russians back.[43]

The asphyxiating gas used, according to a Russian general officer, was derived from burning material 'soaked in arsenic', the fumes of which 'stifled' the defenders.[44] This account appears to be the source of several later works that mention the event.[45]

This undertaking, if it truly took place, was taken to be yet another of the portents of how future war would be conducted that was ignored.[46] It might with equal justification be deemed a backward glance to the techniques of yesteryear. The Japanese, however, denied that they instigated any such method, and in turn accused the Russians of using asphyxiating bombs against them,[47] indicating again the distaste that the use of, or accusations of the use of, poisonous chemicals evoked. Norregard noted laconically that 'in the presence of a war correspondent at any rate, both parties trifle with the truth in a very wanton way',[48] and, in any event, it was by using 'tedious modes of attack' that Fort Chikuan, and eventually Port Arthur, were forced to succumb.

There is perhaps one further point to consider in relation to the subject of what might be inelegantly termed 'pre-chemical warfare' chemical warfare. This concerns the situation in international law, for it is undoubtedly the case that some of the methods that were later to become familiar were addressed in this arena several years before the event. In other words, chemical warfare in certain of its manifestations has the distinction, which if not unique is certainly uncommon, of being banned before it had been invented.

The prohibitions in question were embodied in declarations adopted by the two Hague Conferences on disarmament of 1899 and 1907.[49] The first conference was initiated by Czar Nicholas II, although it was the brainchild of General Alexei Kuropatkin, the Russian minister of war, who had sought a means of limiting the vast expense attendant on keeping up with the arms race of the time. In 1898 the Austrian army, perceived as Russia's main potential adversary at the time, was planning to re-equip its artillery with a rapid-fire field gun. The unbearable cost of following suit was the irresistible force behind Kuropatkin's idea. The Czar agreed, as did, perhaps naturally, the finance minister, Count Witte and the foreign minister, Count Muraviev. The prospect of admitting that Russia was unable to keep up was felt to be too embarrassing, however, and so the stratagem of disguising this fact behind an international conference on disarmament was evolved.

On 29 August 1898 the Czar issued his 'manifesto' to all the nations represented at St Petersburg, much to the surprise, and in some quarters dismay, of the rest of the world. While the various 'peace movements' were delighted and the press generally was favourable, the 'ruling classes' were more sceptical, if not downright hostile, for, substantially, the same reasons: a fear of being tricked, of being caught at a disadvantage. Despite this no country wanted to be seen openly hostile and while none wanted such an idea to succeed all had to present a positive public face. So, in spite of his undoubted knowledge of the true feelings of the various governments, in January 1899 Maraviev sent out his proposed agenda for the conference. It consisted of eight topics; the first proposed agreeing not to increase naval and military forces or budgets for a fixed period. The next three projected the prohibition of methods of warfare as yet conjectured and of devices that were at that time in their infancy, including submarines, asphyxiating gas and aerial bombing ['launching of projectiles from balloons']. The next four concerned themselves with the laws and usages of war and the application of arbitration to disputes between nations.

Despite all the various unspoken objections the conference convened at the Huis ten Bosch on the 18 May 1899 with 108 delegates from twenty-six countries present. The British delegation included Admiral Sir John 'Jacky' Fisher, at the time C-in-C of the Atlantic Station, and was headed by Sir Julian Pauncefote, the British ambassador to the United States. The American contingent included perhaps the most famous and influential personage to attend, Captain Alfred Thayer Mahan, whose published works were obligatory reading for those interested or involved in matters naval, and whose classic *The Influence of Sea Power on History,* published in 1890, was, by personal command of Kaiser Wilhelm II, placed on board all German warships.

As was to be expected from hard-headed delegates nominated by cynical governments whose burgeoning industries included massive and influential names like Krupp, Schneider-Creusot and Vickers-Maxim, there was to be no headway made in the matter of arms limitation. Proposals regarding the rules of warfare extracted, though privately, from Fisher the pungent aphorisms: 'the humanising of war, you might just as well talk of humanising Hell!'[50] and 'moderation in war is imbecility',[51] yet nevertheless managed a few tentative steps forward. On the subject of limiting the use of new or theoretical weapons some progress was made; despite British objections a motion banning the use of expanding or Dum-Dum bullets was carried by majority vote and the launching of explosives from balloons was unanimously condemned. That condemnation lasted only until the next session, however, when, having had time to think about it, the delegates fixed the ban at five years.

The conference circumscribed the use of another uninvented weapon when it adopted 'An International Declaration Respecting Asphyxiating Gases', declaring that:

The contracting Powers agree to abstain from the use of projectiles the sole object of which is the diffusion of asphyxiating or deleterious gases.[52]

The majorities of attendees felt able to agree on this, with one notable exception in Mahan. He explained his rationale in a report to the 'United States Commission to the International Conference':

As a certain disposition has been observed to attach odium to the view adopted by this Commission [the United States] in this matter, it seems proper to state, fully and explicitly [. . .] that on the first occasion of the subject arising in Sub-Committee, and subsequently at various times in full Committee, and before the Conference, the United States naval delegate did not cast his vote silently, but gave the reasons, which at his demand were inserted in the reports of the day's proceedings. These reasons were, briefly:
1. That no shell emitting such gases is as yet in practical use, or has

undergone adequate experiment; consequently, a vote taken now would be taken in ignorance of the facts as to whether the results would be of a decisive character, or whether injury in excess of that necessary to attain the end of warfare, the immediate disabling of the enemy, would be inflicted. 2. That the reproach of cruelty and perfidy, addressed against these supposed shells, was equally uttered formerly against firearms and torpedoes, both of which are now employed without scruple. Until we knew the effects of such asphyxiating shells, there was no saying whether they would be more or less merciful than missiles now permitted. 3. That it was illogical, and not demonstrably humane, to be tender about asphyxiating men with gas, when all were prepared to admit that it was allowable to blow the bottom out of an ironclad at midnight, throwing four or five hundred into the sea, to be choked by water, with scarcely the remotest chance of escape. If, and when, a shell emitting asphyxiating gases alone has been successfully produced, then, and not before, men will be able to vote intelligently on the subject.[53]

Malan thus advanced an observation, echoing, whether consciously or not, Playfair's point made in 1854, and published the same year as the conference convened, concerning the selective interpretation of 'humaneness'. Mahan was actually acting on directions regarding the matter that had been forwarded to the US delegation by Secretary of State John Hay. In opposing the resolution Hay's rationale was that the United States did not wish to deny itself prematurely a means of defence. He was also sceptical that any such agreement would overcome the temptations of a nation at war to use such devices if it deemed it advantageous: 'Considering the temptations to which men and nations are exposed in time of conflict, it is doubtful if an international agreement to this end would prove effective.'[54] Accordingly the US did not vote in favour of adopting the prohibition. Neither did the British.

The conference closed on 29 July 1899 and despite the deep cynicism and lack of desire of most of the participants for any meaningful outcome it was presented to the world as a great new beginning. The results in total were: three conventions were set up – on arbitration, the laws and customs of war on land and extending the Geneva rules to maritime warfare; the three declarations concerning balloons, expanding bullets, and gases were adopted; six wishes concerning future accomplishment were expressed, and a resolution that the future limitation of military expenditure and research was highly desirable and merited future study was announced.

One of the wishes expressed was for a second conference to be held at a time unspecified. Given the negative views of a majority of the participants there seemed little prospect of this, and given the international situation prevailing in the period immediately after the finish of the first conference there seemed little chance of a second, for soon after the British Empire found itself at war with the Transvaal and Orange Free State in Southern Africa. No recourse to international arbitration to settle the dispute there! The early years of the twentieth century saw international tensions grow and the arms race continue unabated, with its most obvious manifestation in the naval rivalry between Britain and Germany. In 1904 war began between Russia and Japan, which, to the surprise of many, saw the Japanese score several stunning victories, most notably the capture of Port Arthur in January 1905 and the annihilation of the Russian Baltic Fleet at Tsushima in May the same year. This fleet, renamed the 2nd Pacific Squadron, had sailed half-way around the world before its rendezvous with Admiral Togo and had nearly precipitated a war with Britain, which had a treaty with Japan, following an incident in the North Sea. Compensations for this incident were, ironically perhaps, settled by recourse to arbitration under the terms of the 1899 Hague Conference.

It was these successes of Japanese arms, though in truth they were as inconclusive in the military sphere as they were decisive in the naval (few now number Field Marshal Oyama in the pantheon of martial genius), rather than the humbling of the Russians, which prompted the American President Theodore Roosevelt to intervene and offer to arbitrate.

Roosevelt had proposed the convening of a second Hague Conference in 1904 but had accepted that it could not be held while two of its participants were at war. The parties negotiated a peace treaty under the aegis of the President at Portsmouth, New Hampshire, in August 1905 and the following month the somewhat chastened Czar issued invitations to a second conference, at The Hague, taking over from Roosevelt with the latter's blessing.

The second conference sat from 15 June to 18 October 1907, at the Dutch Parliament, the Huis ten Bosch being considered too small for the 256 representatives from forty-four states who attended. There was just as much cynicism from the same sources as had attended the first conference – the Kaiser, in one of his recurring belligerent moods, letting it be known that if limitation of armaments were mentioned the German delegation would immediately leave – but the results, on paper, nevertheless seemed fruitful.

Again arbitration became a bone of contention, but several subjects were agreed upon, with the requisite degree of obfuscation in order to accommodate varying interpretations, and fifty-six articles redefining the laws and customs of land warfare were adopted by all the attendant nations.

Once again the discharging of explosives or projectiles from balloons was prohibited for a further five years, and another resolution that sought to regulate 'Means of Injuring the Enemy, Sieges, and Bombardments' was adopted. The parts relevant, if only perhaps obliquely, to the current context were embodied in Article 23, the relevant portions of which read:

It is particularly forbidden:
(a) to employ poison or poisoned weapons.
(e) to employ arms, projectiles, or material calculated to cause unnecessary suffering.[55]

Despite the British delegation, acting on the instructions of a Liberal government 'desirous of promoting the utmost possible unanimity among the nations', retrospectively accepting the 1899 declaration against the use of asphyxiating gases,[56] perhaps the most illuminating, and forthright, comment on the reality of the whole business is that by the Kaiser. His annotation of the notes sent to him concerning the convention on arbitration, during the first conference, reveals both his own and, there is much evidence to suggest, many others' perception of the concept of conferences in total. The 'All Highest's' feelings are self-evident:

> I consented to all this in order that the Czar should not lose face before Europe [. . .] In practice however I shall rely on God and my sharp sword! And I shit on all their decisions.[57]

Much to the distaste of the Kaiser no doubt, but at the instigation of the Americans, a resolution had been introduced that committed the participants to holding another conference within the same time scale as had divided the first two. This would have taken place in 1915 had not other events supervened.

It is of course a moot point as to whether the utilisation of the Dundonald Plan would have breached any of the above articles of international law. However, in judging the legality of an actual usage of chemical warfare, the German attack at Ypres, one post-war writer put it thus: 'no impartial court would today judge Germany guilty of violating the letter of the law of 1899 in staging the chlorine attack [. . .] on 22 April 1915'.[58] Others thought differently.[59] However, it might be argued, with of course the inestimable benefit of hindsight, that Britain would not have been beyond international law had the Dundonald plan come to fruition.

Examination of the available evidence concerning 'pre-chemical warfare' chemical warfare indicates that the idea of such methods had crossed the minds of many, both in the 'for' and 'anti' lobbies, and it may have indeed been put into practice on occasion – on a small scale. Winston S. Churchill stated a universal truth when he put it thus: 'When difficulties and dangers perplex all minds, it has often happened in history that many men by different lines of thought arrive at the same conclusions.'[60]

Many men had indeed arrived at similar conclusions, and the various operations recorded would today fall under the definition of chemical warfare even if the term had not been invented contemporaneously. Why then did the use of noxious fumes, given that the materials to generate them existed and were known for many centuries, not become a more common technique?

It is self-evident that the difficulties of generating a sufficient concentration of noxious fumes in the open air; necessarily at some distance from the object of attack so that the preparations are not subject to disruption, but where they may be apt to disperse before arriving at their desired destination, must be greater than when they can be confined, as in underground operations where the area to be rendered uninhabitable is finite. In conventional military operations a vast amount of material will be needed to achieve the requisite concentration. This has logistical implications, and logistics determine the size, composition, and effectiveness of military forces. The problems associated with lugging thousands of tons of coal, coke, sulphur etc., in the days of animal-based transport are obvious. Further, until the advent of cannon firing explosive ordnance made them obsolete, fortifications consisted of high walls, towers and suchlike. The difficulties of attacking a tall position with a cloud of heavier-than-air fumes are immediately apparent.

When the advent of the railway had, to a degree, solved the problems of logistics, and when advances in ordnance had forced the designers of fortification from their lofty towers, 'thundering artillery [. . .] pointed against the walls and towers which had been erected only to resist the less potent engines of antiquity',[61] in Gibbon's words, then the practical disadvantages to introducing 'chemical' weapons were eroded. It was, however, only when the industrial revolution had added manufacturing and motive power to the arsenals of nations that these 'new' methods of warfare became practically viable.

However, the Secret War Plans of Lord Dundonald were both qualitatively and quantitatively of an altogether different magnitude from those that have been outlined above, and the solution to the logistical conundrum was his proposed employment from ships. Quite simply, what a ship could carry with ease would involve a major logistical effort on land. By way of example, in comparing the gunnery power of Nelson's fleet at Trafalgar (27 ships) with the artillery of Napoleon's Army of the North at Waterloo (366 guns) John Keegan states it thus: 'six times as many guns, of much heavier calibre, could be transported daily by Nelson's fleet as by Napoleon's army, at one fifth of the logistic cost and at five times the speed.'[62] The 12th Earl of Dundonald, writing many years later of his ancestor's schemes, expressed a similar appreciation, though perhaps in a somewhat less scientific manner: 'Marine fortifications in the Admiral's day when the plans were conceived, would get their dose in shiploads, land fortifications in cart loads.'[63] Ships, of course, while in comparison with land-based load carriers being of practically limitless capacity, are very limited as regards the kinds of targets they can engage with. None of the examples sketched as being precursors to chemical warfare involved the type of operations for which Dundonald had evolved his Secret War Plans – operations against maritime fortifications from the sea.

Not only had he produced a unique concept, therefore, but he had also solved the logistical difficulties of putting it into practice; indeed, the very nature of the operations he was advocating minimised them. So while Churchill's phrase is undoubtedly true in the wider sense, it cannot apply to the Dundonald Plans as originally conceived. Proposing the taking of marine fortifications from the sea using poison or asphyxiating gas to kill, disable, or drive out, the defenders was unique; doing something similar on land was not. So while the Secret War Plans of Lord Dundonald can be considered in one context as merely being a manifestation of 'different lines of thought' arriving at similar conclusions, in another they were, and remain, distinct. They were the product of a distinct and singular line of thought; the product of, as their author might have put it, an Imperial Mind.

7

A National Emergency

Lord Dundonald arrived from England. He is studying the conditions of the war in the hopes of being able to apply to modern conditions an invention of his [. . .] grandfather for driving a garrison out of a fort by using sulphur fumes.

Sir Douglas Haig, 11 March 1915

THE criteria, as laid down by Playfair, for resurrecting the plan had been met within three months of the outbreak of the Great War, or so Lord Dundonald was to judge after the conditions and course of the conflict had taken a direction that had not – with certain exceptions – been foreseen. Conventional methods of fighting the enemy were proving ineffectual, in terms of driving them from their position, and remarkably expensive in terms of casualties. The enemy in question was of course the army of Imperial Germany[1] and the position from which they were to be driven was the Western Front in northern France. The seeming stalemate in that area had, as is well known, resulted from the failure of Germany's Schlieffen Plan, the plan for defeating France within six weeks. This dislocation and the subsequent inability of offensive measures to defeat entrenched opposition – trench warfare – baffled those who sought answers to it in the tactical sphere.

Though this had surprised many, if not most, of the military minds in all the nations involved it was a technologically led condition that had been manifesting itself, to somewhat lesser degrees, since the middle of the previous century. The Allied armies before Sevastopol, the Union armies at Richmond and St Petersburg, the British fighting the Boer and the Japanese besieging Port Arthur could all testify to the difficulty of defeating a well-entrenched and tenacious foe. The nub of the matter resolved itself around discovering ways of successfully carrying out that traditionally most unsuccessful of military manoeuvres, the frontal assault against an entrenched enemy. This was the only course of tactical action open to the armies, of both sides, in France because the manpower and industrial resources available had caused a front of previously unknown size and strength to be brought into being. There were no flanks to turn; there were no points, the loss of which would compel the defeat of the attacked force, within attainable striking distance. There were no opportunities to demonstrate any large tactical skill.

This situation had been preceded by a short-lived phase of mobile warfare, from 4 August when seven German armies had crossed the Belgian and French frontiers in conformity with the Schlieffen Plan, which meant a holding action with minimal forces against the Russians in the East, while an overwhelming force enveloped the French forces in a lightning campaign. Once victorious, Graf Alfred von Schlieffen had calculated, these armies could then be sent east to inflict a similar fate on the slower-to-mobilise Russians. The premeditated violation of Belgium resulted in bringing the British into the war, or, according to taste, giving a small claque of politicians an excuse to do so, while the Germans continued their advance until early September when their manoeuvres were entirely dislocated by Joffre's counterstroke at the Marne. Both sides then tried to turn each other's flank in what came to be called 'the race to the sea' and, when they reached the coast, ended up facing each other in entrenched positions along a more or less continuous line across northern France and Belgium. Thus began a phase of the conflict that Sir Douglas Haig had, in his scenario of future war, expounded while chief-of-staff in India. He had termed it 'the wearing out fight'.[2]

Such a situation had been predicted, and with a greater clarity and perception than was the case with Haig, by one Ivan Bloch. Bloch, a former highly successful businessman had made his fortune in railways and banking, then turned his hand to writing, and in 1898 had published in Russia a six-volume work that was to make him (contemporaneously) famous; *The Future of War*.[3] This scholarly work, which drew heavily on his knowledge and experience of business, sought to demonstrate that the rise of the modern industrialised nation-state had made war between such states impossible owing to the immense, virtually unlimited, resources that could be brought to bear. Past conflicts, with the possible exception of the American Civil War, had been mainly limited affairs; limited by the industrial capacity of the warring states and by the size of the armies that could be raised and maintained. Such limitations were, by the last years of the nineteenth century, no longer applicable. The massive industrialisation and population increases had made possible the raising and equipping of armies of previously unimaginable size. These armies would, Bloch reasoned, be unable to achieve a decisive victory on the battlefield and the result would be attrition: both sides fighting until mutual exhaustion prevailed, and total ruin engulfed all. Bloch also sought to explain that because of the rise of industry and its corollaries, finance and trade, no one nation could emerge as victor from a war between them. The dislocation of the above institutions would result in ruin. Furthermore the increase in firepower resultant on the rise in industrial power would make battlefields vastly more deadly for the combatants' engaged and vast slaughter would ensue. To engage in such an enterprise, he argued, would be tantamount to committing national and international suicide, with famine and a breakdown in social order being the end results. Therefore, he concluded, war, meaning, though he never used the phrase, total war, had become impossible.

Just as the Bumblebee flies when technically speaking it is said to be unable to do so, so the soldiers and the nations of the Great War fought when, as Bloch had demonstrated, it was theoretically impossible for them to so do. The difficulties he had predicted accurately enough, though in truth he had understated them. The formidably well-trained and rehearsed German military machine, over 1,500,000 men guided by the best brain that could be devised, the German General Staff, that 'collective substitute for genius',[4] and provided with the best equipment that science and industry could contrive, soon proved that it was not immune to the inertia of war. Though it performed nearly well enough, in the final analysis it failed in its attempt and Bloch's predictions seemed to be realised.

This failure of the Schlieffen Plan had so discomfited the German Chief of the General Staff, General Helmut von Moltke, the nephew of the architect of victory in 1870–71, whose dilution and modifying of it had arguably contributed to its failure, that he suffered a mental collapse and was replaced. The new C-in-C, for that is what the position entailed in the German system, was Erich von Falkenhayn, who found himself in somewhat of a quandary. The Schlieffen Plan having failed, there was nothing in the General Staff pigeonholes to deal with this contingency. The 'collective substitute for genius' had gambled all on one throw. It failed,[5] and if the hallmark of genius is the capacity to take infinite pains, then the collective substitute was found wanting; no thought had been given to what would happen in such an event. The French were undefeated and the Russians still had to be dealt with. With the knowledge that the ammunition supply would be fatally overstretched by any large-scale offensive operations, and confident of the defensive capability of his armies there, Falkenhayn 'closed down' Germany's western front and moved a substantial portion of the forces from there to the east where the Russians were causing great anxiety to Germany's ally, Austria-Hungary, though their attack on German territory had been stymied by a duo of commanders whose names would soon eclipse all others.

In order to make the west secure Falkenhayn ordered strong defences constructed, thus making the British and French armies task doubly difficult, 'mere' field entrenchments having proved impervious beforehand. This decision, metaphorically standing Schlieffen on his head, was to manifest itself in the superiority of German defensive works, which the allies never did match, or try to, considering themselves bound to assault and throw back the invaders who were occupying a large portion of northern France and Belgium. Thus was set the general pattern of the next three years until the Russians had been removed from the scene, although it must hastily be added that the Germans were hardly quiescent during the intervening period.

Colonel Hankey, the Secretary to the Committee of Imperial Defence, in his 'Boxing Day' memorandum, named after the 1914 day upon which it was erroneously supposed to have been written,[6] had expounded upon these matters, remarking upon the 'remarkable deadlock' that had come to prevail, and postulated means of overcoming it.[7] In paragraph seven of the memorandum, Hankey elucidates the fact that where this type of situation has prevailed in the past, an *impasse,* as he calls it, two methods have been employed to overcome it: firstly, a tactical solution or 'special material'; or, secondly, strategic means – 'an attack delivered elsewhere, which has compelled the enemy so to weaken his forces that an advance becomes possible'.[8]

Unfortunately, the examples Hankey provides as to the overcoming of *impasses* are not directly relevant to the situation pertaining in France at the time. Had he perhaps addressed himself to the tactical difficulties encountered in the American Civil War, especially during Grant's final campaigns around Richmond; or the even more recent case of the siege of Port Arthur; even perhaps the Franco-British operations before Sevastopol during the Crimean campaign, he may have come to the conclusion that there was to be no panacea in the form of any special material. This, however, is unfair criticism; these matters are clearer to the armchair critic writing at leisure some ninety years after the event with the enormous benefit of hindsight and, of course, a vast canon of literature on the subject at hand. Hankey and many others were applying their ingenuity to a contemporaneous issue, and seeking solutions to real and pressing problems; problems they could not contemplate at their leisure, but which needed urgent attention by men harassed with a thousand other cares. Men such as the Minister for War, the legendary Field Marshal Earl Kitchener, who on 2 January 1915 had written to the British C-in-C in France, Sir John French, setting out his views:

> There does not appear to be much sign of the contemplated push through on the part of the French Army. Probably they find themselves up against the same problems all along the line as you do in your part, viz. trenches that render attack only a waste of men for a few yards gained of quite worthless ground. The feeling is gaining ground that, although it is essential to defend the lines we hold, troops over and above what are necessary for that service could be better employed elsewhere.
>
> I suppose we must now recognise that the French Army cannot make a sufficient break through the German lines of defence to cause a complete change of the situation and bring about the retreat of the German forces from Northern Belgium. If that is so, then the German lines in France may be looked upon as a fortress[9] that cannot be carried by assault, and also cannot be completely invested – with the result that the lines can only be held by an investing force, while operations proceed elsewhere.[10]

Kitchener then went on to suggest fresh theatres where he thought the British Army would be more profitably employed, 'an attack delivered elsewhere' in

Hankey's analysis. French replied the next day: 'The impossibility of breaking through the German lines by direct attack is not admitted. Recently rain and fog have been the principle difficulty. It is largely a question of larger supplies of ammunition, and especially of high explosive.'[11]

Sir John received a copy of Hankey's memorandum on 6 January courtesy of the First Lord of the Admiralty, Winston Churchill. Churchill received a reply from the C-in-C on the 9th in which he was told that French entirely disagreed with the memorandum's analysis and conclusions. The War Council in turn disagreed with French, and they had concluded on 13 January 1915: 'That if the position in the Western theatre became in the spring one of stalemate, British troops should be despatched to another theatre and objective.'[12]

Sir John could not agree, and the dispute over whether the best place to defeat the Germans was in France, where they were strongest, or another theatre, where it might be easier, was to continue throughout the war, and indeed continues in some circles to this day. However, the British military 'establishment' stuck to its considered view that the Germans could only be defeated by beating their army. That army, or the major portion of it, was in France so therefore that was where the main effort should be concentrated. The tactical problems on the Western Front could not, in their view, be overcome by strategic solutions. Attempts to deliver the strategic solution, such as the Dardanelles and Salonika operations, were indeed not to prove fruitful for a variety of reasons, and the Western Front was to become the main theatre of the war, indeed the only place where it could be won, though it might have been lost elsewhere. This is a point still in academic dispute to this day, although the logic of J.F.C. Fuller is persuasive:

> In what locality could Germany most profitably be struck? The answer depended on the most practical allied line of operations, which, in its turn, was governed by the location of the allied main bases. They were France and Great Britain, and in no other area than France could the ponderous mass armies of this period be fully deployed and supplied in the field. The main bases and the main theatre of war were fixed by geography and logistics, and no juggling with fronts could alter this.[13]

The tactical problem did not have a strategic solution, and the difficulties revolved around discovering ways to successfully carry out an operation rightly categorised as violating every military principle.[14] This was unfortunately not a matter of choice for those commanding any of the armies on that front, and, for the Allied side, there was also the political side of the equation to consider: France had been invaded and the enemy occupied a portion of her soil. The French government and people would hardly countenance making another theatre the focus of the main effort while such a situation prevailed. Also, moving the primary theatre would not necessarily have overcome the tactical problem. Abraham

Lincoln is held to have said, when his generals were facing similar difficulties and were seeking easier places to fight the Confederates, 'Where goes the fighting, so go the trenches.'

The American Civil and Great Wars had many similarities, including the cardinal fact that the winning side only emerged as such after fighting and defeating the opposing army, which had to be fought where it chose, or was forced, to stand. The General in Chief of the Union Army well understood this and made it plain that the opposing army was his target, not any geographical location.[15] The Allied problem on the Western Front was not therefore, what to do? It was; how to do it? The 'wearing out fight', it appeared, would be a lot more wearing for the attackers than the defenders. Superficially the soundest strategy would then have been to allow the Germans to expend themselves on the Allied defences. This they were understandably reluctant to do. As Hankey had said: 'We should ask nothing better than that [they] should hurl fresh masses to destruction on our impregnable positions.'[16] Falkenhayn no doubt would have said the same. It was paradoxical that while industry, technology, and science had provided means and methods of equipping, transporting, and maintaining these armies of millions, it had not at that time evolved any tactical aids with which to carry out an offensive operation against entrenched opposition with any prospect of success. While masses of men could be equipped, transported, and maintained in their positions, if they were to move out of those positions in order to advance upon the enemy then they would have to walk. In the face of the defensive strength provided by industry, technology, and science – magazine rifles, machine guns, barbed-wire, artillery – this was a fearsome prospect; it was pitting men against machines,[17] which, in many of its essentials, was comparable to the nineteenth-century problem of pitting wood against walls. The 10th Earl of Dundonald had addressed that problem and, at least to his own satisfaction, provided a solution; his grandson, having inherited the solution, was equally satisfied that it could answer the analogous problem.

Lieutenant-General the 12th Earl of Dundonald was not the only person whose thoughts turned to the 10th Earl's Secret War Plans at that period and in that context, for an article had appeared in the press concerning them and their possible applicability on 29 September 1914:

Mr. Turpin, the inventor of melinite, declares he has made an invention which will modify all present military tactics and render all defences illusory. The enemy's forces, he says, will be annihilated by its use, and general disarmament will be the result. Moreover, he is reported to have declared that the French Minister of War has decided to use the invention.

A statement like that at the present time must, of course, be taken with more than a grain of salt, for in previous times of stress inventors have hinted at marvellous instruments off destruction that have, as it has turned out,

20 The 12th Earl of Dundonald (1852–1935)
The 12th Earl of Dundonald, shown here *circa* 1880, was a professional cavalry-man of some note, serving in the 2nd Life Guards for nearly thirty years and rising to command the regiment. He had, as had his nautical forefather, a penchant for invention, one of his less martial innovations being the 'Tilting Teapot', which first appeared in 1905. Devised for optimum brewing, he called it the SYP teapot: 'Simple Yet Perfect'.
Information on the 'Tilting Teapot' from: http://www.virtualtea.com/vt/tilt.html
Photograph in the author's collection

proceeded rather from a patriotic wish that did them credit than from actual knowledge and experiment. [. . .]

But although we must discount to a large extent as mere dreams such assertions made in times of excitement, we cannot overlook the fact that there is, or should be, in the possession of our own War Office a plan which its inventor was positive would destroy entire armies at one blow and at very small expense. And that these plans were no visionary invention, although they may now be obsolete, can be proved undoubtedly. Lord Dundonald, otherwise known as Thomas Lord Cochrane, their inventor, first proposed them in 1811, and nothing occurred between then and 1859 to render them impracticable. Lord Dundonald, beside being a seaman of exceptional skill – he was described by Sir Archibald Alison as 'after the death of Nelson the greatest naval commander of that age of glory' – was the inventor of many plans for the greater efficiency of the Navy, and as early as 1843 he was urging the necessity of adapting steam power and screw propellers to ships of the line. [. . .] In the reign of George IV he submitted his war plan to Lord Exmouth and Lord Keith, but they expressed an opinion that for the welfare of the human race it was advisable that the noble lord should carry his secret with him to the grave.

Lord Dundonald, was, however, not easily rebuffed. He induced the Government to submit the plans to a secret committee consisting of three admirals and two scientific persons, who reported that, in their opinion, the plan would be perfectly irresistible, but inhuman, and for this reason they would not advise its being used. All through the Crimean War he and various members of Parliament pressed the Government to give it consideration. At length Lord Palmerston submitted it to Professors Faraday, Playfair, and Graham, who reported favourably, and in May, 1855, Lord Dundonald said he was prepared by the end of June, if his plans were adopted and his services were accepted, without fee or reward, to demolish every Russian fortress in the Baltic at an expense of less than £200,000. But the offer was declined.

The nature of the plan has, of course, never been made public [. . .] It is possible that the secret plans may have been a forecast of some modern high explosive, but there is evidence against this theory, for Lord Dundonald was prepared to carry out his plan at very short notice and at a small cost, while modern explosives require expensive factories and elaborate processes.

[It] may not apply to warfare in 1914, and the secret war plan may long ago have been destroyed by the authorities as valueless and out of date. Yet there is a possibility, however remote, of its still being effective, and of its being in existence, forgotten or overlooked, in some dusty recess at the War Office. One thing, however, is certain, that if the secret plan has been superseded by modern inventions we have descended to depths of inhumanity inconceivable in the past, when it was rejected time after time as too terrible to be employed.[18]

The 12th Earl was a professional cavalryman of some note, serving in the 2nd Life Guards for nearly thirty years and having risen to command that regiment. As a brigadier he had commanded the Mounted Brigade in South Africa under Sir Redvers Buller during the latter's operations in Natal. Known popularly as 'Dundoodle', he was, according to Birdwood, his brigade major (later an army commander in France during the Great War) 'full of verve' and 'a curiously sensitive man living largely on his nerves'.[19] He had, as had his nautical forefather, a penchant for invention, his most successful perhaps being 'The Dundonald Patent Attachment and Galloping Carriage', which was a machine gun portable to cavalry and one of his few inventions to be officially adopted. A modicum of fame had come his way when, in 1884–85, he had commanded the 2nd Life Guards Detachment of the Sudan Camel Corps in the expedition to relieve Khartoum, and had then carried the despatches announcing the death of General Gordon, and a modicum of notoriety when as a lieutenant-general he had first commanded, and then had been dismissed under somewhat acrimonious circumstances from, the Canadian Militia.

He recounted in his autobiography how, on the night of 26 January 1900, he had considered revealing his grandfather's Plan during the Natal campaign in South Africa. The defensive skills of the Boers – invisible in trenches and armed with deadly accurate Mauser rifles – were causing great distress and consternation to the British force attempting to cross the Tugela River and relieve the beleaguered town of Ladysmith:

> I kept turning over in my mind whether I should not go to see Sir Redvers Buller with the object of revealing to him the Secret Plans of my grandfather [. . .] which had been handed to my keeping by Lord Playfair under a solemn promise that they would only be divulged in the event of national emergency.
>
> In my mind's eye I saw the great banks of smoke, producing an atmosphere – to use the words of the plans – 'dark as the darkest night'; then I thought of this same atmosphere impregnated with sulphur. I saw the lines of Boer riflemen in their trenches, waiting for our men, with Mausers useless, for those that held them could not see [. . .] But I restrained myself and kept the secret.[20]

Clearly the situation in South Africa in general, and at the Tugela in particular, did not constitute one of 'national emergency' in Lord Dundonald's opinion. That being so, it comes as no surprise to learn that some two years later, following Britain's victory, at tremendous cost, in the South African campaign he again refused to divulge the 'secret' when asked to by the Admiralty. On 8 July 1902, the First Lord of the time, the Earl of Selborne, wrote to Dundonald after reading the 10th Earl's autobiography:

> In Lord Dundonald's Autobiography, Vol. 2 page 227, there is a very interesting chapter about his secret plans. I have had search made for these plans both at the Admiralty and the Record office, and no trace can be found of them. I should be greatly obliged if you would tell me whether you possess them, and if so, whether the Admiralty might have a look at them.[21]

Selborne, and by extension the British government, did not get them at this time, however. As the 12th Earl put it: 'He wishes to have them but I had given a promise to Lord Playfair only to divulge them in case of National Emergency.'[22] In Dundonald's judgement no such state existed in 1902.

He was to change his mind upon the commencement of the Great War however: 'I felt convinced the time had come when the Secret Plans of my grand-father [. . .] would prove of great value to the nation both at sea and on land.'[23] These words were written more than a decade after 1914, and the author does not tell us what caused his new-found conviction, but whatever the motivation, Lord Dundonald revealed the long-secret plans to the Secretary of State for War:

> I saw Lord Kitchener in the House of Lords in September 1914,[24] after his first address to that assembly as Secretary of State for War, and asked him for an interview. For this interview I took with me all the information I possessed, and told Lord Kitchener that as a soldier I had come to him first, as I thought the Plans could be effectively used against the enemy in Northern France and Belgium.[25]

Kitchener, to adopt the parlance of a later age, brushed him off by immediately pronouncing 'the idea was of no use for land operations, and as it was the invention of an Admiral he advised me to see the Admiralty about it'.[26] This brusque dismissal *may* not however have been genuine. In his *War Memoirs* David Lloyd George, when Minister of Munitions, relates the tale of the official trial of the first prototype tank at Hatfield in February 1916:

> I went with other Ministers, including Lord Kitchener [. . .] to witness the official trial of the first machine [. . .] The experiment was a complete success. [. . .] At last, I thought, we have the answer to the German machine-guns and wire [. . .]
>
> Sir William Robertson was also very favourably impressed, but Lord Kitchener scoffed as the huge, clumsy creature lumbered and tumbled about, though always moving forward, and expressed the opinion that it would be very quickly knocked out by artillery. He certainly gave the impression at the time that he thought little of the invention.[27]

In apparently dismissing the concept of armoured warfare as summarily as he had done chemical warfare, was Kitchener displaying the innate conservatism, closed mind, and military stupidity popularly associated with First World War generals? Lloyd George, who was by no stretch of the imagination an uncritical admirer of the guiding brains of the British military, adds to his account the following letter from General Sir Robert Whigham who had accompanied Kitchener to the trial:

Lord Kitchener was so much impressed [by the performance of the tank] that he remarked [. . .] that it was far too valuable a weapon for so much publicity. He then left the trial ground before the trials were concluded, with the deliberate intention of creating the impression that he did not think there was anything to be gained from them. [. . .] Lord Kitchener was rather disturbed at so many people being present at the trials as he feared they would get talked about and the Germans would get to hear of them. [. . .] I do know [. . .] that he had great expectations of them, for he used to send for me pretty frequently [. . .] and he referred to them more than once in the course of conversation. His one fear was that the Germans would get to hear of them before they were ready.[28]

As Lloyd George put it: 'I can only express regret that he did not see fit to inform me of it at the time [as] I was responsible [. . .] for the manufacture of these weapons.'[29] One can empathise with Lloyd George; Kitchener's unusual methods and mental processes, honed by his long experience 'practically as an Oriental autocrat',[30] have often been remarked upon. The question, then, is: was he being totally honest with Dundonald when dismissing the usefulness of the Secret Plans, or was he adopting similar methodology to that which he used with regards to the tank? There is circumstantial evidence that the latter might have been the case, for on 26 September 'J.M. Woodward' circulated a memorandum, addressed to the Master General of the Ordnance – a member of the Army Council[31] – concerning the 'invention of Lord Dundonald'. It stated:

I have been making enquiries about the invention [. . .] Major Wall (at present confidential clerk to DMO [Director of Military Operations]) states as follows:–

'Some time between 1879 and 1882 the DQMG [Deputy Quartermaster General] (Sir A. Alison) had I believe in his possession a paper or memo. on a combustible or explosive compound invented by Lord Dundonald (or Lord Cokrane [sic]). This was, I think, (or had been) submitted to HM Government, who did nothing at the time as the explosive was too powerful for use in civilized warfare.

On Sir A. Alison retiring from this Department he took all the papers with him. They were indexed by myself and I believe a paper on the subject was with them. MTI the descendant of the old 'Central Section' of the Intelligence Department may have some record among the papers which it took over in 1888, on its separation from the Intelligence Department.'

A further reference to this question is contained in the Panmure Papers (see pp 340 and 341). [The relevant pages were included with the memorandum].

I have a distinct recollection that reference was made to this subject some 12 or 15 years ago when I was serving in the branch now known as MO1. I cannot remember details, but if my memory serves me right either Sir Henry Brackenbury or Sir John Ardagh expressed the opinion that Lord Dundonald's invention was perfectly feasible but that it should only be used in the event of England being at death grips with a powerful antagonist, as the invention had far reaching and deadly effects.[32]

The Master General of the Ordnance initialled this memorandum, indicating he had read it, and two other – unfortunately unidentifiable – individuals, who also received the relevant pages from the Panmure Papers, annotated it. Both annotations are dated 26 September 1914:

The proposal referred to is apparently that described in [. . .] 'The Panmure Papers'. Although it is not suggested that any projectiles should be employed, it is quite likely that the use of the sulphur fumes would be considered an infringement of the Hague Convention of 29th July 1899.[33]

I agree that [. . .] the Hague Convention implies that noxious fumes are not to be used.[34]

As stated, the above evidence is only circumstantial at best in indicating that Kitchener was being disingenuous in dismissing the Plan for land operations. Given Lloyd George's account vis-à-vis tanks it is explicable why he *might* have dissembled, though since, as far as it is possible to ascertain, he was talking on a one-to-one basis with a fellow high-ranking officer it is less easy to discern a motive for so doing on this occasion. Clearly, though, somebody in the higher echelons of the military hierarchy had thought the invention of Lord Dundonald worth investigating for possible use, and the timing of the memorandum might be suggestive of a connection between the Dundonald–Kitchener meeting and the curiosity concerning the 10th Earl's Plans. However, if the possibility of a causal link be considered too tenuous, then coincidence remains the only other explanation, and Kitchener's words to Dundonald can be taken at face value. The 12th Earl certainly took them as such, and 'after meeting Lord Kitchener, I got an introduction from my son-in-law Major the Hon. Ralph Hamilton to his relative Admiral Sir Frederick Hamilton the Second Sea Lord'.[35] Accordingly he took himself and his papers to the Admiralty, calling, again on an unspecified date, on Admiral Hamilton where he 'explained fully the value of the plans for Naval operations, including landing operations, and also for land warfare'.[36] He received a letter from Hamilton on 29 September, which does at least allow his first meeting with him to be placed before that date:

I have talked the matter over with Prince Louis [of Battenberg, the First Sea Lord] and he thinks you had better see Churchill. [...] he agrees with me that at present we can see no probability of naval use, especially seeing that a failure would be giving the whole thing away without any corresponding gain; as for land, when a sufficiently grave crisis arrives there can be no doubt of its use.

He agrees with me that the best thing to ask Churchill for would be a small joint Naval and Military Commission to consider the whole matter and in the meantime to divulge as little as possible.

You had better write a note to Churchill asking him for an interview on a private matter.[37]

Dundonald must have immediately taken Hamilton's advice, for the next day he received a note from the First Lord stating 'I should be glad to see you if could come here [the Admiralty] at 5:30pm on Friday [2 October 1914].'[38] Lord Dundonald kept the appointment and:

Showed the Secret Plans of Admiral Lord Dundonald to Mr. Winston Churchill, who though overwhelmed with work, showed much interest in them, and after he had seen some of my papers sent for the First Sea Lord [Battenberg]; the interview lasted about half an hour.

[...] Churchill told me he wished to consult Admiral Sir Arthur Wilson and desired for the purpose to have the papers I had shown him.[39]

Thus Winston Churchill, at the time 'responsible to Crown and Parliament for all the business of the Admiralty',[40] became *au fait* with the Secret War Plans. He records the matter in his monumental account of the war, *The World Crisis*, quoting at length a letter he had sent to Prime Minister H.H. Asquith on 5 January 1915 and telling him that, with regard to the manufacture of smoke barrels, there are 'other matters closely connected with this to which I have already drawn your attention, but which are of so secret a character that I do not put them down on paper'.[41] He explains how Lieutenant-General Lord Dundonald, 'the grandson of the famous Admiral Cochrane'[42] had visited Lord Kitchener and appraised him of various plans 'left by his ancestor' for making smoke screens and for 'driving an enemy from his position by means of noxious though not necessarily deadly fumes'. Churchill relates his interview with Dundonald during the course of which he asked to see the plans of 'the illustrious Cochrane', which after a few days consideration Lord Dundonald felt justified in revealing in view of the current 'national emergency'. In fact it was not for another two weeks, until 16 October, that the Plans were sent to Churchill:

I enclose the two papers I showed you, which are sufficient to give an outline of the plans: I have others fuller in detail: the information I have is held at your disposal with anything I can do personally.[43]

The 12th Earl also related for Churchill's benefit his philosophy regarding keeping the Plans secret until his criteria concerning a 'national emergency' had been met:

> I may mention that when Lord Selborne was the First Lord he asked me to hand him the secret; shortly after, the War Office asked me;[44] I refused these requests, also I abstained from divulging the Secret when we were trying to cross the Tugela, as I considered it should be reserved for some great emergency in the national life of our country. I had given a pledge not to divulge the secret until a national emergency had arisen.[45]

Churchill relates how he received the papers 'in the middle of October' and, inaccurately, describes them as having 'once before, in the Crimean War [...] been placed at the disposal of the British Government'.[46] The *World Crisis* contains a facsimile of the words inscribed on the 'inner covering of the packet':

> To the Imperial mind one sentence will suffice: All fortifications, especially marine fortifications, can under cover of dense smoke be irresistibly subdued by fumes of sulphur kindled in masses to windward of their ramparts.[47]

This suggests, as does other evidence examined later, that the version of the Plans Churchill received were those presented to the Hastings Committee in 1846,[48] and Churchill, no doubt considering himself the possessor of an 'Imperial Mind', wrote that 'the reader, captivated by the compliment, will no doubt rise to the occasion and grasp at once the full significance of the idea'.[49]

Sir Arthur Wilson, however, who Churchill had decided to consult with regard to the Plans, was not so captivated. Wilson was a past First Sea Lord and one of the few living men who had actually fought in the Crimean War, and later, in 1884, at the second battle of El Teb in The Sudan, gained a Victoria Cross – in the days when there were both naval and military versions – for gallantry. This was earned on the occasion, celebrated – if that is the correct term – in the works of Kipling and Newbolt, when a British square broke. Wilson helped rally the troops and fought the Dervish spearmen with his cutlass and, after that broke in use, his bare fists.[50] He has been described as 'once an outstanding fleet commander and in his later years a consultant on almost every naval enterprise of the First World War'.[51] Churchill describes him as having a 'practical and inventive turn of mind', which 'seemed specially adapted to the task' of assessing the scheme.[52] This assessment is, however, somewhat at odds with his earlier (in the same book) characterisation of

Wilson as 'a man of the highest quality and stature, but, as I thought, dwelling too much in the past of naval science, not sufficiently receptive of new ideas when conditions were changing so rapidly, and of course tenacious and unyielding in the last degree'.[53] This opinion, though written post-war, is consistent with his pre-war appraisal: 'I cannot feel much confidence in Wilson's sagacity.'[54]

Churchill was soon writing to Dundonald, on 18 October, returning the papers to him and appraising him of Sir Arthur's findings:

> Sir Arthur Wilson thought the scheme obsolete on account of modern conditions, and it was useless to pursue it with him. *I* do not share these views and am considering how and when progress may be made.[55]

Sir Arthur Wilson had evidently made his mind up, and being 'tenacious and unyielding in the last degree' Churchill could not persuade him to reconsider. Dundonald was, unsurprisingly, none too happy, replying on 24 October:

> The term obsolete does not describe a novel departure. You, I know, place an accurate value on the criticism [. . .] I feel sure that you will help my wish to conduct land operations under the plan if agreed that the navy is out of it. I much trust that the secret will be maintained by the officers to whom you entrust it [. . .][56]

Churchill himself, not accepting that the 'navy was out of it', and obviously taken with the Plan, sought to pursue it with his customary vigour, giving 'decisive instructions' to make experiments and, in a letter of 1 January 1915, enjoined Dundonald to lay his scheme before Colonel Hankey, the Secretary for the Committee of Imperial Defence, who was, as Churchill stated, 'pursuing considerable investigations in a similar though not identical direction'. Churchill also noted 'with some misgivings' that the German government was attempting 'to purchase sulphur on an exceptionally large scale'.[57] Hankey was of course in pursuit of that 'special material' with which to overcome the tactical *impasse*, and he records how

> Under the seal of the strictest secrecy[58] (removed by subsequent publicity) I became the repository of the secret passed down through several generations of the Dundonald family for using sulphur to asphyxiate an enemy.[59]

Another repository of the 'secret' was Sir Douglas Haig, the future Field Marshal and C-in-C of the British Army on the Western Front, who was visited by Lord Dundonald on 11 March 1915. Curiously Dundonald recounted that the visit was made in the context of utilising only the smoke screen aspect of the Plan. As he was to state it:

I decided to go to France and personally bring before Field Marshal Sir John French the advantages which I felt so certain would follow the use of smoke screens in his operations. I confined myself to this portion of the Plans only, as I had learnt that the use of asphyxiating vapour in our warfare was not considered desirable. [. . .] I [. . .] left London on 5 March 1915.[60]

Haig, however, recorded that Dundonald was 'studying the conditions of the war in the hopes of being able to apply to modern conditions an invention of his great grandfather (sic) for driving a garrison out of a fort by using sulphur fumes. I asked him how he arranged to have a favourable wind.'[61] Perhaps this apparent discrepancy can be explained by Haig's diary having been written contemporaneously,[62] while Dundonald's account, as Churchill's, was not completed for another decade or so.

Dundonald had actually given the matter of favourable winds some thought, and, following research at the meteorological office, had reached the following conclusion:

The successful application of this method of warfare depends on a favourable wind. During the winter and spring months in Western Europe the winds are, [on] two days out of three, from a quarter favourable to an attacker advancing on Berlin. Taking a line from the sea in Holland to Berlin the wind conditions are most favourable to attack in an easterly direction [. . .] during the months November, December, January and February.[63] [64]

He was of course correct in this – the prevailing winds over northwest Europe do blow from the west or southwest – and later in the war the British army especially was to utilise this to launch massive cloud gas attacks. It is a matter of record that no attempts were made to attack the German trenches, or indeed any other targets, with sulphur fumes, and that researches into such matters were terminated by the British, though efforts to perfect and enhance smoke screens were to continue. Confirmation of this came on 21 March 1915 when Churchill ordered the Admiralty Smoke Screen Committee be formed under the chairmanship of the unflagging Earl. It was made clear to him in which direction his, and the committee's efforts should be directed in a letter sent from Churchill's private secretary, James Masterton-Smith, on 31 March:

Mr. Churchill asked me to write and confirm a decision already communicated to you by Colonel Hankey, that while the smoke experiments are to be continued it is not intended for the present to proceed with the more important proposal [i.e. experiments in noxious fumes]. Mr. Churchill agrees that it would not be expedient to introduce into the war elements which might justify the enemy in having recourse to inhuman reprisals. At the same time

Mr. Churchill wishes me to convey to you his sense of deep obligation for the ungrudging manner in which you have placed at his disposal your exceptional knowledge.[65]

Study of his ancestor's Plans, and his attempted upgrading of them with regard to modern warfare, had provided Dundonald's 'exceptional knowledge'. However, despite Churchill's subsequent endorsement that 'there can be no question but that Lord Dundonald had grasped at this time the whole idea of gas and smoke warfare, and that he had derived it directly from the papers of his grandfather',[66] his conception of 'modern' warfare seems somewhat naïve when viewed at this distance in time. For example, Churchill quoted from a paper by Dundonald that stated:

The vehicles with sulphur would be conducted and operated by men in Gas-proof helmets. An attack on miles of entrenchment would be made on sectional fronts by sulphur and smoke, the intervening blocks where sulphur would not be employed being smoked only, in order to blind the hostile artillery.[67]

It is undoubtedly true that these proposed tactics were, superficially at least, much the same as those utilised later in the war, following the outbreak of chemical warfare, but what was not quoted was the description of the vehicles that would generate the sulphur fumes:

For offensive operations on land I suggest the employment of two classes of sulphur vehicles and two classes of smoke vehicles – Class A Light Steam Vehicles; Class B Light Push-Cart Vehicles.[68]

What the effect of the formidable German artillery would have been on these vehicles is not difficult to imagine. Dundonald's undated draft plan for a Secret Attack on the German Fleet at Schillig Roads is perhaps similarly unsophisticated.

The German Fleet sometimes lies at anchor about four miles from the entrance of the estuary leading up to Wilhelmshaven.
The method proposed is to attack this fleet secretly, and without giving any warning to the enemy, by affixing large smoke pots, mines, and tubes containing sulphurous acid, to submarines which would take up their position at the mouth of the estuary.
The tide beginning to flow up the estuary, at given periods of time each submarine would disengage its burden in succession. In order to blow away obstructions in the river the first mines let loose might be rendered contact mines at an early period in their career upwards. In other the contact could be delayed until they got higher up the river. The same methods of delay in

operations could be arranged for the sulphurous acid and smoke pots.

There are narrows some distance up the estuary from where the fleet anchors. In order to escape from the mines, asphyxiating vapour, and smoke, the enemy would doubtless make for these narrows, and if there was enough smoke probably some of the vessels would run ashore.

Later, when the mines have got some way up the river, it might be possible for destroyers to torpedo the enemy ships which had run aground in the confusion.

The wind being favourable some of the enemy's batteries might be masked by flat bottom boats, filled with smoke producing material, run ashore.[69]

This is of course another case of the armchair warrior pontificating at leisure from a comfortable distance, and, with respect to the plan for attacking the German fleet, it will be noted that 'tubes containing sulphurous acid' – sulphur dioxide – were mentioned, as had been proposed by Lyon Playfair in 1855. This at least was a method that might have offered a chance of bringing the Plans, or at least one aspect of them, into a modern context. Why then was this, at least potentially promising, 'special material' abandoned? It is difficult to state with any certitude at this point in time, but the likelihood is that the sheer pressure of events at the time militated against the expenditure of scarce resources in experimentation with measures of uncertain utility. There was also the legal aspect to consider, and Churchill, in retrospect, was to write how 'the use of noxious or poisonous fumes were explicitly prohibited by International Law'.[70] This is a debatable point at least, and he was certainly less legalistic at the time; in Masterton-Smith's words, quoting him: 'it would not be *expedient* [emphasis added] to introduce into the War, elements which might justify the enemy in having recourse to inhuman reprisals'.[71] This was written only twenty-two days before the Germans themselves launched their massive chlorine gas attack on French and Canadian forces at Ypres, manifestly not in retaliation for anything the British or French had done. This begs the question therefore: did the British 'miss the boat' by declining to investigate thoroughly the Dundonald plan? That is, could they have pre-empted the German use of gas, and if so would it have brought any advantage?

The answer to the first part of the question is undoubtedly yes. The British certainly had both the concept and the necessary technology to have started using chemical warfare before the Germans – indeed, they had possessed both for more than a century. While the 12th Earl's 'Class A Light Steam Vehicles' and 'Class B Light Push-Cart Vehicles' might have proved hopelessly anachronistic, he did conceive, develop, and construct a device that was capable of emitting noxious fumes: his portable smoke producer. As he makes clear in his autobiography, he had been 'engaged in making private experiments with smoke screens' before his elevation to the Admiralty committee discharged with investigating that function.[72] His book contains a photograph showing an experiment at Shoeburyness with the portable smoke producers, which, though using oil as their fuel, would also burn sulphur.

> In these the smoke was ejected in an almost horizontal direction, a slight rotary movement being given to the smoke; this gave it time to cool and conform to the surface of the ground.[73]

On 3 June 1915 he had supervised no fewer than forty of these smoke producers at the Shoeburyness experiment, and, if the inventory of goods is to be believed, had burnt over seventy-seven pounds of sulphur in them during the course of the trial.[74] What lessons had been learnt from this trial of the 10th Earl's methods, probably the largest-scale trial that had ever been undertaken, are not recorded.

As regards the second point, the answer is 'probably not,' for the answer to the tactical *impasse* was not to be found in chemical warfare at all, and while poison gas was of utility in piercing the enemy front line, as were many other weapons and tactics, it could not restore mobility to the battlefield, and mobility was, as became apparent later, the crux of the matter. The logistical implications of the scheme would also have tended to militate against its adoption at that time. The 10th Earl himself had calculated, with respect to a land operation, that some thousands of tons of materials would be required. This would have been a difficult, and probably impossible, amount to manage given the logistical problems that the war was causing at that time.

If the British abandoned, for whatever reason or reasons, the concept of utilising gas warfare during the first six months of the war, their opponents were arriving at the opposite conclusion and were seeking to transfer the idea into a useable weapon. The culmination of these efforts was the attack of 22 April 1915 on the Ypres salient, using some 160 tons of chlorine liberated from cylinders, which caused many thousands of allied casualties and virtually denuded the front line of its defenders through having killed or driven them from their positions. Since chlorine gas and sulphur dioxide are somewhat comparable in their effects at similar concentrations, here, it might be argued, at long last and over a century since he had first conceived them, was vindication of the 10th Earl's Secret War Plans. The discharge of poisonous gases would indeed have the effect that he had anticipated and render the object of attack uninhabitable and thus indefensible, and the German methodology in 1915 was merely one that replicated, albeit with a different agent, that proposed by Playfair in 1855 – 'by mechanical means [. . .] fill strong iron boilers with liquid sulphurous acid [. . .] and this liquid acid on the removal of the pressure would assume the form of a gas'.[75]

The history of chemical warfare throughout the rest of the Great War, and it became a major weapon, is beyond the compass of this work. There is, however, one further question relating to the Secret War Plans of Lord Dundonald that needs to be considered: was the German recourse to such methods inspired by the Plans? This question would hardly need to be asked were it not for one curious fact: the 12th Earl believed that the Plans had been stolen by an agent and passed to Germany, and were then adapted for use by the Imperial German armies.

8

Secret No More

The question may well arise in people's minds [. . .] how did the Germans get hold of the essence of Admiral Lord Dundonald's Plans, a secret which had been so religiously kept[?]

Lt.-Gen. the 12th Earl of Dundonald

O NE by-product of war, any war, is the subsequent appearance of the memoirs of those who have participated in it in whatever capacity, and the Great War, as it was known until a later and even greater conflict relegated it somewhat, accordingly produced a great deal of autobiography. One of the most important of these, even with the usual caveats, was the work by Winston S. Churchill entitled *The World Crisis*, which brought a huge number of important documents into the public arena and ran eventually to six volumes. In the second of these, published in 1924, the approach made by the 12th Earl of Dundonald vis-à-vis his grand-father's Secret War Plans was revealed, as were the nature of the Plans themselves, and also reproduced in facsimile were the words inscribed on 'the inner covering of the packet':[1]

> To the Imperial mind one sentence will suffice: All fortifications, especially marine fortifications, can under cover of dense smoke be irresistibly subdued by fumes of sulphur kindled in masses to windward of their ramparts.[2]

Prior to this the nature of the Secret War Plans had not been generally known, even if the existence of the Plans had been alluded to on occasion. An example had occurred some three years previously, when *Punch* magazine, in producing a history of England in its own inimitable style, had this to say on the subject during its treatment of the Crimean War:

> Lord Dundonald's famous 'secret war plan,' originally proposed in 1811, and rejected by a secret Committee presided over by the Duke of York, who pronounced it 'infallible, irresistible, but inhuman,' was revived after the inventor's readmission to the British Navy, and urged on the Admiralty and Government [. . .] It was again rejected on the score of its inhumanity,

21 'To the Imperial Mind one sentence will suffice[:] All fortifications, especially marine fortifications, can – under cover of dense smoke – be irresistibly subdued by fumes of sulphur kindled in masses to windward of their ramparts.' Winston Churchill's *The World Crisis* contained a facsimile of this image, described as being inscribed on the 'inner covering of the packet'. Churchill, considering himself the possessor of an 'Imperial Mind' no doubt, wrote that 'the reader, captivated by the compliment, will no doubt rise to the occasion and grasp at once the full significance of the idea'.
Image from an original document in the Dundonald Papers, GD233/874/84, courtesy of the 15th Earl of Dundonald

though *Punch* welcomed the plan, without knowing exactly what it was, and besought the Government to cast away scruples and use *anything* against such an enemy as Russia. Whatever may have been 'Dundonald's plan' was never divulged, it remained a nameless mystery.[3]

The inscription revealed by Churchill, it may be recalled, had formed the cover to the 10th Earl's submission to Captain Hastings on 10 September 1846, containing 'No 1: Secret Plan For ensuring at one blow the maritime superiority of England'[4] and 'No 2: Origin of the Preceding and Following Secret Plans'.[5] The first Plan, basically put, contained details concerning smoke screens, while the second covered the use of burning sulphur – together with much exposition on related matters. The provenance of this material – Churchill, it appears, had not kept copies of the various missives and documents that had been exchanged[6] – was a file of papers that Dundonald had been engaged in putting together. He wrote concerning this on 7 April 1921, telling Churchill that:

> I have been asked by the War Office if I can furnish an account of the early history of smoke screens for land warfare during the late war. I have collected such papers as I can lay my hands upon, which include correspondence with you, this correspondence rebounds very much to the credit of your foresight, but I would like to have your permission to include my correspondence with you amongst the papers before doing so; there is nothing in it which you could possible have objections, quite the contrary, it is impossible to make the history complete without it. I will send you the file to glance over on hearing.[7]

Churchill replied on the 11th stating that he would be 'much obliged'[8] to be sent the file of papers, and Dundonald duly sent, two days later, 'the file of smoke screen papers for your perusal'.[9] This file was returned to Dundonald on 18 April with a note from Edward Marsh[10] (Churchill was in France) thanking him for sending the 'typescript' and telling him that Churchill 'certainly thinks you would be right to publish it'.[11] In fact the typescript, entitled 'Smoke Screens and the Late War; my Experiences'[12] was not published as such, though the Churchill–Dundonald correspondence contained in it was to form both the basis of Churchill's account of the Secret War Plans, and, later, was also used by the 12th Earl for his account of the matter in his autobiographical *My Army Life* published in 1926.

Neither Churchill nor Dundonald, however, make reference to a curious paragraph in the typescript entitled 'The Germans and Admiral Lord Dundonald's Plans':

> The question may well arise in people's minds after reading these papers,

how did the Germans get hold of the essence of Admiral Lord Dundonald's Plans, a secret which had been so religiously kept[?] When I brought forward these Plans at the commencement of the War, I was unaware of the publication of Lord Panmure's Papers: these in private letters from Lord Palmerston to Lord Panmure, then Secretary of State for War, gave away the secret entrusted to the former, at the time of the Crimean War by Admiral Lord Dundonald. The levity and indifference to the interests of our country displayed in publishing these confidential documents is almost inconceivable.[13]

Despite his admonitions concerning them, however, it may well have been with a good deal of relief that Lord Dundonald discovered, precisely when is not revealed to us, that *The Panmure Papers* had been published in 1908. It might be inferred from the paragraph in question that he conceived of a causal link between the Secret War Plans and the German introduction of gas into the Great War on 22 April 1915 and its subsequent general usage – 'how did the Germans get hold of the essence of Admiral Lord Dundonald's Plans[?]' In fact it was the case that he genuinely feared that he had been the unwitting cause of the 'essence' getting into German hands – that he had been the catalyst whereby the enemy had derived the concept of using poison gas. This is confirmed by a story handed down orally through the Dundonald family over the years: this details how the 12th Earl kept the two parts of the Plan separate: one in his home in Scotland, Lochnell Castle, and the other in his London residence at Mains Lodge, Wimbledon.[14] These two portions were brought together at the second address during the latter portion of 1914 for pressing on the government, before being returned to their owner.[15] Shortly after this they were abstracted by the butler to the household, who was allegedly of German origin and sympathies, and taken or sent to Germany – thus establishing a link between them and the German deployment of gas.

Ian Grimble first revealed the existence of this second Dundonald family secret in his 1978 biography of Admiral Lord Cochrane, *The Sea Wolf*:

Whilst the British government rejected the use of sulphur as an asphyxiant, the Germans had their own plans and introduced gas warfare within weeks of that rejection. The two halves of Cochrane's formula had been stolen from Lord Dundonald's house at Wimbledon (for which he suspected his butler) but its secret could have been discovered in the Panmure papers, as well as by independent research.[16]

Grimble was the first twentieth-century biographer of the 10th Earl to be allowed access to family papers 'that have never been seen by previous biographers'.[17] It seems he had also had the tale from the 14th Earl, who had tried to trace the Plans through the offices of Bernard Quaritch Ltd, 'Dealers in Ancient

Manuscripts, Rare, Artistic and Scientific Books and Works in Standard Litera-ture'. On 5 January 1955 the 14th Earl received the following letter:

> In reply to your letter of the 1st January[18] we think that there is little doubt that the Secret War Plans of your ancestor is that which was Lot 70 in Sotheby's sale of the 2nd June 1924 when it was part of the Melville Papers. This was described by the auctioneer as follows:
>
> Dundonald (Thomas Cochrane, Earl of) His famous [sic] Secret War Plan for Destroying and Enemy's Fleets and Coast Defences, 26pp folio, addressed to HRH The Prince Regent, March 1812, signed by Cochrane in five places. [...][19]

Perhaps the 14th Earl thought that the stolen Plans had been recovered, but while the papers referred to above are obviously concerned with them, including as they did the 'Memorial' of 1811, they are not the whole Plan, for there never was a definitive Secret War Plan, but merely several variations upon a common theme – as this work has hopefully demonstrated.

Given the description, in two parts and with the covering inscription referred to, there seems little doubt that the version shown to Churchill in 1914 was the 1846 variation examined in Chapter 3. Yet the original documents could not have been stolen since they were in the possession of the 12th Earl in 1923[20] when the covering page was forwarded to Churchill for him to have copied and inserted in his book. Dundonald's letter – sent from his Wimbledon address – of 5 September 1923 evidences this:

> The papers were under lock, so kindly excuse the delay in sending the endorsement on the Secret Plans. I add the following thoughts which occur to me in connection with the meaning of the sentence.
>
> West or South West winds are the most prevalent in the neighbourhood of the British Isles.
>
> Marine fortifications in the Admirals day when the plans were conceived, would get their dose in shiploads, land fortifications in cart loads.[21]

This of course begs the question as to exactly what could have been taken by the nefarious butler, which unfortunately seems impossible to answer at this distance in time. Even the name of the alleged felon remains unknown – the identities of members of the Mains Lodge household in 1914 having been lost. It also seems to be the case that the 12th Earl informed no one else of this theft other than members of his family – certainly the contemporaneous police and Home Office files contain nothing remotely appertaining; likewise the Churchill archive and even the Dundonald family papers. The current holder of the Dundonald title, the 15th Earl, can only reiterate the oral history passed down to him:

I am afraid I cannot shed any more light on the loss of the papers other than what I was told by my father. The 12th Earl, his grandfather, held the two parts of the plan in geographically separate areas [. . .] When he went to see Churchill he brought both papers together and held them in the London safe. Unbeknown to him his butler had German blood and sympathies and he stole the plan after the 12th Earl had exhausted his enquiries. The plan was then sent to the German side by the said butler. History does not relate whether the authorities were involved; I would doubt it owing to the nature of the plans.[22]

Given the lack of any other available evidence the story cannot be independently corroborated, and yet on the other hand it is impossible to believe that the 12th Earl's tale is fiction; it would be surely untenable to posit that he might have manufactured such a story merely to mislead his own family. It follows therefore that the tale is true, or that the 12th Earl at least believed it to be true, and something went missing, perhaps a copy of the 1846 Plans,[23] or perhaps notes he had made with a view to bringing them up to date. Lord Dundonald then conceived that these had been responsible for stimulating the Germans to move to gas warfare. If such is the case, and we can only hypothesise, his state of mind subsequent to the German gas attack at Ypres – following which 'A feeling of anger and horror ran through the whole nation'[24] – can be well imagined, particularly given the outrage expressed by many of his contemporaries. The Military Despatch of the Commander in Chief of the British Expeditionary Force, Sir John French, published on 10 July 1915, encapsulates this:

Following a heavy bombardment, the enemy attacked the French Division at about 5pm, using asphyxiating gases for the first time. Aircraft reported that . . . thick yellow smoke had been seen issuing from the German trenches [. . .]

What follows almost defies description. The effect of these poisonous gases was so virulent as to render the whole of the line held by the French Division [. . .] practically incapable of any action at all. It was at first impossible for anyone to realise what had actually happened. The smoke and fumes hid everything from sight, and hundreds of men were thrown into a comatose or dying condition, and within an hour the whole position had to be abandoned, together with about 50 guns.

All the scientific resources of Germany have apparently been brought into play to produce a gas of so virulent and poisonous a nature that any human being brought into contact with it is first paralysed and then meets with a lingering and agonising death.

As a soldier I cannot help expressing the deepest regret and some surprise that an Army which hitherto has claimed to be the chief exponent of the chivalry of war should have stooped to employ such devices against brave and gallant foes.[25]

Yet Lord Dundonald had been urging essentially similar methods on the British only a matter of months previously, and there is no escaping the conclusion that the destruction described by Sir John French as being visited on the French troops was an exact replication of those that the Secret War Plans were designed to inflict – though in reverse, as it were. For such 'a curiously sensitive man',[26] the thought that he was responsible must have been excruciating. However, if there is no corroborating evidence for the tale of the untrustworthy butler, and thus, as it were, Lord Dundonald's secondary responsibility for the attack on the British side, what of the 'other side of the hill' and the German account of how poisonous gas came to the battlefield?

Prior to the Great War the German chemical industry led the world, a pre-eminence based on the 1856 British discovery of aniline, a coal tar derivative. From this arose a whole new business, the dyestuffs industry, which, for reasons outside the scope of this work, was particularly taken up by the scientists and businessmen of Germany. At the beginning of the twentieth century, these had achieved a dominant position in the world market through the IG cartel, or *interessen gemeinschaft* (community of interest), created in 1903:[27]

> In 1913 the world production of dyes reached approximately 150,000 tons, of which Germany controlled three-quarters, producing at the same time something over 85 per cent of the intermediates entering into the finished dyes.[28]

Aside from the staple of dyestuffs, these corporations produced many other pioneering products, including heroin, and, perhaps of more lasting benefit, artificial fertilisers based on the synthetic production of nitrates. This last achievement was to have massive import following the outbreak of the Great War, for with that conflict came the British naval blockade of Germany and thus the severing of the trade route between Germany and Chile, the world's primary source of natural nitrates. This was of such importance because the other main use of this raw material was the production and manufacture of explosives. However, because of German reliance on rapid victory through the putting into operation of the Schlieffen Plan, and with no other contingencies having been taken into account, the stockpile of this raw material was estimated to be adequate for only six months of hostilities. Thus, within about three months of the beginning of the war, 'every expert [all those with knowledge of the parlous state of the German armaments industry] recognised the necessity of ending the war in the spring of 1915'.[29]

Fortunately for the German Army, and particularly for the reputation of the Great General Staff, though perhaps not for the general benefit of the human race, the chemical industry, the IG, was able to overcome the shortage by putting the artificial substitutes into large-scale production. As the report of the British Mission, appointed after the war to investigate the German chemical industry and its contribution to the military effort, put it:

> It was largely owing to the efforts of this combination [the IG] that Germany was enabled to continue the war in spite of the blockade. The IG works produced the bulk of the synthetic ammonia and nitric acid needed for the production of fertilisers and explosives, all the poison gas (with the exception of some chlorine and phosgene), and a large proportion of the high explosives.[30]

This, though, was inevitably a process that could not be extemporised overnight, and in the meantime, as related in an earlier chapter, it was necessary to 'close down' the fighting in France and send the troops thus released to deal with the Russians.

There were, in the current context, really two side effects to all of this: firstly, the outbreak of war had seen the disappearance of the export markets that the German chemical combines relied on – a manifestation of the dislocation to the international world of trade and commerce that Bloch had warned of; secondly, the necessity to co-ordinate military requirements with industrial capacity had led to a significant degree of liaison between the industrialists and the army. Falkenhayn, whom it may be remembered had succeeded Moltke following the breakdown of both the Schlieffen Plan and his own (Moltke's) health, had assigned Major Max Bauer as the High Command's link with heavy industry, and it was this officer who discovered that the now virtually redundant dyestuffs industry had vast quantities of poisonous chemicals at hand, but no present use for them. Given that conventional methods were prohibited by the shortage of the requisite materials, or at least until the chemical industry could catch up with the shortfall caused by the British blockade, it occurred to Bauer that here might be a possible solution to the problem. Carl Duisberg, the 'recognised spokesman' of the dyestuffs industry, was approached and, unsurprisingly, enthusiastically embraced the idea of utilising the stockpile of otherwise useless material at his industry's disposal. Further, if the project was found to be worthwhile then a new 'market' for the industry was assured. It was undeniably found worthwhile and the 'market' duly materialised; indeed, the German dyestuffs industry prospered, as a letter written to Bauer from the head of one of the companies on 24 July 1915 demonstrates:

> You should see what things look like here in Levrkusen,[31] how the whole factory is turned upside down and reorganised so that it produces almost nothing but military contracts [. . .] As the father and creator of this work, you should derive great pleasure.[32]

The German chemical industry provided the means; the will, the element generally lacking as regards the Dundonald Plans, was forthcoming through the need for an alternative to conventional explosives. Bauer – 'the father and creator' – provided the remaining factor, the concept, so the question arises of where he got the idea. Had he, and by extension 'the Germans', somehow got hold of 'the essence' of Admiral Lord Dundonald's Plans as the 12th Earl feared?

The first attempt to transfer chemical warfare on to the battlefield was made in October 1914 – that is, during the time when the 12th Earl of Dundonald was attempting to interest Winston Churchill and the British Admiralty in the methods evolved by his grandfather. In a book published in Berlin in 1920, General Max Schwarte, formerly of the Imperial German Army, relates it thus:

> The essential principle in the construction of the first effective German chemical shell consisted in the use of an accessory load of irritant material which was blown into dust on the explosion of the shell, thus creating a cloud of dust that so irritated the mucous membrane that for the time being the enemy could not fight in the cloud. The shell was [...] a shrapnel whose balls, instead of being imbedded in explosive were imbedded in closely packed sternutatory[33] powder.[34]

Three thousand of these modified devices were fired at the British positions at Neuve Chapelle on 27 October 1914, with no effect discernible to either the attackers or the attacked. However, the crucial point is surely this: a device used in battle by the German Army on 27 October cannot reasonably have owed its existence to papers stolen, at the very earliest, on 18 October in London. Not even the much-vaunted efficiency of the Germans could have achieved such a rapid transition from concept to realisation, and thus it is clear that the idea must have originated independently of the activities of the 12th Earl of Dundonald or his butler in the autumn of 1914. If it be deemed permissible to employ a legal metaphor, had Lord Dundonald been charged with, albeit unwittingly, supplying the thought behind the German chemical warfare scheme, he would, on the evidence, have been found 'Not Guilty'.

The failure of the first gas shells did not deter further attempts to realise a workable weapon, and more powerful chemical agents were tried in a shell, known as the T-shell, that was dedicated to their use. These were used on the Eastern Front against the Russians, again with no discernible effect, on 31 January 1915 and again on the Western Front during March with similar non-results. Schwarte relates that these experiences were the reason why the technique was changed to the type used at Ypres on 22 April:

> It appeared very difficult to put in the very small space of the artillery shell the necessary quantity of gas to create, in a short time, a sufficiently dense

cloud over the target. [. . .] The arms in use at that time were not suitable –
both from the standpoint of kind and number – for the large-scale use of gas.
The number of cannon and *minenwerfer* was too limited for the terrain to be
bombarded, and the capacity of the shell [. . .] was too small for gas. [. . .] As
an illustration we may say that in order to gas effectively a square surface, 100
metres on a side, about 50 shots of the 15cm. T-shell were required. At the
same time there was scarcely one heavy field howitzer battery for each kilo-
metre of front.

So if we were to achieve any decisive means in breaking through the stabi-
lised front, which we had in the trench warfare of 1915, then we had to make
ourselves independent of the weapons in use and find new and simple means
which were more suitable for large scale use and which at the same time
could be produced quickly and in large numbers.[35]

These 'new and simple means' were to be found in the use of chlorine gas – as
related, a plentiful substance, rendered of otherwise little utility with the demise of
the dyestuffs industry, and one moreover that was, as a matter of course, stored
and transported in robust metal cylinders. Simply put, then, little more needed to
be done than to transport these cylinders to a suitable spot and await favourable
weather conditions – consisting in the main of a breeze in the required direction. A
total of 5,730 of these cylinders, containing 168 tonnes of chorine, were duly
transported to a six-kilometre stretch of the Western Front near Ypres in Belgium,
and the meteorological conditions were adjudged suitable on 22 April 1915. The
results were as related by Sir John French. There were, according to Schwarte,
more advantages to using chlorine than those occasioned by its availability:

> A decisive factor in the selection of this substance is that it possesses an
> important military property; namely, as a result of its great volatility it leaves
> no after effects in the zone that is gassed. Hence the cloud could be followed
> by infantry assaults. Short experiments confirmed this superiority and
> showed further that we can mix large amounts of chlorine gas with a steady
> current of air without changing the current in any essential manner.[36]

The rationale behind the move to a different method of application of chemical
warfare to the battlefield, from gas shell to gas cloud via cylinder discharge, can
thus be delineated, and, as already stated, the initial impetus behind the resort to
gas shell cannot have owed anything to events that occurred in London in October
1914. There is, however, one telling sentence in Schwarte's writings, which
suggests that the 'essence' of Lord Dundonald's Secret War Plans had indeed
become known to the Germans. While writing of the cylinder-discharge option, or
'making use of the driving power of the wind to carry the chemical substance from
our own positions to those of the enemy', in his words, he went on to state:

We did not learn enough in this respect before the World War to enable us to send over chemical substances in great masses and in sufficiently high combat concentrations. Instead of the burning sulphur of Lord Dundonald-son, [sic] Germany had at her disposal large quantities of chlorine gas in liquefied form.[37]

Unfortunately, he does not tell us which 'Lord Dundonaldson' he was referring to, but we can calculate that since his work was published in 1920 he could not have learned of the 12th Earl's proposals vis-à-vis Churchill from information in the public domain – the latter being the first to publicise the matter in 1924 via volume II of *The World Crisis*. There are then only two possible sources for knowledge of 'the burning sulphur of Lord Dundonaldson' that the German high command possessed, if it be accepted that it was not General Schwarte alone who possessed this information. It could have derived from reading *The Panmure Papers*, or from information acquired during the course of the conflict; conceivably, in that case, the work of the dastardly butler.

However, the point he makes concerning 'we did not learn enough in this respect *before* [emphasis added] the World War' is surely relevant, and this, taken together with his mention of 'the burning sulphur', is suggestive, to put it no stronger, of German knowledge of the Dundonald Plans prior to 1914. If this is indeed the case then it seems probable that *The Panmure Papers* were the source, given that this work constituted the only sure supply of information concerning the Plans as far as even the British were concerned – as is evidenced by the memorandum of 26 September 1914 referred to in the previous chapter. If all this be granted, then the 12th Earl had indeed been correct in his admonition, and the publication of Lord Panmure's papers had gratuitously given away the secret to the Germans, albeit, of course, that by the time they were published the techniques they described were probably obsolete.

Courtesy of Schwarte, then, we can establish at least a tentative link between Germany and the Secret War Plans of Lord Dundonald, or at least that version of them that pertained in 1855. It is quite another matter, however, to argue that this was a causal factor in the German recourse to chemical warfare, for to make that case it would have to be shown that Bauer used them as the basis for his ideas. There is absolutely no evidence that this was so, and in any event the factors already mentioned that pertained vis-à-vis Germany during the early part of the Great War provided impetus enough for resort to unconventional methods. Chemical warfare, to reiterate, commenced with the use of gas-shells, and then, because of their unsuccessful nature at the time, these were temporarily abandoned for the cylinder-discharge methods. It might plausibly be argued that the discharge of a chemical agent from cylinders bore a similarity to the methods espoused by the 10th Earl, but brought up to date, as it were, by technological progress so that the weapon arrived at the point of application in a ready-to-use state, rather than being manufactured *in situ*. Indeed, sulphur dioxide and chlorine are, in some essentials, rather similar; both have a fatal effect at a concentration of 1,000 parts per million of air (1,000 ppm) and both are more than twice as heavy as air – chlorine being 2.45 times, and sulphur dioxide 2.21 times, heavier. This figure relates of course to sulphur dioxide in its pure form, and the methods proposed by Lord Dundonald were hardly conducive to purity, though whether creating it by burning crude and impure sulphur in masses of coal, charcoal, and so on would have made it more or less effective is difficult to say. It would certainly have made a very bad mixture, as Michael Faraday had commented,[38] and though, in whatever degree of purity, it was never seriously used as a battlefield chemical agent it would have fallen into much the same category as chlorine using the classification system that pertained at the time.

However, the evolution of gas shell into gas cloud, as Schwarte and others explained it, required no intervention from any long-dead admiral or indeed his still-living grandson; it was a logical progression in the search for an effective weapon, in an entirely similar manner as the later switch back to gas shell. Thus, it can also be argued that even though the Germans might have in fact got 'the essence of Admiral Lord Dundonald's Plans' from *The Panmure Papers*, it made no difference. The Germans would have resorted to chemical warfare in any event, simply because they had the need, and the means, to do so. To resort to the legal metaphor again; if *The Panmure Papers* were facing the charge of giving the concept of chemical warfare to the Germans, then the peculiarly Scottish verdict of 'Not Proven' would be likely to apply.

All this of course begs the question of exactly what is the truth concerning the story of the butler and the stealing of the Plans from the 12th Earl's house in Wimbledon. Clearly, having assigned a 'Not Guilty' to Lord Dundonald as regards responsibility, via negligence, for chemical warfare being adopted by Germany, the corollary as far as the butler is concerned must be 'Unsuccessful'. If he was engaged in espionage for Germany his haul was worth very little, and it is difficult to conceive of some sort of professional spy being tasked to keep an eye on a retired Lieutenant-General whose last major post was commander of the Canadian Militia. If one accepts that the butler was responsible for making off with some paperwork associated with Admiral Lord Dundonald's Plans, then it seems logical to assume that it was an opportunist crime, motivated, if indeed he was of German extraction as suspected, by patriotic impulses.

Unfortunately, the truth behind all this remains as elusive as ever; it is a situation that will undoubtedly continue unless and until further evidence comes to light. Perhaps the last word on the matter should go to the current Earl of Dundonald:

I guess that it is very unlikely that we will ever know the truth of the matter, unless I stumble across some as yet undisclosed missives from my great-grandfather on the subject.[39]

Thus the second and final mystery concerning the Secret War Plans of Lord Dundonald remains – inviolate and secret still.

APPENDIX

SHORT BIOGRAPHICAL NOTES ON THOSE WHO STUDIED OR WERE APPRAISED OF DUNDONALD'S SECRET WAR PLANS

Anglesey, Marquis of. Henry William Paget, Marquis of Anglesey (1768–1854)

Now chiefly remembered for losing his leg at the Battle of Waterloo, when, anecdotally, hit by a cannonball while alongside Wellington. He is said to have exclaimed 'By God, sir, I've lost my leg!', to which Wellington replied, 'By God, sir, so you have!'

In 1827 he became Master-General of the Ordnance and a year later, under the Duke of Wellington's administration, Lord Lieutenant of Ireland. He served in this post again 1830–33 and was Master-General of the Ordnance once more between 1846 and 1852, when he retired with the rank of Field Marshal.

Auckland, Lord. George Eden, Earl of Auckland (1784–1849)

In 1830 he became President of the Board of Trade and Master of the Mint. During a brief tenure as First Lord of the Admiralty in 1834 he commissioned an expedition to the East Indies, resulting in the naming of the New Zealand town after him.

As Governor-General of India in 1838 he launched the first Anglo-Afghan war, which, following the success of early operation, led to him being granted the title of Earl of Auckland.

In 1846 he was again appointed First Lord of the Admiralty, holding the position until his death in 1849.

Berkeley, Admiral. Maurice Frederick Fitzhardinghe Berkeley (1788–1867)

Berkeley entered the Navy in 1802, was promoted Lieutenant in 1808, Commander 1810 and Captain 1814. He reached Flag-Rank as Rear-Admiral in 1849, achieved Vice-Admiral 1856 and was promoted Admiral in 1862.

In 1840–41 he commanded the *Thunderer* in the Mediterranean, during which time Britain became involved in helping the recently acceded Ottoman Sultan Abd-ul-Mejid (Abd ül-Mecid, Abdülmecit) defeat the Pasha of Egypt, Mehemet, or Muhammad, Ali who was in revolt and campaigning in Syria.

The Sultan asked the Great Powers for help, and was rewarded with European intervention, including participation by the Royal Navy. The *Thunderer* was involved in several operations along the Syrian coast, including the bombardment and taking of St. Jean d'Acre (Acre, Akko) in November 1840, for which Berkeley received a medal.

This action was his last service at sea though he remained engaged in naval administration, holding a seat at the Board of Admiralty, with short interruptions, from 1833 to 1857, culminating with the position of First Sea Lord from 1854 to 1857. He was also the Liberal MP for the City of Gloucester for the periods 1831–33, 1835–37, and 1841–57.

Burgoyne, Lieutenant-General Sir John. John Fox Burgoyne (1782–1871)

John Fox Burgoyne was the son of General John Burgoyne, of American Revolutionary War fame, and was commissioned into the Royal Engineers in 1798. He fought in the wars against Revolutionary France and in the Anglo-American War of 1812.

In 1838 he became a Major-General and in 1845 was named Inspector-General of Fortifications before being promoted to Lieutenant-General in 1851. Before the outbreak of the Crimean War he went to Constantinople to advise on fortification. He went to the Crimea as Lord Raglan's chief engineering officer during the siege of Sevastopol.

Upon his return to England in 1856, he received a baronetcy (hereditary knighthood[1]) and was made the Commander of the Tower of London. He retired in 1868 as Field Marshal.

Colquhoun, Lieutenant-Colonel J.S.

No biographical details.

Congreve, Colonel. Sir William Congreve (1772–1828)

His most famous invention was the rocket that bore his name, first used against the French fleet at Boulogne-sur-Mer in 1806. Fired from specially designed boats, with a land version being developed in 1812, the rockets were used throughout the Napoleonic Wars.

His rank derived from being gazetted Lieutenant-Colonel in the Hanoverian artillery in 1811, he being a particularly close friend of the Prince Regent within whose gift such appointments lay. He published a number of works, including treatises on *The Congreve Rocket System* and *An Elementary Treatise on the Mounting of Naval Ordnance.*

Congreve, General. Lieutenant-General Sir William Congreve RA (1741–1814)

Congreve was Colonel-Commandant of the Royal Artillery and Comptroller of the Royal Laboratory in Woolwich. His son, Sir William Congreve, was the inventor of the Congreve Rocket.

Exmouth, Lord. Edward Pellew, Viscount (1757–1833)

Pellew entered the navy in 1770 and served in both the American Revolutionary War and the subsequent conflicts with Revolutionary and Napoleonic France. He was given command of the Mediterranean fleet in 1811 and was created Baron Exmouth in 1814. In 1816 a combined force of British and Dutch ships under his command bombarded Algiers, thereby compelled its Turkish ruler to abolish Christian slavery. As a reward for his achievement at Algiers, he was created Viscount Exmouth.

Faraday, Michael (1791–1867)

Michael Faraday went on to become an eminent scientist despite having received little formal education, being apprenticed to a bookbinder at the age of 14, though always demonstrating a ferocious interest in science. In pursuit of this interest he attended, in 1812, Humphry Davy's last four lectures at the Royal Institution, took notes, and later obtained an interview with Davy where he asked him for a position. At first refused this was, by dint of good fortune, granted him in 1813 and he became Davy's assistant at the Institution, thereby commencing a second apprenticeship. In 1821 he was promoted in the Royal Institution to be Superintendent of the House, and later in the year he undertook a set of experiments, which culminated in his discovery of electro-magnetic rotation – the principle behind the electric motor. In August 1831 he discovered electro-magnetic induction – the principle behind the electric transformer and generator. These discoveries were of fundamental importance in allowing electricity to become the powerful technology it did.

Between 1830 and 1851 Faraday was Professor of Chemistry at the Royal Military Academy in Woolwich, and during his tenure the Admiralty frequently solicited his advice on various matters. It is then perhaps unsurprising that Sir Thomas Byam Martin should have sought his opinion on Lord Dundonald's plan to attack Kronstadt.

A member of an obscure Christian sect, the Sandemanians (sometimes known as Glasites), Farady declined offers of knighthood and ennoblement.

Graham, Sir James. Sir James Robert George Graham (1792–1861)

A politician who held numerous seats as a Whig member of Parliament: Hull 1818–20, St Ives 1820–21, Carlisle 1826–29, Cumberland 1829–32, and East Cumberland 1832–37.

In 1837 he joined the Tory Party and, again, became an MP for a number of constituencies: Pembroke 1838–41, Dorchester 1841–47, Ripon 1847–52, and, lastly, Carlisle 1852–61.

He held cabinet posts on three occasions: First Lord of the Admiralty 1830–34 (resigned over the 1833 Church of Ireland Act), Home Secretary 1841–46, First Lord of the Admiralty 1852–55.

While Home Secretary, in 1844, his authorising the interception and opening of letters written by those considered subversive, to either the UK or foreign states, made Graham a controversial figure. As Charles Greville put it: 'It lit up a flame throughout the country. Every foolish person who used papers and pens fancied their nonsense was read at the Home Office.'[2]

He has been reckoned, justifiably so in all probability, as a political figure of the second rank.

Graham, Sir Thomas. Thomas Graham (1805–1869)

Born in Glasgow and educated at Glasgow University followed by postgraduate study in Edinburgh, where he presented his first lectures in chemistry. In 1830, he became one of the first professors of Anderson's University, Glasgow, taking up the Chair of Chemistry.

Graham is often considered the father of colloid chemistry. His other major area of contribution was in the diffusion of gases. In 1833 Graham published an article, 'On the Law of the Diffusion of Gases', in which he explicitly stated what is now known as Graham's Law of Gaseous Diffusion.

He is commemorated by a statue in George Square, by the Thomas Graham Building at the University of Strathclyde, and, more prosaically, by the kidney dialysis machine, the antecedent of which he invented.

Hastings, Sir Thomas

Few biographical detail of Sir Thomas Hastings have been unearthed. He was President of the Commission for Coast Defences, under Sir Robert Peel's government, during the tenure of which he was appointed, in 1845, Storekeeper of the Ordnance, remaining in that position until the Board was abolished in 1855.

The Board of Ordnance was responsible for warlike stores for both the Navy (the Sea Service) and the Army (the Land Service), and its history can be traced back to the fifteenth century.

It took over responsibility for artillery in 1682 and, from 1792, military

engineering. It changed from being an army institution to a civil department in
1683. From then on it was responsible for barracks, surveying (Ordnance Survey),
fortifications, and contracts. It also had the care of armament factories and instal-
lations, such as the Royal Arsenal, Royal Academy and Royal Laboratory at Woolwich, and the powder mills at Faversham and Waltham Abbey.

By the nineteenth century, the Board of Ordnance was the second largest
Department of State, next only to the Treasury, with the Master General of the
Ordnance holding a cabinet position. The other members of the Board were: the
Surveyor-General of the Ordnance, the Storekeeper of the Ordnance, and the
Clerk of the Ordnance.

The Board was finally abolished in 1855 and its duties merged with those of the
War Office.

Keith, Lord. George Keith Elphinstone, Viscount (1746–1823)

After serving as a captain in the American Revolution and early French Revolutionary Wars, he was appointed Vice-Admiral in 1795. He suppressed the muti-
nies at Nore and Spithead in 1797 and commanded the Mediterranean Fleet
between 1798 and 1801, the North Sea Fleet between 1803 and 1807, and the
Channel Fleet from 1812 to 1815. He received Napoleon's surrender after
Waterloo. He won no notable battles but was a skilled administrator and
commander.

Martin, Sir Byam. Thomas Byam Martin (1773–1854)

Martin entered the Royal Naval Academy at Portsmouth in 1785. In 1815 he was
appointed Deputy-Comptroller of the Navy. In 1816 he became Comptroller,
which office he held till the reorganisation of the Navy Board in 1831. From 1818
to 1831 he sat in Parliament as member for Plymouth. He became a Rear-Admiral
in 1811 and in 1819 he was promoted Vice-Admiral, then Admiral in 1830. The
honorary title of Vice-Admiral of the United Kingdom was granted in 1847, and
he was made an Admiral of the Fleet in 1849.

He was eulogised by Joseph Conrad in *The Mirror of the Sea* (1906):

Departing this life as Admiral of the Fleet on the eve of the Crimean War, Sir
Thomas Byam Martin [. . .] was [. . .] A brilliant frigate captain, a man of
sound judgment, of dashing bravery and of serene mind, scrupulously
concerned for the welfare and honour of the navy, he missed a larger fame
only by the chances of the service.

Minto, Lord. Gilbert Murray Kynynmound, Earl of Minto (1782–1859)

Ambassador to Berlin from 1832 to 1834, First Lord of the Admiralty from 1835
to 1841 and Lord Privy Seal from 1846 to 1852.

Palmerston, Lord. Henry John Temple (1784–1865)

The son of an Irish peer, he was born at Broadlands, Hampshire. He succeeded to the Irish peerage on his father's death in 1802, and being an Irish peer meant he was eligible to sit in the House of Commons. Aged twenty-two he achieved this, originally by the simple expedient of paying £1,500 to became the MP for Horsham. He remained in politics all his life and was then vastly experienced when, after the fall of Lord John Russell's government in 1855, he became, at the age of 70, Prime Minister for the first time for a term lasting three years.

He saw Britain emerge from the Crimean War as one of the victors, and his correspondence with Lord Panmure, and other documents quoted in the text, reveal that he was 'economical with the truth' when dealing with questions in the House of Commons.

Panmure and Palmerston, despite the latter's denials, were it seems, prepared to action the use of Lord Dundonald's Secret War Plans in an attempt to terminate the siege of Sevastopol.

Panmure, Lord. Fox Maule Ramsay, 11th Earl of Dalhousie and 2nd Baron Panmure (1801–1874)

Originally named Fox Maule, he was born at Brechin Castle, the Panmure family home in Angus, Scotland. His plethora of names were acquired through him inheriting the Barony of Panmure from his father in 1852, and, from his cousin in 1860, the Earldom of Dalhousie. In 1861 he also assumed the Dalhousie family surname of Ramsay.

Panmure was appointed Secretary of State for War (1855–58) under Palmerston. Nicknamed 'The Bison' because of his brawny physique and bullish temperament, he was not a success in the office and indulged in nepotism by attempting to secure advancement for a relative. He was also held responsible for the conduct of the latter part of the Crimean War and ended up shouldering much of the blame for its disastrous execution.

Parker, Admiral Sir William. William Parker (1781–1866)

William Parker entered the navy in 1793 as a captain's servant on the *Orion*, which, as part of the Channel fleet under Lord Howe, participated in the 'Glorious First of June', 1794.

In 1798 he was appointed as acting Lieutenant to the *Queen*, flagship of Sir Hyde Parker (no relation) and attained post rank in October of 1801 as Captain of the *Alarm*, which he commanded briefly before transferring to the *Amazon*, which he commanded for nearly eleven years. The *Amazon* was part of Nelson's command, and participated in the chase after Villeneuve across the Atlantic and back before the two admirals met at Trafalgar; *Amazon*, though, had been sent on a lone mission and missed the battle.

In 1830 Parker was promoted to Rear-Admiral and became second in command of the Channel squadron the following year. He was appointed First Sea Lord in 1846 by Lord Auckland, but held the position only briefly before returning to command the Channel fleet.

In 1852 he attained the rank of Vice-Admiral and returned ashore, being promoted to Admiral in 1862. He may be regarded as performing a singular service to the Royal Navy when, on 13 July 1854, a certain John Arbuthnot Fisher entered the service via a nomination from him. In 1863 Parker became Admiral of the Fleet.

Playfair, Lyon. (1818–1898)

Born at Chunar, Bengal, Lyon Playfair was educated at St Andrews University, the Andersonian Institute in Glasgow, and Edinburgh University. He became private laboratory assistant to Thomas Graham at University College, London, and in 1839 went to work under Justus Liebig at the University of Giessen.

After returning to Britain he was, in 1843, appointed Professor of Chemistry at the Royal Manchester Institution. Two years later, he was made chemist to the Geological Survey, and subsequently became Professor in the new School of Mines. In 1848, he was elected to the Royal Society, and three years later was made Special Commissioner and a member of the executive committee of the Great Exhibition. In 1853 he was appointed Secretary of the Department of Science, in which capacity he advocated the use of poison gas against the Russians in the Crimean War, and studied the methods proposed by Lord Dundonald in his Secret War Plans.

Lord Dundonald passed his papers relating to his Secret War Plans to Playfair, who kept them until he in turn gave them to the 12th Earl of Dundonald, probably in 1896. Lyon Playfair was knighted in 1883 and enobled in 1892 as Baron Playfair.

Prince Regent, The. George, Prince of Wales (1762–1830)

In 1811 George III was deemed to be suffering from an incapacitating mental illness, and his eldest son George, the Prince of Wales, was appointed Regent. He continued in this position until the death of his father in 1820, whereupon he became king as George IV.

By then however his physical health was deteriorating, he being greatly obese and addicted to alcohol and opium. His mental health also declined and he became reclusive. He died at Windsor Castle in 1830.

York, Duke of. Prince Frederick Augustus, Duke of York and Albany (1763–1827)

The second eldest child, and second son of King George III, he was created Duke of York and Albany in 1804, and from 1820 until his own death in 1827 was the heir presumptive to his elder brother, King George IV.

He served as the Commander-in-Chief of the British Army during the unsuccessful 1793–98 Flanders campaigns against Revolutionary France. He resigned as C-in-C of the Army in 1809 as a result of a scandal caused by the activities of his mistress who had been selling army commissions.

He was acquitted of having accepted bribes and, in 1811, reappointed by his brother. He remained as C-in-C of the Army until his death. He is popularly remembered in the nursery rhyme *The Grand Old Duke of York*.

NOTES TO THE TEXT

Chapter 1, pp. 1–16

1. Carl von Clausewitz, *On War*, trans. J.J. Graham, rev. edn (London: Wordsworth Classics, 1997), p. 40.

2. A.C. Benson and Viscount Esher (eds), The *Letters of Queen Victoria: 1837–1861*, 3 vols (London: John Murray, 1907), vol. III, p. 9.

3. Anthony Price, *The Eyes of the Fleet: A Popular History of Frigates and Frigate Captains, 1793–1815* (London: Hutchinson. 1990), p. 99.

4. Thomas Cochrane, 10th Earl of Dundonald, *The Autobiography of a Seaman*, 2 vols (London: Richard Bentley, 1860), vol. II, p. 159.

5. Admiral Sir R.H. Bacon, *The Life of Lord Fisher of Kilverstone: Admiral of the Fleet*, 2 vols (London: Hodder & Stoughton, 1929), vol. I, p. 121.

6. Price, *Eyes of the Fleet*, p. 137.

7. John B. Hattendorf, in 'Introduction' to Christopher Lloyd, *Lord Cochrane: Seaman, Radical, Liberator* (London: First Owl Books, 1998), p. xi.

8. Thomas Barnes Cochrane, 11th Earl of Dundonald, and H.R. Fox Bourne, *The Life of Thomas, Lord Cochrane, 10th Earl of Dundonald*, 2 vols (London: Richard Bentley, 1869), vol. II, p. 246.

9. Donald Thomas, *Cochrane: Britannia's Last Sea King* (New York: Viking, 1978), p. 69.

10. Ibid., p. 72.

11. Cochrane, *Autobiography*, pp. 185–6.

12. Price, *Eyes of the Fleet*, p. 135.

13. Cochrane, *Autobiography*, p. 202.

14. Ibid., p. 205.

15. Ibid., p. 206.

16. Ibid., p. 216.

17. William Richardson, *A Mariner of England: An Account of the Career of William Richardson from Cabin Boy in the Merchant Service to Warrant Officer in the Royal Navy (1780 to 1819) as told by himself*, ed. Col. Spencer Childers (London: John Murray, 1908). Extracts appear in John E. Lewis (ed.), *The Mammoth Book of Life Before the Mast: Sailors' Eyewitness Accounts from the Age of Fighting Ships* (London: Robinson, 2001), p. 259.

18. Cochrane, *Autobiography*, p. 208.

19. Ibid., p. 224.

20. Ibid., p. 224.

21. Richardson, *A Mariner of England*, pp. 260–1.

22. Cochrane, *Autobiography*, p. 226.

23. Ibid., p. 229.

24. Richardson, *A Mariner of England*, p. 264.

25. Robert Harvey, *Cochrane: The Life and Exploits of a Fighting Captain* (London: Constable & Robinson, 2002). p. 129.

26. Ian Grimble, *The Sea Wolf: The Life of Admiral Cochrane*, rev. edn (Edinburgh: Birlinn, 2000), p. 95.

27. Ibid., p. 95.

28. Harvey, *Cochrane*, p. 123.

29. Cochrane, *Autobiography*, p. 211.

30. Ibid., p. 244.

31. Quoted in Thomas, *Cochrane*, p. 188.

32. Quoted in ibid., p. 178.

33. Brian Vale, *The Audacious Admiral Cochrane: The True Life of a Naval Legend* (London: Brasseys, 2004), p. 62.

34. Nicholas Tracy, in Nicholas Tracy and Martin Robson (eds), 'Editorial' in *The Age of Sail: The International Annual of the Historic Sailing Ship* (London: Conway, 2002), p. 10.

35. Vale, *The Audacious Admiral Cochrane*, p. 58.

36. Lady Georgiana Chatterton (ed.), *Memorials, Personal and Historical of Admiral Lord Gambier* [. . .], 2nd edn, 2 vols (London: Hurst and Blackett, 1861), vol. II, p. 342.

37. 'Memorial' from Cochrane to the Prince Regent dated 2 March 1812, The Melville Papers, the Papers of Henry Dundas, 1st Viscount Melville, British Library, Add. MSS 41083 (2nd series), vol. V, sect. 2, fo. 164.

38. Horatio Nelson to Lord Hood, 29 July 1794. Quoted in Sir George Sydenham Clarke, *Fortification: Its Past Achievements, Recent Developments, and Future Progress*, 2nd edn (London: John Murray, 1907), p. 231.

Chapter 2, pp. 17–33

1. Thomas Cochrane, 10th Earl of Dundonald, *The Autobiography of a Seaman*, 2 vols (London: Richard Bentley, 1860), vol. II, p. 169.

2. Ibid., p. 171.

3. Ibid., p. 179.

4. Ibid., p. 180.

5. Dundonald Papers, Papers belonging to the Dundonald family, National Archives of Scotland, GD233/874/85.

6. Sir George Douglas and Sir George Dalhousie Ramsay (eds), *The Panmure Papers*, 2 vols (London: Hodder & Stoughton, 1908), vol. I, pp. 340–1.

7. Dundonald Papers, GDD233/874/75.

8. This phenomenon may have misled him somewhat. See Chapter 4.

9. Dundonald Papers, GD233/874/85.

10. Augustin M Prentiss, *Chemicals in War: A Treatise in Chemical Warfare* (New York: McGraw-Hill, 1937), p. 3.

11. Writing in 1855 of this, Cochrane was to state that the date of the 'Memorial' was 12 April. See *The Panmure Papers*, vol. I, p. 341.
12. 'Memorial' from Cochrane to the Prince Regent dated 2 March 1812. The 'Melville Papers', the Papers of Henry Dundas, 1st Viscount Melville, British Library, Add. MSS 41083 (2nd series), vol. V, sect. 2, fo. 163.
13. Ibid., fo. 163.
14. Melville Papers. There are some twenty-three folio sheets in the collection, fos 163–186, but unfortunately it is not always easy to discern the folio numbers on the photocopied documents in my possession. Accordingly, where it has not been possible to identify individual sheets the reference is to the collection.
15. Melville Papers.
16. Ibid.
17. Ibid.
18. Ibid.
19. Ibid.
20. Ibid.
21. Ibid.
22. Ibid.
23. Ibid., fo. 166.
24. Ibid., fo. 168.
25. Melville Papers.
26. A wine pipe is a large cask, equal to four barrels, holding 105 imperial gallons.
27. Melville Papers, fo. 168.
28. Melville Papers.
29. The terms 'Temporary Mortars' and 'Explosion Ships' are, in this context, interchangeable.
30. Melville Papers.
31. Ibid.
32. Ibid.
33. Ibid., fos 169–78.
34. *The Panmure Papers*, vol. I, p. 341.
35. Thomas Barnes Cochrane, 11th Earl of Dundonald, and H.R. Fox Bourne, *The Life of Thomas, Lord Cochrane, 10th Earl of Dundonald*, 2 vols (London: Richard Bentley, 1869), vol. II, p. 247.
36. Melville Papers.
37. Cochrane, *Autobiography*, p. 127.
38. Dundonald Papers, GD 233/96.
39. E.H. Nolan, *The History of the War against Russia*, 2 vols (London: James S. Virtue, 1857), vol. II, p. 366.
40. Melville Papers, fo. 180.
41. A.T. Mahan, *The Influence of Sea Power upon the French Revolution and Empire*, 2 vols (Boston: Little, Brown & Co., 1893), vol. II, p. 118.

42. Anthony Price, *The Eyes of the Fleet: A Popular History of Frigates and Frigate Captains, 1793–1815* (London: Hutchinson, 1990), p. 45.

43. Ibid., p. 45.

44. Melville Papers, fo. 176.

45. Christopher Lloyd (ed.), *The Keith Papers, 1803–1815.* 3 vols (London: Navy Records Society, 1955), vol. III, p. 316.

46. Cochrane, *Autobiography*, p. 228.

47. Ibid., p. 228.

48. Ibid., p. 229.

49. Ibid., p. 229.

50. Ibid., p. 231.

51. Ian Grimble, *The Sea Wolf: The Life of Admiral Cochrane*, rev. edn (Edinburgh: Birlinn, 2000), p. 152.

52. Edward L. Beach, *The United States Navy: A 200 Year History*, reprint (Boston: Houghton Mifflin, 1986), p. 70.

53. Grimble, *The Sea Wolf*, p. 153.

54. Cochrane and Bourne, *Life of Thomas, Lord Cochrane*, p. 247.

Chapter 3, pp. 34–54

1. Thomas Barnes Cochrane, the 11th Earl of Dundonald, and H.R. Fox Bourne, *The Life of Thomas, Lord Cochrane, 10th Earl of Dundonald*, 2 vols (London: Richard Bentley, 1869), vol. II, p. 248.

2. Ian Grimble, *The Sea Wolf: The Life of Admiral Cochrane*, rev. edn (Edinburgh: Birlinn, 2000), p. 351.

3. The greatest drawback to 'secret' weapons is that they tend to remain secret only until they are used. Retaliation in kind, two playing the same game, then becomes a possibility. The writer Isaac Asimov has argued that Greek Fire, in its original form at least, was the only truly 'secret' weapon to have existed: '[of] weapons that are secret even after being used, and that technologically equivalent enemies do not adopt even though they are being defeated by them [...] there is only one that is truly secret [Greek Fire]. It was used by a single nation on a number of different occasions spread over a substantial period of time and was never duplicated by any other nation. [...] One can understand the reason why Greek fire was secret. It was a complicated chemical mixture that others saw only as it was burning. Without an unburned sample to study and with chemical technology still in an embryonic stage, it is not surprising that no one could duplicate it, or even dream of duplicating it.' Isaac Asimov, 'The Unsecret Weapon', in *The Sun Shines Bright* (London: Granada Publishing, 1984), pp. 212–15.

4. Cochrane and Bourne, *Life of Thomas, Lord Cochrane*, vol. II, p. 250.

5. Ibid., p. 250.

6. *House of Lords Journal* (1844), LXXVI, p. 640; House of Lords Record Office, ref. HL/PO/JO/2/76.

7. I am indebted to Mr Paul Gibbons of the House of Lords Record Office for this information.

8. Cochrane and Bourne, *Life of Thomas, Lord Cochrane*, vol. II, p. 251.

9. Ibid., pp. 250–1.

10. Ibid., p. 251.

11. Ibid., p. 251.

12. Ibid., pp. 251–6.

13. *House of Lords Journal* (1846), LXXVIII, p. 1194; House of Lords Record Office, ref. HL/PO/JO/2/78.

14. Cochrane and Bourne, *Life of Thomas, Lord Cochrane*, vol. II, p. 257.

15. Dundonald Papers, GD233/184/13.

16. By Winston Churchill in volume 2 of *The World Crisis*, published in 1924. Churchill reproduced the words in facsimile in this book. See Chapters 7 and 8.

17. Dundonald Papers, GD233/874/84.

18. Ibid.

19. Dundonald Papers, GD233/874/85.

20. Ibid.

21. Dundonald Papers, GD233/184/12.

22. Dundonald Papers, GD/233/874/77.

23. Dundonald Papers, GD233/184/11/

24. Dundonald Papers, GD233/184/14.

25. Data on Cherbourg Breakwater taken from Billy L. Edge, Orville T. Magoon, Pierre-Yves Liagre, and Stéphane Macquet, 'Technical Discoveries from the Cherbourg Breakwater', obtained from http://www.pubs.asce.org/WWWdisplay.cgi?0101102 [accessed on 8 April 2005].

26. The document is annotated at this point, presumably by, one of the Hastings Commission: 'I do not understand by what process we are to land and take possession, being enveloped in the same [clouds] of smoke and sulphur vapour.'

27. This sentence, from the word 'annihilate' was annotated: 'I doubt that fact, and if correct surely no civilised nation would be the first to apply such a mode of proceeding.'

28. Annotated: 'It would be more easy of application and more generally available on shore than afloat.'

29. Annotated by Dundonald: 'Any number of ships.'

30. Dundonald Papers, GD233/184/14.

31. Dundonald Papers, GD233/184/15–16.

32. Lord John Russell Papers, PRO 30/22/6, p. 202.

33. Lord John Russell Papers, PRO 30/22/6, p. 228.

34. Lord John Russell Papers, PRO 30/22/6, pp. 228–9.

35. *House of Lords Journal* (1847–8), LXXX, pp. 199–200; House of Lords Record Office, ref. HL/PO/JO/2/76.

36. Dundonald Papers, GD233/874/77.

Chapter 4, pp. 55–73

1. *Encyclopaedia Britannica*, 14th edn (London: Encyclopaedia Britannica, 1929).
2. A.C. Benson and Viscount Esher (eds), *The Letters of Queen Victoria: 1837–1861*, 3 vols (London: John Murray, 1907), vol. III, p. 9.
3. Sir George Sydenham Clarke, *Fortification: Its Past Achievements, Recent Developments, and Future Progress*, 2nd edn (London: John Murray, 1907), p. 231.
4. Ibid., p. 177.
5. Ibid., pp. 245–6.
6. Martin Papers, the Papers of Sir Thomas Byam Martin, British Library, Add. MSS 41370, fos 291–2.
7. Ibid., fos 293–5.
8. Ibid., fo. 295.
9. Ibid., fo. 302.
10. Ibid., fo. 304.
11. Ibid., fo. 305.
12. Ibid., fo. 306.
13. Ibid., fo. 308.
14. Ibid., fo. 309.
15. Ibid., fo. 310.
16. Ibid., fo, 321.
17. Ibid., fo. 322.
18. Ibid., fo. 322.
19. Ibid., fo. 323.
20. Ibid., fo. 331.
21. Ibid., fo. 332.
22. Ibid., fo. 332.
23. Ibid., fo. 331.
24. Ibid., fos 328–30.
25. Ibid., fos 326–8.
26. Ibid., fos 333–6.
27. Ibid., fos 333–6.
28. Ibid., fos 333–6.
29. Ibid,. fos 333–6.
30. Ibid., fo. 337.
31. Thomas Barnes Cochrane, the 11th Earl of Dundonald, and H.R. Fox Bourne, *The Life of Thomas, Lord Cochrane, 10th Earl of Dundonald*, 2 vols (London: Richard Bentley, 1869), vol. II, p. 343.
32. Ibid., p. 343.
33. Martin Papers, fo. 339.

Chapter 5, pp. 74–91

1. *Punch*, issue 724 (26 May 1855), p. 211.
2. *Punch*, issue 731 (14 July 1855), p. 19.
3. *Punch*, issue 731 (14 July 1855), p. 15.
4. *Punch*, issue 735 (11 August 1855), p. 60.
5. *Punch*, issue 738 (1 September 1855), p. 94.
6. I am indebted to Mr A. Khan of the House of Lords Record Office for the information about Col. French.
7. *Hansard*, 4 May 1855, cols 115–16.
8. *Hansard*, 10 May 1855, col. 295.
9. *Hansard*, 18 May 1855, cols 768–9.
10. *Hansard*, 29 June 1855, col. 300.
11. Sir George Douglas and Sir George Dalhousie Ramsay (eds), *The Panmure Papers*, 2 vols (London: Hodder & Stoughton, 1908), vol. I, p. 308.
12. Ibid., p. 340.
13. Ibid., p. 340.
14. The Melville Papers, the Papers of Henry Dundas, 1st Viscount Melville, British Library, Add. MSS 41083 (2nd series), vol. V, sect. 2, fo. 164.
15. Douglas and Ramsay, *The Panmure Papers*, vol. I, pp. 341–2.
16. Granville Papers, PRO 30/29/19/9.
17. Ibid.
18. Dundonald Papers, GD233/874/95.
19. Ibid.
20. Dundonald Papers, GD233/874/82.
21. Martin Papers, Add. MSS 41370.
22. Dundonald Papers, GD233/874/82.
23. Ibid.
24. Dundonald Papers, GDD233/874/75.
25. Ibid.
26. Ibid.
27. Ibid.
28. Ibid.
29. Thomas Cochrane, 10th Earl of Dundonald, *The Autobiography of a Seaman*, 2 vols (London: Richard Bentley, 1860), vol. II, p. 236.
30. Colin Armstrong, 'Introduction' to Thomas Wemyss Reid, *Memoirs and Correspondence of Lyon Playfair*, reprint (Jemimaville: P.M. Pollak, 1976), unpaginated.
31. Reid, *Memoirs of Playfair*, pp. 160–1.
32. Dundonald Papers, GDD233/8/4/75.
33. Reid, *Memoirs of Playfair*, p. 161.
34. Lt-Gen. the 12th Earl of Dundonald, *My Army Life* (London: Arnold, 1926), p. 330.

Chapter 6, pp. 92–111

1. See, for example: Major Joseph B. Kelly, 'Gas Warfare in International Law', in *Military Law Review: Department of The Army Pamphlet 27–100–9* (Washington, DC: Headquarters Department of The Army, July 1960), p. 3.

2. Thucydides, *History of the Peloponnesian War*, trans. Rex Warner, reprint (Harmondsworth: Penguin Classics, 1954), p. 172.

3. Ibid., p. 325.

4. *The Encyclopaedia Britannica*, 14th edn (1929).

5. Isaac Asimov, 'The Unsecret Weapon', in *The Sun Shines Bright* (London: Granada Publishing. 1984), pp. 212–15.

6. Lord Hankey, *The Supreme Command*, 2 vols (London: George Allen & Unwin, 1961), vol. I, p. 228.

7. Edward Gibbon, *The Decline and Fall of the Roman Empire*, 8 vols (London: The Folio Society, 1998), vol. VII, pp. 29–30.

8. Hankey, *The Supreme Command*, vol. 1, p. 230.

9. Steven Runciman, *The Fall of Constantinople 1453* (London: Cambridge University Press, 1965), p. 97.

10. Though Fuller disagrees, saying that sulphur was used to 'gas-out' the garrison. J.F.C. Fuller, *The Decisive Battles of the Western World*, 3 vols (London: Cassell & Co., 1956), vol. I, p. 512.

11. Ibid., vol. I, p. 517. Also Runciman, *The Fall of Constantinople*, p. 119.

12. Antonia Fraser, *Cromwell: Our Chief of Men* (London: Methuen, 1985), p. 377.

13. Thomas Wemyss Reid, *Memoirs and Correspondence of Lyon Playfair*, reprint (Jemimaville: P.M. Pollak, 1976), p. 159.

14. Ibid., p. 159.

15. Ibid., pp. 159–60.

16. Wyndham D. Miles, 'The Chemical Shells of Lyon Playfair, 1854', *Armed Forces Chemical Journal* (1957), p. 40.

17. Robert V. Bruce, *Lincoln and the Tools of War* (New York: Bobbs-Merrill, 1956), p. 244.

18. Ibid., p. 244.

19. Ibid., p. 244.

20. Ibid., p. 244.

21. Scott D. Bennion and Kathy David-Bajar, 'Cutaneous Reactions to Nuclear, Biological, and Chemical Warfare', Chapter 5 in 'Military Dermatology, Part III: Disease and The Environment', in Brigadier-General Russ Zajtchuk (ed.), *Textbook of Military Medicine* (Washington, DC: Office of The Surgeon General Department of the Army, 1994), p. 74.

22. Bruce, *Lincoln*, pp. 247–8. See also Francis Lord, *Civil War Collectors Encyclopedia* (New York: Castle Books, 1965), p. 79.

23. Jeffrey K. Smart, 'History Notes: Chemical & Biological Warfare Research & Development During The Civil War', *Chemical and Biological Defense Information Analysis Center (CBIAC) Newsletter* (Washington, DC: Defense Technical Information Center, Spring 2004), vol. 5, no. 2, p. 3.

24. *The War of the Rebellion: A Compilation of the Official Records of the Union and Confederate Armies*, Series I, 53 vols; Series II, 8 vols; Series III, 5 vols; Series IV, 4 vols (Washington, DC: Government Printing Office, 1880–1901), Series I, vol. XXXVI, part III, pp. 888–9.

25. Ibid., p. 889.

26. Augustin M. Prentiss, *Chemicals in War: A treatise in Chemical Warfare* (New York: McGraw-Hill, 1937), p. xvi.

27. Translated into English, Moltke's philosophy in matters military was distilled into two statements: 'No plan survives contact with the enemy'; and 'War is a matter of expedients'. Therefore, because only the opening moves of military operations could be planned in advance, affairs after that could only be understood in terms of a series of options. Accordingly, the main task of military leaders consisted in the consideration of, and extensive preparation for, all possible outcomes. Moltke conceived that the chaos attending military operations following 'contact with the enemy' was not totally unpredictable, but rather unpredictable only within certain limits. This allowed a reduction in the number of possible outcomes, thus reducing the matter to manageable proportions. The instrument whereby these options were considered and put into practice was the Prussian, and later German, General Staff, a body specifically formed for the scientific study of military matters.

28. Alistair Horne, *The Fall of Paris: The Siege and the Commune 1870–71* (London: Macmillan, 1965), pp. 131–2.

29. *Cassell's History of the Franco-German War*, 2 vols (London: Cassell, 1895), vol. I, p. 362.

30. Frank Jellinek, *The Paris Commune of 1871* (London: Gollancz, 1937), p. 269.

31. Ibid., p. 269.

32. *Cassell's History of the Franco-German War*, vol. I, p. 362.

33. The Military Correspondent of The Times, *The Foundations of Reform* (London: Simpkin. Marshall, 1908), p. 137.

34. See, for example, Rayne Kruger, *Goodbye Dolly Gray* (London: Cassell, 1959), pp. 128, 138, 145, 243, 245, 256, 359.

35. R.K. Lochner. *The Last Gentleman of War*, trans. Thea and Harry Lindauer (London: Arrow Books, 1990), p. 202.

36. Arthur Anderson Martin, *A Surgeon in Khaki* (London: E. Arnold, 1916), pp. 210–11.

37. After the chemist Masachika Shimose. This explosive was adopted in 1893.

38. B.W. Norregaard, *The Great Siege: The Investment and Fall of Port Arthur* (London: Methuen, 1906), p. 1.

39. Ibid., p. 205.

40. Ibid., p. 210.

41. Ibid., p. 210.

42. Ibid., p. 211.

43. Ibid., pp. 211–12.

44. Lt-Gen. N.A. Tretyakov, *My Experiences at Nan-Shan and Port Arthur with the Fifth East Siberian Rifles* (London: Hugh Rees, 1911), p. 287.

45. For example, Hargreaves, who tells of the Japanese burning 'rags soaked in arsenic', in Reginald Hargreaves, *Red Sun Rising* (London: Weidenfeld & Nicolson, 1962), p. 152,

and Connaughton, who states that the Japanese 'set fire to arsenic', in Richard Connaughton, *The War of the Rising Sun and Tumbling Bear* (London: Routledge, 1991), p. 204. John Buchan later stated that the idea of chemical warfare had been suggested to the Japanese by a British chemist. He gives no source for this statement and it is unverifiable. See John Buchan, *A History of the Great War*, 4 vols (Boston: Houghton & Mifflin, 1922), vol. II, p. 43.

46. Fuller, *Decisive Battles*, vol. III. p. 168.

47. Norregaard, *The Great Siege*, p. 212.

48. Ibid., p. 212.

49. The best concise account of the conference is undoubtedly that given in Barbara Tuchman, *The Proud Tower* (London: Hamish Hamilton, 1966), pp. 229–91. A fuller and more academic version can be found in Frederick W. Holls, *The Peace Conference at The Hague* (London: Macmillan, 1914).

50. Robert K. Massie, *Dreadnought: Britain, Germany and the coming of The Great War* (London: Pimlico, 1993), p. 431.

51. Admiral Sir R.H. Bacon, *The Life of Lord Fisher of Kilverstone: Admiral of the Fleet*, 2 vols (London: Hodder & Stoughton, 1929), vol. I, p. 121.

52. War Office, *Manual of Military Law*, 7th edn (London: HM Stationery Office, 1929), pp. 356–7.

53. 'Report of Captain Mahan to the United States Commission to the International Conference at the Hague, on Disarmament, etc., with Reference to Navies'. Available from http://www.yale.edu/lawweb/avalon/lawofwar/hague99/hag99–06.htm [consulted on 10 April 2005].

54. 'Instruction from Secretary of State Hay to the American delegates at the first Hague Conference', *Foreign Relations of the United States, 1899* (Washington, DC: US Gov. Printing Office, 1901), pp. 511–12.

55. *Manual of Military Law*, p. 379.

56. Kelly, 'Gas Warfare in International Law', p. 23.

57. Tuchman, *Proud Tower*, p. 266.

58. Prentiss, *Chemicals in War*, p. 688.

59. See Kelly, 'Gas Warfare in International Law', pp. 1–68 for a discussion of this.

60. Winston S Churchill, *The River War: The Reconquest of the Sudan*, abridged reprint (London: Four Square, 1964), p. 41.

61. Gibbon, *Decline and Fall*, vol. VIII, p. 135.

62. John Keegan, *The Price of Admiralty* (London: Arrow Books, 1990), p. 67.

63. Letter from Lord Dundonald (12th Earl) to Churchill, 5 September 1923. The Churchill Papers. IZ CHAR 2/126/38–39.

Chapter 7, pp. 112–31

1. Though it is perhaps permissible to write of the 'army of Imperial Germany' there was no Imperial German army as such. Each of the individual states of the German Empire raised its own military force, the largest being the Prussian contingent. For the sake of simplicity, however, references in this work to the military force available to Imperial Germany will be without this qualification.

2. John Terraine, *Douglas Haig: The Educated Soldier*, republished edn (London: Leo Cooper, 1990), p. 48.

3. Ivan S Bloch, *Is War Now Impossible?*, trans. W.T. Stead, abridged edn of *The War of the Future in its Technical, Economic and Political Relations* (New York: Doubleday & McClure, 1899).

4. B.H. Liddell Hart, *The Other Side of the Hill: Germany's Generals, Their Rise and Fall, with Their Own Account of Military Events, 1939–45*, reprint (London: Macmillan, 1983), p. 32.

5. And was, in any event, fatally flawed and thus bound to fail. For an analysis of this, see John Keegan, *The First World War* (London: Pimlico, 1999), pp. 31–40.

6. It is actually dated 28 December 1914.

7. Lord Hankey, *The Supreme Command 1914–1918*, 2 vols (London: George Allen & Unwin, 1961), vol. I, p. 244.

8. Ibid., p. 246.

9. According to Sun Tzu: 'The worst policy of all is to besiege walled cities.' *Sun Tzu on the Art of War*, trans. Lionel Giles, facsimile reprint (Singapore: Graham Brash, 1998), p. 18. The analogy is not exact, of course, for while the inhabitants of a walled city or fortress will probably be defeated once the defences are breached, the German army had space to trade and the process would have to begin over again at a new position.

10. Terraine, *Haig*, p. 127.

11. Hankey, *The Supreme Command*, vol. I, p. 261.

12. Ibid., p. 267.

13. J.F.C. Fuller, *The Conduct of War 1789–1961* (London: Eyre & Spottiswoode, 1961), pp. 161–2.

14. Stephen Roskill, *Hankey: Man of Secrets* (London: Collins, 1970), p. 286.

15. Grant's order to Meade of 9 April 1864: 'Lee's army will be your objective point. Wherever Lee's army goes you will go also.' *The War of the Rebellion*, vol. LIX, p. 827.

16. Hankey, *The Supreme Command*, vol. I, p. 245.

17. At the Battle of Omdurman on 2 September 1898, Winston Churchill observed that, with the Anglo-Egyptian's technological superiority, destroying the enemy 'was a matter of machinery'. The Dervish army numbered some 52,000. Of that around 9,700 were killed and somewhere between 10,000 and 15,000 wounded: a casualty rate of around 50 per cent caused by a superiority of 'machinery'. The Anglo-Egyptian force under Kitchener suffered 482 men killed or wounded. This disparity was to be severely adjusted when both sides possessed the 'machinery'. See Winston S. Churchill, *The River War: The Reconquest of the Sudan*, abridged edn (London: New English Library, 1985), p. 262.

18. H.I. Whitaker, 'A Secret Plan of War', *Pall Mall Gazette*, 29 September 1914.

19. The Marquess of Anglesey, *A History of the British Cavalry*, 6 vols (London: Pen & Sword, 1973–85), vol. IV, pp. 74–5.

20. Lt-Gen. the 12th Earl of Dundonald, *My Army Life* (London: Arnold, 1926), p. 135.

21. Dundonald Papers, GD233/177/111.

22. Ibid.

23. Dundonald, *My Army Life*, p. 329.

24. Dundonald dates this meeting no more precisely. However, Lord Kitchener's maiden speech to the House of Lords took place on 25 August 1914, so the interview Dundonald asked for 'after his first address' could not, unless memory betrayed him, have taken place on that day. The phrasing of Dundonald's account with regard to timing is somewhat ambiguous, and whether the interview took place on the day it was asked for, or later, is not easily ascertained.

25. Dundonald, *My Army Life*, p. 331.

26. Ibid., p. 331.

27. David Lloyd George, *War Memoirs*, 2-vol. edn (London: Odhams Press, 1938), vol. 1, p. 383.

28. Ibid., pp. 383–4.

29. Ibid., p. 384.

30. Hankey, *The Supreme Command*, p. 186. 'He had not endured an English winter for thirty years.' John Pollock, *Kitchener* (London: Constable and Robinson, 2001), pp. 416–17.

31. The Army Council consisted of four Military Members: the Chief of the General Staff (Sir Charles Douglas); the Adjutant General (Sir Henry Sclater); the Quartermaster General (Sir John Cowans); and the Master-General of the Ordnance (Sir Stanley Von Donop). There was also a Finance Member and a Civil Member. The members of the Army Council were responsible to the Secretary of State for the performance of such duties as he might assign to them.

32. War Office, Adjutant General's Department Papers, PRO WO162/8.

33. Discussed in Chapter 6.

34. War Office, Adjutant General's Department Papers, PRO WO162/8.

35. Dundonald Papers. GD233/167/4, p. 4.

36. Dundonald, *My Army Life*, p. 331.

37. Dundonald Papers, GD233/167/4, p. 5. Also in Dundonald, *My Army Life*, pp. 331–2.

38. Dundonald Papers, GD233/167/4, p. 6.

39. Dundonald Papers, GD233/167/4, pp. 6–7.

40. Winston S. Churchill, *The World Crisis 1911–1918*, 2-vol. edn (London: Odhams Press, 1938), vol. 1, p. vii.

41. Ibid., p. 511.

42. Ibid., p. 516.

43. Dundonald Papers, GD233/167/4, p. 7.

44. Documents relating to this have not been traced. However, note Woodward's 26 September memorandum, where he states that he had a 'distinct recollection that reference was made to this subject some 12 or 15 years ago'. Given the former time period, the reference would have been in 1902, and Selborne's request was dated 8 July 1902.

45. Dundonald Papers, GD233/167/4, p. 7.

46. Churchill, *World Crisis*, vol. 1, p. 517.

47. Ibid., p. 518.

48. See Chapter 3.

49. Churchill, *World Crisis*, vol. 1, p. 517.

50. Andrew Gordon, *The Rules of the Game: Jutland and British Naval Command* (London: John Murray, 1996), p. 208.

51. Alan Palmer, *The Banner of Battle: The Story of the Crimean War* (London: Weidenfeld & Nicolson, 1987), p. 251.

52. Churchill, *World Crisis*. vol. I, p. 517.

53. Ibid., p. 60.

54. This followed Wilson's inept performance at a meeting of the Committee of Imperial Defence, which Churchill had attended as Home Secretary, on 23 August 1911. The meeting had been called to consider the question of 'Action to be taken in the event of Intervention in a European War'. This event revealed the fundamentally divergent plans of the army and navy, or rather the complete lack of such in the case of the latter. See Hankey, *The Supreme Command*, vol. I, p, 102.

55. Dundonald Papers, GD233/167/4, p. 8. Also quoted in Churchill, *World Crisis*, vol. 1, p. 517.

56. Dundonald Papers, GD233/167/4, p. 9. Also quoted in part in Churchill, *World Crisis*, vol. 1, p. 517.

57. Dundonald Papers, GD233/167/4, p. 15. Also quoted in Churchill, *World Crisis*, vol. 1, p. 519.

58. The secrecy concerning the Plans had been comprehensively breached by the publication of the Panmure Papers in 1908. This was a fact obviously unknown to Dundonald, Hankey, and the Admiralty, but not to the War Office, as evidenced by the Woodward memorandum, or the Germans (see Chapter 8).

59. Hankey, *The Supreme Command*, vol. 1, p. 230.

60. Dundonald, *My Army Life*, p. 332.

61. John Terraine, *White Heat: The New Warfare 1914–1918* (London: Guild, 1982), p. 161, n. 7.

62. Though the degree to which this primary source was subsequently interfered with in order, it is claimed, to reflect well on its author is a subject of some debate. For an account of the 'fiction' included in the Haig Diary, see Denis Winter, *Haig's Command: a Reassessment* (Harmondsworth: Penguin, 1992), pp. 230–9, 311–14.

63. Dundonald Papers, GD233/184/44.

64. These months, though, were hardly the ideal ones for military campaigning.

65. Churchill, *World Crisis*. vol. 1, p. 519.

66. Ibid., p. 519.

67. Ibid., p. 519.

68. Dundonald Papers, GD233/184/44.

69. Dundonald Papers, GD233/168/18.

70. Churchill, *World Crisis*, vol. 1, p. 519.

71. See Chapter 6 for an account of the contemporary state of international law.

72. Dundonald, *My Army Life*, p. 335.

73. Ibid., pp. 335–6.

74. Dundonald Papers, GD233/168/14.

75. Dundonald Papers, GDD233/874/75.

Chapter 8, pp. 132–44

1.   Winston S. Churchill, *The World Crisis 1911–1918*, 2-vol. edn (London: Odhams Press, 1938), vol. I, p. 517.

2.   Dundonald Papers, GD233/874/84.

3.   Charles L. Graves, *Mr. Punch's History Of Modern England in Four Volumes* (London: Cassell, 1921), vol. I (1841–1857), pp. 78–9.

4.   Dundonald Papers, GD233/874/85.

5.   Dundonald Papers, GD233/874/86.

6.   The Churchill Archive contains none of the 1914 correspondence.

7.   Churchill Papers, IZ CHAR 2/114/130.

8.   Churchill Papers, IZ CHAR 2/114/144.

9.   Churchill Papers, IZ CHAR 2/114/145.

10. Churchill's long-time Private Secretary.

11. Churchill Papers, IZ CHAR 2/114/153.

12. There are three copies of this work in the Dundonald Papers at the National Archives of Scotland in Edinburgh.

13. Lt-Gen. the 12th Earl of Dundonald, 'Smoke Screens and the Late War' (unpublished), p. 72.

14. A site now occupied by the tennis club's out courts.

15. We know Churchill had them until 18 October. Dundonald Papers, GD233/167/4, p. 8, and Churchill, *World Crisis*, vol. I, p. 517.

16. Ian Grimble, *The Sea Wolf: The Life of Admiral Cochrane*, rev. edn (Edinburgh: Birlinn, 2000), p. 367.

17. Ibid., Acknowledgments page.

18. Not traced.

19. Dundonald Papers, GD233/100/72/3.

20. And are in the Dundonald Papers still.

21. Churchill Papers, IZ CHAR 2/126/38–39.

22. Personal communication, 24 April 2000.

23. There are two typewritten copies currently in the Dundonald Papers.

24. David Lloyd George, *War Memoirs*, 2-vol. edn (London: Odhams Press, 1938), vol. I, p. 117.

25. Military Despatch, 15 June 1915, published in *Supplement to the London Gazette*, No. 29225, 10 July 1915.

26. The Marquess of Anglesey, *A History of the British Cavalry. 1816–1919*, 6 vols (London: Pen & Sword, 1973–85), vol. IV, pp. 74–5.

27. More accurately, there were two cartels formed by the six dominant German companies: BASF, Bayer, and Hoechst formed one, while Agfa, Cassella, and Kalle made up the other. These six, together with another two, Ter Meer and Greisham, formed a single, more integrated group in 1916, and eventually merged formally in 1925, to form *Interessen Gemeinschaft Farbenindustrie Aktiengesellschaf*, or the, post-World War Two, infamous I.G. Farben.

28. Augustin M. Prentiss, *Chemicals in War: A Treatise in Chemical Warfare* (New York: McGraw-Hill, 1937), p. xvi.

29. Fritz Haber, 'Chemistry in War', *Journal of Chemical Education*, p. 528. Also quoted in Joseph Borkin, *The Crime and Punishment of IG Farben* (London: André Deutsch, 1979), p. 14.

30. Report of British Mission Appointed to visit Enemy Chemical Factories in the Occupied Zone Engaged in the Production of Munitions of War. 1919. Quoted in Prentiss. *Chemicals in War*, p. 638.

31. This plant, by the end of the war, had produced in total some 10,682 tonnes of phosgene, 3,616 tonnes of diphosgene, and 4,500 tonnes of mustard gas. It was thus one of Germany's most important chemical warfare establishments.

32. Letter from Karl Duisberg (Bayer) to Bauer, Bauer Papers, Bundesarchiv, Koblenz. Quoted in Borkin, *IG Farben*, p. 20.

33. A sternutatory agent is a substance that irritates the respiratory tract. Such agents are also known as 'sneeze gases'.

34. M. Schwarte (ed.), *Die Technik im Weltkrieg* (Berlin: Mittler & Sohn, 1920), p. 273. Also quoted in translation in Prentiss, *Chemicals in War*, p. 434.

35. Schwarte, *Die Technik*, p. 273. Prentiss, *Chemicals in War*, p. 433.

36. Schwarte, *Die Technik*, p. 273. Prentiss, *Chemicals in War*, pp. 433–4.

37. Schwarte, *Die Technik*, p. 273. Prentiss, *Chemicals in War*, p. 433.

38. See Chapter 4.

39. Personal communication, 4 December 2000.

Appendix, pp. 146 & 148

1. James VI of Scotland and I of England, in order to raise funds for the for the upkeep of military forces in Ireland and the colonisation of Ulster, invented baronetcies in 1611 and sold them to the untitled landed gentry. Queen Victoria considered baronetcies useful for 'ennobling the middle class'.

2. C.C.F. Greville (H. Reeve, ed.), *The Greville Memoirs: A Journal of the Reigns of King George IV. And King William IV. & A Journal of the Reign of Queen Victoria from 1837 to 1852 & from 1852–1860*, 2nd edn, 8 vols (London: Longmans, Green, & Co., 1874), vol. V, p. 182.

BIBLIOGRAPHY

Documents and Collections

Unpublished

Leopold Amery Papers. Churchill College, Cambridge. GBR/0014/AMEL

The Churchill Papers. Papers of Sir Winston Churchill. Churchill College, Cambridge. IZ CHAR

The Dundonald Papers. Papers belonging to the Dundonald family. National Archives of Scotland. GD233

Granville, 1st Earl's Papers. Public Record Office. PRO 30/29

The Martin Papers. The papers of Sir Thomas Byam Martin. British Library. Add. MSS 41370, fos 291–367

The Melville Papers. The papers of Henry Dundas, 1st Viscount Melville (Miscellaneous correspondence). British Library. Add. MSS 41083 (2nd series), vol. V, sect. 2, fos 163–186

Lord John Russell Papers. Public Record Office. PRO 30/22

War Office. Adjutant General's Department Papers. Public Record Office. PRO WO 162

Published

Billy L. Edge, Orville T. Magoon, Pierre-Yves Liagre, and Stéphane Macquet, *Technical Discoveries from the Cherbourg Breakwater*. Obtained from http://www.pubs.asce.org/WWWdisplay.cgi?0101102

'Instruction from Secretary of State Hay to the American delegates at the first Hague Conference'. *Foreign Relations of the United States, 1899*. Washington, DC: US Gov. Printing Office, 1901

The Keith Papers. Perrin, W.G. (ed.), vol. I. Lloyd, Christopher (ed.), vols II and III. 3 vols. London: Navy Records Society, 1926, 1950, 1955

The Panmure Papers. Douglas, G. and Ramsay, G.D. (eds). 2 vols. London: Hodder & Stoughton, 1908

The War of the Rebellion: A Compilation of the Official Records of the Union and Confederate Armies. Series I, 53 vols. Series II, 8 vols. Series III, 5 vols. Series IV, 4 vols. Washington, DC: Government Printing Office, 1880–1901. Available online at: http://cdl.library.cornell.edu/moa/browse.monographs/waro.html

'Report of Captain Mahan to the United States Commission to the International Conference at the Hague, on Disarmament, etc., with Reference to Navies'. Available from: http://www.yale.edu/lawweb/avalon/lawofwar/hague99/hag99-06.html

Periodicals, Journals, and Newspapers

Armed Forces Chemical Journal
Chemical and Biological Defense Information Analysis Center (CBIAC) Newsletter
Hansard
House of Lords Journal
Journal of Chemical Education
London Gazette
Military Law Review
Pall Mall Gazette
Punch
The Times

Books

Anglesey, The Marquess of. *A History of British Cavalry 1816–1919*. Vol. 4, *1899–1913*. London: Pen & Sword, 1986

Asimov, Isaac. 'The Unsecret Weapon', in *The Sun Shines Bright*. London: Granada Publishing, 1984. [This article first appeared in *The Magazine of Fantasy and Science Fiction*, June 1980.]

Bacon, Admiral Sir R.H. *The Life of Lord Fisher of Kilverstone: Admiral of the Fleet*. 2 vols. London: Hodder & Stoughton, 1929

Baker, Mark. *The Rise and Fall of Gwrych Castle, Abergele and Winifred, Countess of Dundonald – A Biography*. Llandudno: Mark Baker, 2004

Beach, Edward L. *The United States Navy: A 200 Year History*. Reprint Boston: Houghton Mifflin, 1986

Bennion, Scott D. and David-Bajar, Kathy. 'Cutaneous Reactions to Nuclear, Biological, and Chemical Warfare', Chapter 5 in 'Military Dermatology, Part III: Disease and The Environment', in Brigadier-General Russ Zajtchuk (ed.), *Textbook of Military Medicine*. Washington, DC: Office of The Surgeon General Department of the Army, 1994

Benson, A.C. and Esher, Viscount (eds), *The Letters of Queen Victoria: 1837–1861*, 3 vols. London: John Murray, 1907

Bloch, Ivan S. *Is War Now Impossible?* Translated by W.T. Stead. Abridged edition of *The War of the Future in its Technical, Economic and Political Relations*. New York: Doubleday & McClure, 1899

Borkin, Joseph. *The Crime and Punishment of IG Farben: the Birth, Growth and Corruption of a Giant Corporation*. London: André Deutsch, 1979

Bridge, Admiral Sir Cyprian. *Sea-power, and Other Studies*. London: Smith, Elder, 1910

Bruce, Robert V. *Lincoln and the Tools of War*. New York: Bobbs-Merrill, 1956

Buchan, John. *A History of the Great War*. 4 vols. Boston: Houghton Mifflin, 1922

Cassell's History of the War Between France and Germany 1870–1871. 2 vols. London: Cassell, 1894

Chatterton, Georgiana, Lady. *Memorials, Personal and Historical of Admiral Lord Gambier, G.C.B. With Original Letters from William Pitt first Lord Chatham, Lord Nelson, Lord*

Castlereagh, Lord Mulgrave, Henry Fox, first Lord Holland, the Right Hon. George Canning, etc. Edited from family papers. 2nd edn, 2 vols. London: Hurst & Blackett, 1861

Churchill, Winston S. *The River War: The Reconquest of the Sudan.* Abridged reprint. London: Four Square, 1964

Churchill, Winston S. *The World Crisis 1911–1918.* 2 vols. London: Odhams Press, 1938

Clausewitz, Carl von. *On War.* Trans. J.J. Graham. Rev. edn. London: Wordsworth Classics, 1997

Cochrane, Thomas, 10th Earl of Dundonald. *The Autobiography of a Seaman.* 2 vols. London: Richard Bentley, 1860

Cochrane, Thomas Barnes, 11th Earl of Dundonald, and Bourne, H.R. Fox. *The Life of Thomas, Lord Cochrane, 10th Earl of Dundonald.* 2 vols. London: Richard Bentley, 1869

Colomb, Vice-Admiral P.H. *Naval Warfare: Its Ruling Principles And Practice Historically Treated.* 3rd edn. London: W.H. Allen, 1899

Connaughton, Richard. *The War of the Rising Sun and Tumbling Bear: A Military History of the Russo-Japanese War 1904–5.* London: Routledge, 1991

Cowper, Henry. *World War One and its Consequences – The Nature of the War.* Milton Keynes: The Open University, 1990

Dundonald, Lt-Gen. the 12th Earl of. *My Army Life.* London: Arnold, 1926

Encyclopaedia Britannica. 14th edn. London: Encyclopaedia Britannica, 1929

Fraser, Antonia. *Cromwell: Our Chief of Men.* London: Methuen, 1985

Fuller, J.F.C. *The Conduct of War, 1789–1961.* London: Eyre & Spottiswoode, 1961

Fuller, J.F.C. *The Decisive Battles of the Western World.* 3 vols. London: Cassell & Co., 1956

Fuller, J.F.C. *Grant & Lee: A Study in Personality and Generalship.* London: Spa, 1933

Gibbon, Edward. *The History of the Decline and Fall of the Roman Empire.* 8 vols. London: The Folio Society, 1998

Gordon, Andrew. *The Rules of the Game: Jutland and British Naval Command.* London: John Murray, 1996

Grant, Ulysses S. *The Personal Memoirs of US Grant.* New York: Konecky & Konecky, 1886

Graves, Charles L. *Mr. Punch's History Of Modern England in Four Volumes.* Vol. I, 1841–1857. London: Cassell, 1921

Grimble, Ian. *The Sea Wolf: The Life of Admiral Cochrane.* Rev. edn. With a Postscript by Charles Stephenson. Edinburgh: Birlinn, 2000

Hankey, Lord. *The Supreme Command 1914–1918.* 2 vols. London: George Allen & Unwin, 1961

Hargreaves, Reginald. *Red Sun Rising: The Siege of Port Arthur.* London: Weidenfeld & Nicolson, 1962

Harvey, Robert. *Cochrane: The Life and Exploits of a Fighting Captain.* London: Constable & Robinson, 2002

Holls, Frederick W. *The Peace Conference at The Hague.* London: Macmillan, 1914

Horne, Alistair. *The Fall of Paris: The Siege and the Commune 1870–71.* London: Macmillan, 1965

Jellinek, Frank. *The Paris Commune of 1871.* London: Gollancz, 1937

Keegan, John. *The First World War.* London: Hutchinson, 1998

Keegan, John. *The Price of Admiralty.* London: Arrow Books, 1990

Kruger, Rayne. *Goodbye Dolly Gray: The Story of the Boer War.* London: Cassell, 1959

Liddell Hart, B.H. *The Other Side of the Hill: Germany's Generals, Their Rise and Fall, with Their Own Account of Military Events, 1939–45.* Reprint. London: Macmillan, 1983

Lloyd, Christopher. *Lord Cochrane: Seaman, Radical, Liberator. A Life of Thomas, Lord Cochrane, 10th Earl of Dundonald, 1775–1860.* London: First Owl Books, 1998

Lloyd George, David. *War Memoirs.* 2-vol. edn. London: Odhams Press, 1938

Lochner, R.K. *The Last Gentleman of War.* Translated by Thea and Harry Lindauer. London: Arrow Books, 1990

Lord, Francis. *Civil War Collectors Encyclopaedia.* New York: Castle Books, 1965

Mahan, A.T. *The Influence of Sea Power upon the French Revolution and Empire.* 2 vols. Boston: Little, Brown & Company, 1893

Martin, Arthur Anderson. *A Surgeon in Khaki.* London: E. Arnold, 1916

Massie, Robert K. *Dreadnought: Britain, Germany and the Coming of The Great War.* London: Pimlico, 1993

Military Correspondent of The Times, The (Col. Charles a'Court Repington). *The Foundations of Reform.* London: Simpkin, Marshall, 1908

Nolan, E.H. *The History of the War against Russia.* 2 vols. London: James S. Virtue, 1857

Norregaard, B.W. *The Great Siege: The Investment and Fall of Port Arthur.* London: Methuen, 1906

Palmer, Alan. *The Banner of Battle: The Story of the Crimean War.* London: Weidenfeld & Nicolson, 1987

Pollock, John. *Kitchener.* London: Constable & Robinson, 2001

Prentiss, Augustin M. *Chemicals in War: A Treatise in Chemical Warfare.* New York: McGraw-Hill, 1937

Price, Anthony. *The Eyes of the Fleet: A Popular History of Frigates and Frigate Captains, 1793–1815.* London: Hutchinson, 1990

Reid, Thomas Wemyss. *Memoirs and Correspondence of Lyon Playfair.* Reprint. Jemimaville: P.M. Pollak, 1976

Richardson, William. *A Mariner of England: An Account of the Career of William Richardson from Cabin Boy in the Merchant Service to Warrant Officer in the Royal Navy (1780 to 1819) as told by himself.* Edited by Col. Spencer Childers. London: John Murray, 1908. Extracts appear in Lewis, Jon. E. (ed.), *The Mammoth Book of Life Before the Mast: Sailors' eyewitness accounts from the age of fighting ships.* London: Robinson, 2001

Roskill, Stephen. *Hankey: Man of Secrets.* London: Collins, 1970

Runciman, Sir Steven. *The Fall of Constantinople, 1453.* London: Cambridge University Press, 1965

Schwarte, M. (ed.), *Die Technik im Weltkrieg.* Berlin: Mittler & Sohn, 1920

Spaight, J.M. *Air Power and War Rights.* London: Longmans, Green & Co., 1947

Sun Tzu on the Art of War. Trans. Lionel Giles. Facsimile reprint. Singapore: Graham Brash, 1998

Sydenham Clarke, Sir George. *Fortification: Its Past Achievements, Recent Developments, and Future Progress.* 2nd edn. London: John Murray, 1907

Taylor, A.J.P. *The First World War: an Illustrated History.* Harmondsworth: Penguin, 1966

Terraine, John. *Douglas Haig: The Educated Soldier.* London: Leo Cooper, 1990

Terraine, John. *White Heat: The New Warfare 1914–18*. London: Guild, 1982

Thomas, Donald. *Cochrane: Britannia's Last Sea King*. New York: Viking, 1978

Thucydides. *The History of the Peloponnesian War*. Translated by Rex Warner. Reprint. Harmondsworth: Penguin Classics, 1954

Tracy, Nicholas and Robson, Martin (eds), *The Age of Sail: The International Annual of the Historic Sailing Ship*. London: Conway, 2002

Tretyakov, Lieut.-General N.A. *My Experiences at Nan Shan and Port Arthur with the First East Siberian Rifles*. Translated by Lieutenant A.C. Alford. London: Hugh Rees, 1911

Tuchman, Barbara. *The Proud Tower: A portrait of the world before the war 1890–1914*. London: Hamish Hamilton, 1966

War Office, The. *Manual of Military Law*. 7th edn. London: HM Stationery Office, 1929

Winter, Denis. *Haig's Command: a Reassessment*. Harmondsworth: Penguin, 1992

Internet

Billy L. Edge, Orville T. Magoon, Pierre-Yves Liagre, and Stéphane Macquet, *Technical Discoveries from the Cherbourg Breakwater*. Obtained from: http://www.pubs.asce.org/WWWdisplay.cgi?0101102

Masachika Shimose: http://www.ndl.go.jp/portrait/e/datas/109.html?c=0

'Report of Captain Mahan to the United States Commission to the International Conference at the Hague, on Disarmament, etc., with Reference to Navies'. Available online at: http://www.yale.edu/lawweb/avalon/lawofwar/hague99/hague99-06.htm

The War of the Rebellion: A Compilation of the Official Records of the Union and Confederate Armies. Series I, 53 vols. Series II, 8 vols. Series III, 5 vols. Series IV, 4 vols. Washington, DC: Government Printing Office, 1880–1901. Available online at: http://cdl.library.cornell.edu/moa/browse.monographs/waro.html

The 'Tilting Teapot': http://www.virtualtea.com/vt/tilt.html

INDEX